James W Taft

(Read aug 26 - 28, 1960)

VICE PRESIDENT
IN CHARGE OF REVOLUTION

KARSH

Murray D Lincoln

VICE PRESIDENT

IN CHARGE OF

REVOLUTION

by Murray D. Lincoln

AS TOLD TO DAVID KARP

McGraw-Hill Book Company, Inc.

NEW YORK   TORONTO   LONDON

MURRAY D. LINCOLN is fond of saying that what every big organization needs is a "vice president in charge of revolution"— somebody on the staff who'd spend full time keeping everybody and everything stirred up; somebody who knew when to nag and when to inspire and who could do both equally well; a kind of professional needler who, by timely reminders of the organization's fundamental objectives, would keep leadership on its toes and on the right track.

In effect, Murray Lincoln himself has played this role, regardless of the organization he's worked for or the spot he might have occupied on the organization chart. As New England's first county agricultural agent back in 1914 he was no less a "vice president in charge of revolution" than he is today as president of some fifteen different business enterprises. Indeed, it's been said of him that when he goes to Heaven he'll take one look around, decide the place could stand some straightening up, and ask St. Peter for a broom.

Mr. Lincoln's thought and experience have led him to become one of the world's foremost advocates of consumer cooperation as an economic way of life. In consumer cooperation he sees the surest route to a world of peace and abundance. He first came to national recognition as the executive secretary of the cooperatively centered Ohio Farm Bureau Federation. Today he is head of Nationwide Insurance, which has assets of more than three hundred and fifty million dollars, and a group of other companies whose activities span such diversified fields as broadcasting, manufacturing, credit, finance, and building. He was the first president of CARE, and, since 1941, has been president of the Cooperative League of the U.S.A. He was a lay representative of American agriculture on the five-member U.S. delegation to the United Nations Conference on Food and Agriculture at Hot Springs, Virginia, in 1943. An early consultant to the United Nations Economic and Social Council, he is now a member of the executive committee of the U.S. Committee for the United Nations. He has also served, or is serving, on such bodies as President Truman's Commission on Higher Education, the National Commission for Adult Literacy, the National Child Labor Committee, and the National Planning Association. Whatever his job or title, his role has always been that of the creative and controversial leader—a man impatient with the *status quo,* eager to change things for the better, and convinced that things *can* be better if people will only work together to make them so.

This book is the personal recollection
of the life of Murray Danforth Lincoln,
born in 1892. It represents a remarkable
feat of recall by a man who has never
kept a diary, who wrote few letters, and
even fewer articles for publication.
In so far as it has been possible or practical,
names, dates, figures, facts have been
checked and corrected. However, because
this is a personal record of one man's life
and times, there are bound to be some errors and
omissions. For what Murray Lincoln thought,
felt, saw, and remembers, I offer no apology
nor explanation. For what I have failed to
elicit from him, I beg your indulgence.

David Karp

To those men and women who, by simple acts of faith and cooperation, have pointed the way toward the goal of freedom, plenty, and peace for all men, everywhere.

Part One

CHAPTER 1

I WAS BORN in Raynham, Massachusetts, on April 18, 1892. I was the second son in a family that ultimately numbered five boys and one girl.

All of us were born on a stony little New England farm. The focus of our early lives was the small country store that Grandfather Lincoln owned and where my father worked. In those days, the crossroads grocery store served as a meeting place, council hall, and general community center. It had no fixed closing hour. It closed when the last person had nothing more to say but "good night."

The firmest facts about Raynham, just as hard and unrelenting as the rocks which filled its ground, were that it was Protestant, Republican, and insular. The differences between Republicans and Democrats have become so softened over the years it's hard to remember that in Massachusetts in the 1890s it was almost considered sinful to be a Democrat. In Raynham it was assumed that the Democratic party was composed solely of immigrant Irish and Italian Catholics who had been brought into Boston and Fall River, and no self-respecting rural white Protestant would have anything to do with it. New England Yankees of that period were a hard-nosed lot of Protestants. I can still recall the to-do in our family when a second cousin married a Catholic. We children, who learned our prejudices a little at a time and hadn't yet learned to acquire any anti-Catholicism, couldn't understand what the adults were fussing about. Especially when the bridegroom, when we met him, turned out to be a happy-go-lucky station agent from Mansfield who doted on children and who had a vital sense of fun that was missing in our dour elders.

Raynham was studded with prejudices, big and little, and as a child I picked them all up, as children will. The most innocent prejudice is one which has lasted longest with me. It has to do with cigarettes. Cigarettes were then a new fad for the dudes and the debauched. Grandfather would sell clay pipes, plug tobacco, corncob pipes, and cigars, but he drew the line at cigarettes. The first neighbor who took to smoking cigarettes was a man who had already gone to the dogs, so I suppose cigarettes had little to add to his downfall. I retain that prejudice against cigarettes to this day and indulge in a cigar only when I feel particularly dashing.

The economic difference between farmers and city folk was brought home to me sharply when my Uncle Arthur and Aunt Edith came out summers and brought my cousins with them. They spent the summers on Grandfather's farm. Uncle Arthur taught school in Boston and I don't suppose they paid teachers any better than they do now, but farmers—New England stone farmers, anyway—were making out even poorer, and the contrast between the way in which Uncle Arthur and Aunt Edith dressed and the way in which my father and mother dressed upset me. Aunt Edith, in particular, keeps coming back to mind—especially a hat she wore. It was a fancy hat, a hat draped with roses, a far grander hat than my mother ever could afford. I suppose, in a way, Aunt Edith's Boston-bought hat became a symbol for me. Every time I saw her wearing it, I asked myself why it was a schoolteacher's family could dress so much better than a farmer's family. It just didn't seem right somehow.

Raynham was in bad straits economically. Once the trolley

system linked it with nearby communities, it became a dying town. Farming was hard and it was a good deal easier for people to pick themselves up and go to Brockton, Taunton, or Fall River and Middleboro, and find work in the factories there than to stay on and try to earn a living from unrewarding soil. Raynham was mortally wounded by the industrial revolution, and it was a wound few of us saw or understood before it was too late. Not long before I was born most folks there had made their own shoes. That home craft persisted even until the time I was a youngster delivering groceries. In the small room off the kitchen, or in the woodshed, you could still see tools for the making of shoes. But the coming of a shoe factory doomed that home craft, and then the coming of the trolley, which made manufacturing more profitable in Fall River and Brockton, doomed the shoe factory. The factory, run by Zeno Kelly, went into bankruptcy when I was four or five years old.

The farmers around Raynham had come to depend on work in Zeno Kelly's factory to supplement their meager incomes. They had also come to depend on Grandfather's store to supply them with everything they needed to live on except the things they were able to raise or make themselves, and they bought mostly on credit. It was the custom in those days for farmers to pay the grocer two or three times a year, after they'd harvested or sold their crops of potatoes or strawberries. In the depression of '93, the shoe factory was closed down and Grandfather began to incur indebtedness—indebtedness that he was never able to pay off. For my own part, it wasn't until 1926 that I was able to pay off some of the debts that the industrial revolution had inflicted upon our family.

If Grandfather had been a man of different stripe he could have saved himself and his family from worry about debt by going into bankruptcy. It would have been the smart thing to do. But Grandfather was a moral man and bankruptcy was a course a man of his fiber couldn't take. We respected his feelings and worked for many years paying off his debts.

With all the first-hand evidence I had that farming was not what it should be, I don't know why I insisted on becoming a farmer. Maybe it was simply because I wasn't very smart. At least I used to think I wasn't very smart. When I compared myself with my older brother Edward, who got nothing but "A's" and who grew up to be the educator in the family, I felt I was a real dumb cluck. I didn't like school and I had no use for books. There was a long spell in my life when I could honestly say that the only book I'd ever read was *Black Beauty*.

Why farming then? I don't know. Maybe, odd as it seems, it was because farming was such *hard* work that I felt I could do it well. I remember telling myself that while I wasn't as bright as others, I could make up for it by working harder than anybody I knew. And Lord knows there was plenty of opportunity for hard work on a farm. Then too, I loved being around livestock, horses especially. I enjoyed being on a farm. I had the feeling that feeding people was more important than anything else in the world. So, as much as I resisted formal schooling, I made up my mind early to go on to agricultural college because I felt that there were right and wrong ways of farming and I was determined to learn the right ways.

That determination, however, was almost undermined by a sudden excess of wealth.

Stones, as I've mentioned before, were New England's curse. But in 1906 a stone crusher was located in Raynham and the clamor for better roads led to a demand for crushed stone. And it suddenly appeared, to me at least, that the stones of Massachusetts might be the making of a fortune. I was fourteen years old then, tall and thin for my age, but strong and ambitious. Dad had one old mare named Foxtail and an ordinary farm wagon, and so I went into the business of hauling stone. Since I had no tip cart, I had to lift the stone onto the wagon, take the stone to the crusher, and there unload it. The going rate was fifty cents a ton—which meant man-handling up and down that wagon two tons of stone for each half dollar I made. I got into a

4

routine of work. I arose in the morning, loaded the stone, drove ten miles to high school, came home, hauled the load of stone four miles to the crusher, and unloaded it. I returned to do the chores every farm boy was expected to do, did some studying, and got to bed as early as I could to get up the next morning to repeat the process. In my ambition and youthful greed I decided the wagon and the one horse were not enough, so I contracted with our blacksmith to rebuild our wagon, to strengthen it to take a heavier load of three tons rather than one, and bought a horse to make up a team. The horse I bought, on credit, was an outlaw shipped from the West, where all our team horses came from. It had contracted something they used to call "shipping fever," which, I suppose, is a form of influenza. His name was Major and he was a sick horse. I sat up night after night, nursing him and trying not to dwell upon the awful picture of what I had done. I had gone into debt to the tune of a hundred dollars to the blacksmith, and I had paid a hundred and fifteen dollars (sixty-five of which I had yet to earn) for a Western outlaw who looked as though he was not going to live. If Major died, I wouldn't earn a dime, and what was worse, I'd be in debt both to the blacksmith and the horse dealer. You cannot conceive of the New England Yankee's horror of debt or mortgage. They constituted a form of sin and here, at fourteen, I had committed the dreadful sin of going into debt. As I watched that poor beast heave and labor with his breathing I wondered about my own folly. Our family weren't ardent churchgoers but we did fear God and I had learned to pray, and I prayed over that horse with a fervor I hadn't shown before nor probably haven't felt since. God, who is likely a little bit of a Yankee Himself, spared that horse and saved my bacon for me.

I teamed the horses and plunged into stone hauling with a passion that enabled me to pay off my debts to the blacksmith and the horse dealer and earn a surplus of a hundred and twenty-five dollars carting stone while I was going to high school. The process of loading in the morning and unloading in the afternoon went on without interruption. Saturdays, of course, I worked doubly hard, getting in as many as three loads. I was making so much money, and managing to ignore the fact that my father was feeding the horses, that I might never have gone on to agricultural college if the two horses and my buggy had not been stolen. Providence, using the strange device of a horse thief (probably the last in New England) put an end to my career as a stone hauler.

As a youngster I took a rather straight and prim view of things. I saw little to admire in thinkers or readers. While I loved my dad, he was a thinker, a reader, and not a doer. He seemed to me to lack affirmative values. Grandfather, on the other hand, was always instructing me in the simple, practical arts of living. There were two things Grandfather gave me that have lasted throughout my life. One was a proper respect for things. A proper respect for things, he believed, required that they be returned to their proper place. I remember his telling me that it didn't take any longer to put a tool back where it belonged than it did to hunt high and low for it the next time I wanted it. I took that lesson to heart. It seemed to have little or no effect upon my brothers, or even my father. The other thing Grandfather insisted upon was good housekeeping, and generally on Saturday, because Sunday was the day for our relatives to visit, he wanted us to sweep the yard, rake up, and generally make things tidy.

Father had a different sense of order and whenever I swept and straightened up I could hear him muttering that he wished I had left things the way I had found them.

This sense of the proper care of things and this taste for good housekeeping have persisted with me to this day. In the twenties, when the Farm Bureau Mutual Automobile Insurance Company was still a modest operation in Columbus, Ohio, I used to raise Ned regularly with the staff about its bad housekeeping habits. When we had finally grown large enough so that I could have a company car I made up my mind that this was one thing, at least, which would be properly cared for—washed, cleaned, oiled, greased, and gassed for use whenever it was needed. I had to fire one man and threaten another before this respect for company property could become automatic. Today, of course, we keep a fleet of executive cars for our vice presidents and other staff people. I am still enough my grandfather's child to check these cars from time to time and to warn my vice presidents that if they are given company cars they ought to appreciate them well enough to take care of them.

Children, I presume, always prefer to know what's expected of them and to have their elders lay down the law to them. Not brutally, of course, but as a matter of fair discipline. Children are interested in certainties, in blacks and whites. They aren't equipped to understand or cope with uncertainties or shades of gray in opinions. I was big for my age, and in my teens I was man-sized and doing a man's job and earning a man's wages. It seemed wrong for me to give up such a role to become a child again—that is, to become a student. But when those horses were stolen, my role as a man in a man's world was stopped. I think it was Mark Twain who once said that when he was twenty years old he was disgusted at the stupidity of his father but when he reached twenty-five he was amazed to discover how much the old man had learned in five years. When I was in my teens I was puzzled with the lack of decision I saw in my father. I know now, of course, that he granted me that rarest of all privileges—the opportunity to make my own decisions and my own mistakes. He granted me that privilege for two reasons. One of them was that he wasn't certain himself that what he would advise me to do would be any better than what I had decided to do for myself. The other reason was that he was afraid that if he told me what to do he would be damaging my independence, my spirit, and my willingness ever to make up my own mind. I have, over the years, tried to treat my own executives in the same way. I think one of the hardest things for me is to let people do their jobs as they like and make up their own minds. But I know for their own good, and for the good of the enterprise in which we're engaged, that this freedom for a man to make his own mistakes, and to see them as mistakes, is essential.

When I entered the Massachusetts Agricultural College in Amherst in 1910, I was dubious about the whole matter of education. I wanted to be a farmer and I wasn't sure, then, that a farmer needed schooling. For another thing, education cost money, and the hundred and twenty-five dollars I had earned hauling stone was not going to be enough to pay my way through agricultural college. My folks certainly were in no position to help me. I had to earn whatever money I could, however I could.

I went to work on the college farm cutting corn at ten cents an hour. It was heavy corn and hard work and I wasn't making money in any quantity or with any speed. My work in the cornfield took me up to the college barns because it was there we went to pick up our tools at the beginning of the day and there we went in the evening to deposit them. I went through the horse barn at every opportunity because I loved horses and still missed Major—the horse who had, in a sense, put me in college.

It seemed sinful to me to stand around the horse barn, admiring those splendid animals, without doing something. Then, too, I didn't know what sort of an explanation I could give to anyone who found me loitering there. I was too much of a Yankee to admit frankly that I loved horses. That's why I picked up a broom and swept out the barn. When I had about finished, the superintendent of the farm came in and saw me.

"Hello," he remarked. "You don't work here, do you?"

"No," I replied.

"Then why are you sweeping out the place?"

I wet my lips and thought a moment. "Well," I finally said, "I thought the barn didn't look as good as a college barn ought to look."

He took off his hat and laughed. "Well, do you like to clean up?"

"Yes, I do, and I like being around a barn." Strictly speaking, of course, that was stretching the point. I didn't like the cleaning but I did like being around horses and cows. He looked me over carefully for a moment and then said, "Well, you come to see me next Saturday."

I showed up at the horse barn bright and early the following Saturday. "Now, look, if you really like to clean up, I'd like to hire you," the superintendent said. "To tell you the truth," he went on, "some of the trustees have been unhappy about the looks of the place, and I can't get anyone to do the job as well as I'd like to have it done. I'll pay you fifteen cents an hour to clean up, on two conditions. The first condition"—he held up a warning finger—"is that you don't tell any of the other boys how much you're making. The second condition is that you really keep the place clean." I promised to keep both conditions faithfully, and they were easy enough to observe. Keeping the barn clean was a lot easier than cutting corn and it paid 50 percent more. Picking up that broom paid off for me in a way I hadn't expected, and even that didn't end it.

The job I did must have pleased Mr. Elwin Forristall, the superintendent, because one day he asked me if I would like to help Mrs. Forristall with her spring house cleaning. I managed as big a false smile as I could and said I'd love to. If there was one thing I hated to do more than anything else it was to take up carpets and beat them. But that's what I did, and I did it with as much energy as I could, partly because I wanted to get the job done with and partly because I took out my irritation on the carpets. Mr. Forristall was so pleased with the way I worked that he recommended me as janitor to a little fix-it shop in Amherst, owned by a Mr. Thompson.

Mr. Thompson wanted somebody to come down in the morning to clean up the shop and start the old gas-burning engine. I got up before daylight, went down to the shop, and lit the gas. It took about an hour before the engine would get warm enough to start and run all the machinery in the place. During the course of

9

my work there, I cleaned out the attic and came across a piece of machinery I'd never seen before. I brushed it off and brought it downstairs.

"What's this thing?" I asked Mr. Thompson.

He glanced at it and said, "Oh, it's a mimeograph."

"What does it do and how does it work?"

The proprietor scratched his head. "It's to duplicate writing but I'm not sure how it works. We've got some stencils for it here. Some fellow left it here for demonstration and never did come back for it. You type on the stencils and then run the stencils through the machine and make copies of what you typewrite."

The moment he said that I was struck with an idea. "Well, can I take it home and fool with it?" He said, "Sure."

A Yankee's consent means nothing without a price, so I agreed to pay fifty cents a month rental on the mimeograph and fifty cents a month rental on a typewriter. Language had always been difficult for me and in botany I was having trouble with the variety of Latin names. It was rumored throughout the sophomore class that you could get through botany if you had a good notebook. I made up my mind to have a good one and I toyed with the idea of duplicating the professor's lectures and selling them to my classmates.

Lewis Howard, with whom I shared a two-dollar-a-week room, had his doubts about the whole thing but he was patient enough and helped me with the stencils. The problem, of course, lay in the wax coating on the stencil. These were early, primitive stencils and the wax wasn't all it should have been. We had a large kerosene study lamp in our room, and I experimented by holding the stencil so many inches away from the lighted lamp to soften the wax. I also warmed the ink so that it spread evenly. The machine itself worked perfectly. We made some remarkably good copies with that makeshift technique.

It seemed to me that it would help if we could talk the botany professor into handing over his lecture to me so I could type it and run off copies on the mimeograph. These copies, of course, could be sold. Lewis Howard listened to my plan with something like astonishment. Then he flushed and shook his head. "Oh, Murray, they'll just laugh you out of town. Don't do it." He pleaded with me not to make a fool of myself but I couldn't shake the idea from my head. It seemed good and logical.

I went to our botany professor and tried a little flattery on him. I told him how important his lectures were to us and that the boys would be pleased to have his lectures to keep. Verbatim lectures, that is—word for word, including all those grand Latin names. I could see that he was touched by what I had to say and I felt a little guilty about my approach. I would have felt guiltier if I hadn't already invested a dollar in the month's rental on the mimeograph and the typewriter, and I would have felt even guiltier if I hadn't needed the money to keep myself in college. He listened and I spoke about as fast and convincingly as I could. Finally he looked at me and said, "Well, Murray, do you really think they'd be interested?"

"Yes, sir. I'm sure they would be. In fact, I'll put the proposition to them and let them vote on it."

"Well," he said with a grin, "it's all right with me if the gang wants it."

Next day when the class ended, he held up his hand and said, "I want you to stay where you are for a few moments. Lincoln has a proposition he wants to put to you for a vote." With that he grinned at me and walked out of the room. I got up to the rostrum, confronted the hundred and one budding botanists, cleared my throat, and began to speak.

"Well now, we all know that botany is a mighty important subject to agriculturists, but I have trouble remembering those Latin names. Half the time I forget them and the other half I misspell them. What with forgetting and misspelling, I can't manage to keep a very good notebook in this class. And I think every one of you knows that one of the most important things you can have in this class is a good notebook. Now, I'm assuming that at least some of you are having as much trouble as I am. So,

11

here's an idea I've got and I'd like to make this proposal. What would you fellows think of my getting the professor's lecture and mimeographing it and selling it to you at two cents a sheet?"

Well, they just exploded into a roar of ayes that probably rocked the foundations of the Massachusetts Agricultural College. I knew it was a good idea but I hadn't realized it was that good. The idea so impressed them that now and then when I meet old classmates, they still remember me as the one who sold them copies of the professor's lectures. Lewis Howard and I shared the work of typing the stencils and running off the copies. Typing took about two hours and mimeographing another hour. The lectures ran about four pages and we ran off a hundred copies, so we got eight cents a student. I gave Lewis two dollars and kept six for myself. That led to my doing other lectures for other classes and typing theses and other papers, and I did well during my sophomore and junior years. Lewis and I cooked our own meals the first two years and I think my expense per year was about three hundred dollars, so I could get through on room and board at a little over three dollars a week.

When I look back on it now, I realize that this opportunity came about because I had picked up a broom and swept out the college barn without being asked to. I surprised someone by my action and woke him up to my existence. I don't think the world is ever going to give much to the young man who doesn't surprise it now and then. Our respectable young people these days try so hard to fit themselves into precut patterns that they become about as interesting as gingerbread men stamped out of the same cookie cutter. Even our juvenile delinquents run to the same pattern. They dress alike, they talk alike, they travel in gangs. They're terribly afraid of standing out alone, desperately worried that if they do something on their own they will appear foolish. My own feeling is that the fear of appearing foolish has created more nonentities in American life than I'd care to count. I suppose it is nicer, safer, securer to be just like the man who lives next door. But if you want to live and die like the man next door, why go through all the pain and upset and trouble that life from birth to death entails?

My major interests at college were animal husbandry and dairying, but to graduate, you had to have a certain number of prescribed credits and when our junior year rolled around we looked for courses that would give us credits but wouldn't take much time nor tax our brain power. The students' name for them was "gut" courses. I suppose the newer generation has its name for them and it may be different. In searching about for such a course I found out about a new one called Agricultural Education. I knew nothing about the course except that it was taught by Professor William Hart, a dear old man who was always called "Pop" and who had a reputation for being easy on students. Four of us signed up for it, not knowing what to expect but certainly not expecting much. It turned out to be the single most significant course I ever took in college. The heart of the course was the basis for the county agent or extension service.

Farmers today approach agriculture in such a scientific fashion that we forget that farming in the early part of this century was a fairly haphazard operation. Tillage, tools, farming methods hadn't been changed in thousands of years. The farmer who broke ground in the cradle of civilization in Mesopotamia a couple of thousand years before the birth of Christ wasn't doing a much worse job than the farmers who were breaking ground in New England in 1913. And yet, a great deal had been learned about tillage, about insecticides, about new crops, and so on. The trouble was, this information, which was available in experiment stations and at agriculture colleges like ours, just wasn't being used. Pop Hart said that the only way to get farmers to use it was by demonstration. It wasn't enough just to talk about new tools and methods. You had actually to show them working and prove how superior they were to the old in practice.

Like all college students of all times we spent a good deal of time talking about what we would do once we were out of school. I knew that what I wanted to do was to go back to our farm, but

13

my brothers were there and I knew that those thirty-eight acres couldn't support all of us. I had decided to get a job managing a farm somewhere or working for some farmer. Of the hundreds of occupations we discussed, the two which we decided most vehemently we would have nothing to do with were selling insurance and selling books. Many students detested bookselling because they had tried it and knew what a fruitless occupation it was. Insurance, of course, was for the weakling who could do nothing else. During two summer vacations I trimmed apple trees and did like jobs to escape the effete horrors of selling insurance. And now here I am, in the insurance business.

But in those days insurance was far from my mind. I was interested in the newer, scientific ways of farming. At the time there was a joke going the rounds which, though it was innocent enough, said a good deal that wasn't very flattering about the farmers who told it.

A young college man, so the story went, approached a farmer to extol the virtues of an encyclopedia he was selling. The farmer listened patiently to the young man's long and detailed praise of the set and then said, "What use would I have for them?"

"Why," the young salesman said, "this set of books contains the latest, up-to-date information on farming. If you'll read these books and learn the modern way of farming you'll do twice as well as you do now."

"Heck, son," the farmer said, "I ain't farmin' half as well now as I know how!"

The uncomfortable truth this joke hid was that farmers weren't willing to believe that there were better ways of farming, and the point of Pop Hart's course was that they had to be shown and convinced in a way that would leave no loose ends.

In my senior year, Pop Hart called me in to his office one day and said, "Murray, I'd like you to go down to New London, Connecticut, to apply for a job."

"A job? What sort of job?"

"I don't know much about it," Pop said, "but it sounds like just the thing we've been talking about in class. A group of people are organizing an improvement league down there and they are looking for a young man who knows something about modern farming and wants to help the farmer. Now, you've seemed interested in what we've been talking about. Are you interested?"

"Well, sure," I said, and agreed to go down.

I got up early one morning and took the old Central Vermont Railroad coach down to New London and went up to the Chamber of Commerce building where the applicants for the job were being interviewed. There were seven applicants. One by one each applicant was called into a room where there was a board of men asking questions, and as each man went out and another entered, the rest of us moved our chairs closer to the door to hear what sort of questions were being asked. I hadn't the slightest idea of what they were up to, or what they wanted and, I suspect, neither did anyone else in the room. Since I was the last applicant to arrive, I had a good long time to puzzle my mind as to what they would ask and what I would reply.

The job that had to be filled was that of the county agricultural agent. It was a brand-new job. It was, in fact, the first such job created in New England, and there had been a considerable amount of publicity about it.

I sat there, racking my brain and doing what I could to eavesdrop without much success. The outer room finally emptied except for me. I went as close to the door as I dared and listened. The applicant before me was finally asked by a Mr. Davis, "Well, young man, if you got this job what would you do the first year?"

I can still hear that young man's voice as he answered clearly and honestly, "Well, sir, I think I'd have to spend the first year just riding around and getting acquainted with the farmers in the county."

I shook my head and thought to myself, "Well, maybe that's just what you'd have to do—but that's the wrong answer." And

I knew that when they asked me that question I wasn't going to give that answer. Not if I wanted the job at all, and I suddenly discovered that I did want that job.

My turn came and my mind suddenly bristled with the idea that I could solve the whole farm problem by getting the farmers to go into business for themselves, buying and selling as well as using modern methods of production. I don't know, to this day, why that popped into my head or where it came from. Certainly I had never heard of a cooperative, and if I had, I hadn't the slightest idea of how it worked. It may be that without knowing it, I was indebted to Grandfather for the idea. We used to have long talks every time I came home on holidays. He always wanted to know what I was learning. He read the *New England Homestead* and the *Rural New Yorker* and he had a streak of experimentalism in him. At a time when most farmers were indifferent to soil improvement, he was experimenting with alfalfa. As a matter of fact, he was the first to try alfalfa in Raynham.

When Mr. Davis put the fateful question to me, I can't recall exactly what I said but I talked fast and I talked hard. The substance of what I said had to do with the ways farmers could be taught to help themselves. I outlined enough projects to solve most of the farmers' problems of this century. As I've so often said later, I've been trying to catch up with those suggestions ever since.

One of the suggestions had to do with the fact that the farmer always did better when he distributed his own products than when he merely turned them over to the distributor. I hadn't realized that until I'd analyzed the difference between my grandfather's position and that of his brother, my great-uncle Charles. Uncle Charles was a neighbor of ours and distributed milk in Taunton, which was about four miles away. We sold our milk to him. Uncle Charles was, financially, far better off than my grandfather, a fact that never struck home so hard as when Uncle Charles bought his grandson a new tip cart. Now my cousin and I were both hauling stone, but with a new tip cart he didn't have to unload his stone from the wagon. He could just dump the whole load at the crusher where he pleased. It saved half the work. He had new horses, a new harness, and a new tip cart and should have done twice as well as I did in hauling stone, except for two things. My cousin didn't want to work that hard, and I went to the trouble to train my horses to walk faster so as to get in extra loads.

One day it suddenly dawned on me that the reason Uncle Charles was doing better was that he was going to the city with his milk. As a distributor, he was getting as much as we did for producing the milk, since in those days the retail price was generally just twice the amount the farmer got.

Uncle Charles enjoyed other advantages that I greatly envied. One of them was a manure spreader. It was one of the first in the community. It made the job of spreading manure a lot easier and more pleasant and I was always asking father to go down and borrow it. Although the family relationship was good, father hesitated about borrowing the spreader and so only once in a while would we ever use it.

Early in my life the three things I wanted more than anything else in the world were, an engine to pump water (for I surely did hate the chore of doing a hundred strokes on the pump handle), an indoor toilet (for reasons that ought to be fairly obvious to anyone who has ever had to use a privy), and a manure spreader. Whenever I have confessed this, I have had to admit that the great symbols which moved me were mighty homely objects. And when I stood before that committee headed by Mr. Davis, those symbols were somewhere behind what I said and thought.

I don't know what those men made of me or what I had to say but I must have said something that reached them.

I got the job.

2

THE MERE ANNOUNCEMENT that I had the job of the first paid county agricultural agent caused much interest in two places. The first place was among the regional boosters of the state of Connecticut. It seemed to them to be an infringement upon the good name of Connecticut to have to hire a young man from Massachusetts to improve the farming methods in New London County. The other commotion took place in the faculty of the Massachusetts Agricultural College. I had to start on the job immediately and so had to leave before I had fully completed my senior year. A number of my professors balked and were not going to agree to granting me a degree. Protocol in academic life is rigid, even in an agricultural college, and I wasn't going to be graduated. But Professor Hart, who had encouraged me to go down to New London, and Dr. John McLean, who had been my professor in animal husbandry, stood fast by my side. This job, they said, was an honor. It was a new one and an important one and the faculty of the Massachusetts Agricultural College ought to be glad that a Massachusetts boy was chosen for it. They further maintained that other professors ought to show their pride and trust in me by waiving the requirements. There was a good deal of heated discussion and nay-saying, but in the end those good men won their fight for me and I was graduated and received my Bachelor of Science degree in Agriculture.

Upon assuming my duties as agent for the New London County Improvement League I was put under the supervision of Profes-

sor C. D. Jarvis of the State Agricultural College at Storrs. He
was a fine, easygoing professor.

"What am I going to do, Doc?" I asked him.

Old Professor Jarvis scratched his head. "Well, I don't know.
Can you drive a car?"

"No, not really."

"Well, you'd better learn," he said. "I understand the New
London County Improvement League is going to be given a Ford
by the First National Bank, and you'll need that to get around
with. I don't know where your office will be—but that'll be
found. As soon as you can, go on down there and find out what
the farmers want and go ahead and do it."

I nodded my head and went to work. I learned soon enough
to drive the car. My salary, a hundred dollars a month, came from
three sources, each of which contributed a third: the United
States Department of Agriculture, the State of Connecticut, and
the New London County Improvement League. The New York,
New Haven and Hartford Railroad cleaned out its attic at 82
Shetuckett Street in Norwich and I had an office. Now all I had
to do was to go out and save the farmers.

Well, the first thing I found out was that the farmers didn't
want to be saved. In fact, a lot of them didn't want to talk to me.
They certainly didn't want any young man out of college telling
them how to farm.

The dilemma of many farmers of the area was best expressed
in my visit to the farm of a prominent Grange member in Stonington. Doctor Jarvis had told me to go out and find out what the
farmers wanted and how to improve their source of income.
Stonington, Connecticut, was well named. Before it was taken
over to become a summer resort for wealthy New Yorkers, it was
a county filled with stone. I think it was there that the good Lord
dumped the remainder of stone that He had left over from a
previous distribution in Massachusetts, Vermont, and New Hampshire.

To get to the Grange member's farm I had to open the gate

and go through some scrub oak and pitch pine. I saw some animals running through the brush that I judged to be goats at first. They turned out to be Jersey cows. By the time I got up to the barnyard where the farmer was standing, I guess I felt he was in real trouble because of the stony land. I blurted out to him, all sympathy, "Good heavens, man, what in the world is your source of income?"

"Source of income, young man?" he said. "Hell, we don't have any up here. We live on lack of expense."

And so he did. I think the answer is important since 80 percent of the world's people still must get by on lack of expense.

Now many of the fruit farmers in the area had respect for Doc Jarvis. He had run a number of demonstrations on the pruning and fertilizing of fruit trees, saving trees which in the past many farmers would have cut down for firewood. They had respect for him. But he wasn't the county agent. I was and I was something less than twenty-one years old when I signed my contract of employment. I was clean shaven, gangling, and so young that my joints looked green. I was just aching to save the farmers, but the benighted creatures kept escaping from my grasp. Those who had nothing to do with me were the easiest. There were quite a few who had nothing but bad words to say about me. One in particular was the master of the New London County Pomona Grange. It was public knowledge that he had announced he wasn't going to have any young whippersnapper come out to his farm and tell him how to farm.

I might still be in New London trying to convince farmers they ought to be saved if the army worm had not come out in full force in one part of New London County. The first man who called to report the attack was a little excited. He said worms were eating everything in sight. "What are they?" he wanted to know. "What can you do about it?" He told me that the worst infestation was on the farm of the Grange master. He said he was calling really on his behalf because the Grange master had publicly expressed so little confidence in the county agent idea that he didn't have the nerve to ask me for help himself.

Whatever the Grange master had said about me, it wouldn't be right for him to lose his crops. So I hurried out, although I didn't have the faintest idea what to do. I had never met the army worm. It is a voracious little monster and it moves in waves of thousands, stripping everything clean in its path. Like some kinds of locusts, it shows up only once in many years. This variety was a seventeen-year scourge. I went out and watched armies of these worms—tens of thousands of them—move across a field. I saw something that I wouldn't have believed if I hadn't seen it with my own eyes. I saw a wave of them come to a stone wall, wheel in a military movement, march through an opening in the wall, and enter another field. Worms that smart scared me. I sprinted for a phone and called the State Agricultural College. I described the worm as best I could.

"It's the army worm," came the reply.

"What do you do for it?" I shouted.

"Plow furrows around the uninfested fields and fill the furrows with a mixture of Paris green and bran mash. They'll eat that and die."

I passed the instructions along as quickly as possible. I directed one group to mix the poisoned mash and put another to work plowing furrows around the fields. I got on the phone and called nearby communities and told them what to do. We were at it for a few days but we licked the army worm. And I think I won a small measure of confidence among that group of farmers—although that Grange master never did come over and make friends. But the county agent system in that county, in my opinion, probably owes part of its existence to the army worm. It was the most dramatic demonstration of what the agricultural college could do for the farmer, and demonstration was the magic word in those days.

But farmers are a hard lot to convince and I found that you

had to demonstrate over and over again. In order to make a dramatic visual demonstration I got a farmer at one of the crossroads to let me use an acre of his land near the main road. I top-dressed half of that acre with fertilizer and let the rest shift for itself. When haying time came, the unfertilized grass was a little above the knee; the fertilized grass, of course, came up above the waist. Every time one of the farmers came down the road and saw that tall grass he was a little more willing to believe that maybe the skinny county agent knew what he was up to.

Trying to tell people what to do is sure to keep you from making friends. Being obviously younger than the men you're trying to help is also a drawback.

In those days I was up at dawn and out till dark, hardly ever sitting down at all. Lawrence Dodge, a representative of the United States Department of Agriculture, came down to see how I was doing. Dodge wanted us to go into a hotel and have some lunch but I begged off. I said I didn't have the time. Actually, I didn't have the money to pay for a hotel lunch. Instead, I stopped at a country grocery store, bought a five-cent package of Uneeda Biscuits and a half pound of cheese, and sat my luncheon guest down on the ground under a tree and invited him to dig in. We talked a lot. I presume I did all the talking since that's a habit I haven't changed. Dodge ate the cheese and crackers and listened to me and smiled a bit. He was amused at all the plots and plans I was bursting with. Finally, he said, "Well, Murray, you're having a great time, aren't you?"

"Sure I am." I nodded. "I sure have a lot of fun."

Dodge laughed and then looked at me. "How old are you?"

I had signed my employment contract shortly before I was twenty-one, and I told Dodge so. His face fell and he looked alarmed.

"What's the matter, Larry?" I asked.

"Why, good grief, fellow, you aren't old enough to be an employee of the U.S. Department of Agriculture."

I thought about it for a moment. "Well, no one asked me my age. I didn't volunteer it. Did I do wrong?"

Dodge thought about it for a moment and looked at me. "I'll tell you what to do—you raise a mustache. You're big enough so you could have a mustache and nobody'd ever think to question your age again."

So I raised a mustache. It made no visible difference in the way I was treated, and although I've worn one from time to time ever since, I doubt whether it has done me any good. But I do believe that I have the distinction of growing the only mustache ever decreed by the United States Department of Agriculture.

The threat of war in Europe was growing stronger and in the United States ripples of that threat were being felt by the farmer. Fertilizer prices were starting to go up because munitions factories were buying the chemical components of farm fertilizer. I told the farmers they could save themselves a good deal of money if they would home-mix their chemicals and make their own fertilizer. I showed them how to do it, and we figured it would save them seventeen dollars a ton to mix their own. I went from township to township spreading the gospel of mixing your own and saving money—and what was more, undercutting the prices of the local fertilizer company.

I was rooming at the time at the home of the secretary of the Chamber of Commerce, Mr. Elmer Jewett, who was also the manager of the American Thermos Bottle Company in Norwich. His wife was a great cook and was especially good at making apple pies. She had bet me that I couldn't get the farmers of every township to order a carload of fertilizer and had staked one of her wonderful apple pies—I suppose as a sort of friendly incentive.

I had found a fertilizer company that hadn't been doing much business in Connecticut and was willing to sell chemicals to others. I signed a contract with them to sell me potash at forty-eight dollars a ton. I was determined to get farmers in each township to buy a carload. Well, the president of the local fertilizer company started following me about like a beagle, telling the farmers that I didn't know what I was talking about. He kept telling them that since the company itself had to pay seventy dollars a ton for potash, and since that price was a special one for bulk purchases, it was simple common sense that farmers themselves could not do any better. But when the first carload of potash came in and we paid no more than forty-eight dollars a ton, the news spread over Connecticut like a fire before the wind. It wasn't long before I was appearing before farm groups all over the state and as a result each county soon had an improvement league. I won my bet and the apple pie. And my last meeting took place after the spring rains had come and my new Ford was mired in the mud. It took a yoke of oxen to haul it three miles out of the mud. I presume present-day county agents have their own different problems and rewards, but those were mine and I got a kick out of them.

I could not forget my great uncle Charles's success as a private milk distributor, and it was this that started me talking about setting up a milk-distributing plant that would be owned by the farmers who produced the milk. A Mr. Rogers, a local newspaperman who owned a dairy herd, thought it was a good idea and encouraged me. It was he who brought Dr. Knott, a milk specialist, from New York. Dr. Knott had made a study of milk plants from the standpoint of hygiene, and he too told me that I had hit on a good idea and to stick with it. Mr. C. D. Whitman was the head of the New London County Improvement League. He had been superintendent of the Ferguson estate on Fisher's Island, a country schoolteacher, a farmer, and a milkman as well. He was as interested in the milk-plant idea as I was and encouraged and helped me all he could. I was told to set up a cow-testing association, and Karl Musser, who later became secretary of the American Guernsey Breeders Association, was sent into New London County from Washington to help me.

There was just one great trouble with the scheme—the farmers didn't want their cows tested, nor did they want to join the association. Karl Musser and I trudged from farm to farm, trying to convince farmers they ought to join and have their cows tested. We made pests of ourselves and feelings ran high. They ran so high, in fact, that the nearest I've ever come to being chased off a farm at the point of a pitchfork arose over the cow-testing association. But one association finally did get organized. In later years, when I was working for the Ohio Farm Bureau and pushing farmers to set up their own machinery to buy and sell and perform other services, the Extension Service of Ohio State University kept telling me that I was being too aggressive in these matters—that I was exceeding the limits of the Extension Service. I was told that the function of the Extension Service was only to find out what the farmers wanted done and to do it for them— not to insist upon their doing something they didn't want to do. I countered their arguments by recalling the days when Karl Musser and I had been instructed by the United States Department of Agriculture to press for a cow-testing association.

We tried to set up a farm management club to try to get farmers to keep records, but that was a hard one to swallow. Farmers have a congenital hatred of paper work and, while they must do a good deal of it now, in those days they would have nothing to do with it. Whatever else I was doing, I constantly propagandized for the milk plant. It was at this point that I got a call from Washington informing me that someone was being sent out to see me.

That warm spring day, as Lawrence Dodge and I sat under the tree and had our country grocery lunch of biscuits and cheese, I knew that he had been sent for some specific reason. After a long while, he turned to me and said, "Murray, you've got to stop doing some of the things you're doing."

"What do you mean?" I asked, never more surprised in my life and wondering whether he was referring to one thing I had done, or everything.

"Well, you're going too far. You've gotten these guys to buy fertilizer in carload lots, you've been talking to them about setting up a milk plant. That stuff's out. You better just stick to telling the farmer how to grow two blades of grass where one grew before. You can tell him how and why and when to spray his apple trees, and the cow-testing association is okay, but you lay off those economic things."

My temper began to rise and I started to protest. "Why, that's what the farmers wanted. My job was to do what they wanted. They wanted cheaper prices for their fertilizer and I got it for them. They want better prices for their milk and I'm going to try and get it for them with the milk plant."

Dodge's voice got a lot sharper. "I said you've got to junk those things and I mean it."

We argued for a few moments and I could see Larry Dodge's color was changing. Finally he said, "Now, look, don't argue with me. You've got to quit it and that's final."

I was so furious I didn't trust myself to go on talking. I mulled over the matter for a full week. The first weekend I could get away, I cranked up the Ford and drove up to Amherst to consult old Pop Hart. I went to see him because one of the last things he said to me before I went down to New London was: "You'll run into a lot of problems, Murray—but you've got your books with you. There will always be somebody to tell you what to do if you get stuck. And if you ever get into trouble, come back and see me."

I came back and told Pop my troubles, feeling deeply aggrieved. "What's going on down there?" I asked him. "You turned me loose to do what the farmers want, I start to do it, and now they tell me I can't."

He laughed and put his hand on my shoulder. "Well, now, look. You're just beginning to run into a little reaction. You remember that in physics there's a law which states that for every action there's a reaction. You've stepped on somebody's toes and they've hollered 'ouch' to the U.S. Department of Agriculture. That's why they sent that fellow down to see you to tell you to quit. Well, you do as they say and be a good boy. But don't give up your ideas. Because you're right. Keep on using your head and we'll find some way of helping you to do what you ought to be doing."

Not long after, I got a letter from Pop written on the letterhead of the Plymouth County Trust Company in Brockton, Massachusetts. The bank in Brockton wanted to set up an agricultural department and wanted to hire a full-time agent. Pop Hart told me in his letter that he thought I ought to go up to Brockton and look the proposition over carefully. If he thought that much of it, I knew I would take the job if it was offered to me.

There was another inducement for taking that job that Pop Hart hadn't considered but which sprang into my mind the moment I saw the name Brockton. Brockton wasn't far from Easton, and that was where Miss Anne Hurst lived.

Anne and I will be celebrating our forty-fifth wedding anniversary shortly after publication of this book, so I want to pause to detail somewhat the manner of our courtship. I think now would be a good time to say those things about Anne that I may have neglected in the course of a busy, perhaps too busy, life to mention.

Like most great events, our courtship had a small beginning. Anne, whose memory is better than my own, recalls that her mother and mine knew one another through a mutual friend who also happened to be one of Anne's relatives. Anne's recollection is that my mother came to call upon her mother and brought me along. I was eight or nine years old and, in the manner of eight- or nine-year-olds, a poor visitor to have at a social call between ladies. I wouldn't enter the house but insisted upon walking back and forth on the stone wall out front. This sort of skylarking was intended, I suppose, to show my indifference for the little girl who lived within as well as to demonstrate my masculine powers of balance, bravery, and brains. Anne recalls the incident but she makes no comment on her feelings. I presume she was not much impressed. My older brother was in high school with Anne's sister

Rhoda, and those two went out together once or twice. Family legend has it that I once inquired after Rhoda's sister and announced that this was the girl I would one day marry. I claim no powers of clairvoyance or prophecy.

When the time came for me to attend high school I chose to go to the school in North Easton. It was closer home than the one in Taunton and in bad weather I could stay overnight with my grandmother. It also enabled me to see Anne frequently enough to confirm my opinion that she was the best-looking girl in the class. Since I was going to attend college, the principal of the high school, Mr. Thayer, encouraged me, along with the other two prospective college students, to spend as much time as possible in the laboratory in order to gain an enrichment of the work we were getting in the classroom. The high schools in our area were not accredited and graduates of such high schools had to take college entrance examinations. It was to help us to pass those college entrance examinations that Mr. Thayer encouraged us to work in the laboratory, although no teacher was provided. The absence of a teacher was too much temptation for Carlton Haywood, one of the boys who was something of a cut-up anyway, and after several sessions I began to see that my education wasn't getting much enrichment. The only advancement I could see had to do with Carlton's sense of humor.

Anne wasn't taking the college course, and opportunities to see her in school were limited. To make them less limited, I took typewriting and gave up enrichment in the laboratory. Anne's high-ranking scholastic ability in the commercial course was the topic of conversation at my grandmother's house, principally because Anne's commercial teacher boarded there. I suppose, like the eight-year-old who had to walk a stone wall waving his arms and his ego, I simply had to prove to the prettiest girl I'd ever seen that I was better than she. And so I grimly tackled the business of being the best typist in class. I managed, in some of the speed tests, to come out Number One and so proved the point of superiority. After these vast outbursts of energy on my part, Anne simply went on being the best in the class.

Carlton Haywood had been seeing Anne's best friend, Doris Morse, with some regularity but—to Carlton's annoyance—not without having Anne tag along. Social activities for young people in those days centered about the church, and since there was no church in my home community that my family attended regularly, I was left out of most social activities. Carlton, who was aware of this, invited me one day to come along to a church social. I don't think Carlton's motives were purely humane. I think he simply wanted to pry Anne loose from Doris and thought I would do.

The first night Anne and I went out we very properly walked on opposite sides of the road. That same distance held for the next two or three nights we went out together. I used to go to church on Sundays but Anne wouldn't let me walk her home. Visiting a girl on Sundays was almost completely out of the question unless you were pretty serious. If young people reading this account of a small-town courtship are astonished, I should remind them that everything went slower in those days. It was not until Anne and I had been going together for four years or better that we dared stay up until midnight to see the New Year in. Normally it was unheard of to stay with a young lady longer than ten o'clock. Staying up until midnight to see the New Year in struck us both as being almost wicked. I think I had been seeing and writing to Anne for nearly six years before I kissed her, and at that she objected. Well, now, I am not saying that I was the slowest swain in Massachusetts, but I certainly wasn't anywhere near the fastest. Since Anne and I have been happily married for nearly forty-five years I can't say that a slow beginning hampered our happiness much. I wish young people would think a little longer about marriage than they do. I am not advocating that a young man wait six years before he kisses a likely-looking girl, but it might be better for both of them if the time were closer to six years than six minutes.

The chance to go to Brockton was attractive, then, for one important reason—it gave me a chance to see Anne. That chance flowered into a decision on our part to marry, and the first check

I got from the Brockton bank I spent completely on an engagement ring.

The president of the Brockton bank was a fine, farsighted man named C. P. Holland. I learned later that he became interested in establishing an agriculture department because he felt something was wrong with agriculture. Just what was wrong, he wasn't quite sure. In any case, the farmer's situation was, at the time, a matter of considerable discussion. So much discussion that the federal government had established a special committee called the Country Life Commission. I can recall that in my junior year at the Massachusetts Agricultural College our president had been appointed to that commission. The whole student body turned out to see him off when the commission went to Europe as part of its investigation of farm life. Myron Herrick, who was later to be my employer at the Cleveland Society for Savings, was also involved with the work of that commission as the American ambassador to France.

My first interview with Mr. Holland after I got the job gave me a new-found sense of power. He said, "Now, young man, you just do whatever you think ought to be done around here." I just beamed over that invitation. Whenever I wanted to do anything in Connecticut, it cost money. Since the farmers had no money, I rarely was able to do what I wanted. Now, I thought, I've got a real chance. The bank's got money to lend. They bought me a new Ford. I was mighty proud of that Ford. It was the first Ford in Brockton with demountable rims and a self-starter. I was able to live with Grandmother Andrews, close enough to see Anne regularly, and I had this shiny new Ford and worked for a bank. I generally considered myself a very lucky young man.

One of the first projects I undertook was the establishment of a pig club. George Farley, who was superintendent of schools for Brockton, worked with me on this, I think the first such pig club in New England. The idea was simple. The bank bought feeder pigs that children were to buy on money borrowed from the bank. The children were to raise the pigs, sell them, and repay the bank from the proceeds. The pig club motives were multiple: to provide the market with more pigs; to teach the school children care of animals and the virtues of thrift; and to provide the bank with the benefits of a neatly handled public relations stunt.

It would seem that an idea as clear and simple as that should have been easy to execute but for some reason or another it brought on a few dozen headaches, most of which I've forgotten over the years. They seemed terribly important at the time.

After much scouring of the country, a suitable load of feeder pigs was found. The whole squealing load, carried in a truck and a wagon, was photographed in front of the bank, after which the pigs were driven to the rear of the Baptist Church where scores of children were lined up for the delivery.

The whole affair had been well publicized and there was a festive air to the proceedings. Most of the prospective pig farm-ers were little boys who had brought baby carriages, wheelbar-rows, and sacks to take their pigs away. Right in the midst of the proceedings a grand, gleaming Pierce-Arrow limousine drove up. The whole crowd of children and adults gaped as a liveried chauffeur dismounted, circled the limousine, and opened the door. A little towheaded girl with a pink ribbon in her hair, wearing a little blue coat, got out and, accompanied by the chauffeur, stepped up, solemnly signed a note to the bank, and took title to her little pig. The chauffeur carried the animal to the Pierce-Arrow as the little girl, as prim and proper and ladylike as a grand duchess, preceded him. He put her into the car and started to hand her the pig. The newspapermen and photographers there clicked away, took notes, fired questions, and the pig and the little girl disappeared with the limousine. The picture of the pig that rode away in a Pierce-Arrow limousine was published na-tionally and put our little bank on the map.

While pig clubs were fun, I was interested in the farmers in the area and so was Mr. Holland. This was, after all, my own country and I knew it pretty well. What was more, I knew its problems. One of its problems had to do with dairy cows.

31

In those days, farmers didn't borrow much from banks when they wanted dairy cows. They would instead, go to the cow dealers, borrow money from them, buy cows, and sometimes give mortgages on their farms. And the quality of the cows that the dealers offered for sale was generally poor. They were culled cows out of Maine, New Hampshire, and Vermont. I told Mr. Holland that what farmers really needed was better cows. He looked at me and said, "Well, let's find out if we can get them something better than what the old cow dealers have been selling them."

The plan we worked out called for farmers to pay one third of the purchase price of the cow in cash and then later pay the balance out of the proceeds from the sale of the cow's milk. To my knowledge, this was the first such plan offered farmers by a bank anywhere in the country.

The old cow dealers were annoyed. We were invading their bailiwick. There was a good deal of muttering on their part but they bided their time, expecting us to fall flat on our faces.

We brought two or three carloads of cows down from Vermont. Though they were pretty wild, they were good producers and you can still, to this day, see the effect they had on dairy herds. Then someone tipped me off to go out to New York and see Dorr MacLaury, a Scotsman whose kin-folk were among the biggest cow dealers in Oneonta, New York. After I met MacLaury I knew here was a man to trust. I had so much faith in MacLaury that if he said a cow would give ten thousand pounds of milk I not only believed it, I was willing to guarantee it. I was cautious enough at first and wrote to the magazine that every dairy farmer read—*Hoard's Dairyman*. I told them what I had done and asked them if I ought to guarantee that each cow would give ten thousand pounds of milk. The editor replied that he would hesitate to give such a guarantee since it was highly unlikely. But there was something so rough and honest and convincing about Dorr MacLaury that I took the gamble. In the ads we used I guaranteed that each and every cow would give ten thousand pounds of milk. What I should have added to that guarantee was the little phrase, "if you feed them right."

That guarantee raised more trouble than I care to remember. What happened, of course, was that some of those wily old cow dealers, who had been waiting for us to put our foot in our mouth, bought a couple of those cows, did not feed them right, and then paraded the dried-out, sickly beasts before other farmers with a good deal of sneering at our guarantee. A few old farmers took pity on me and tried to bail me out. There was one little old dried-up New Englander, named Mr. Witcher, who had bought four or five of Dorr MacLaury's cows. He was a good cowman and did so well with what he bought that whenever I got a complaint about our cows I'd always retort, "Why, you go to see Mr. Witcher and see what he's done with those cows."

Despite the pressures I was under, I was spending as much time with Anne as I could, now that we were engaged. On October 9, 1915, we were finally married. We went for our honeymoon to Rangeley Lakes in Maine, a place to which we often return to this day. Anne's complaint was that I worried more about cows and dairy problems on our honeymoon than I did about her. We stayed about a week and a half, which was about all the time I thought I could possibly spare. Anne and I returned and moved into my grandmother's home. Grandmother moved upstairs and left the newlyweds to start their life downstairs. I plunged right back into the business I had left ten days before.

I was being harried on all sides, especially by the old cow dealers. What they had to say stung me a bit, perhaps more than I was willing to admit, but an unlikely cow named Molly shut them up once and for all.

William N. Howard, a businessman and farmer in North Easton, came to me one day and said, "Murray, the next time you go to New York, you buy me two of the best cows you can find. I don't care what you pay for them."

When I next saw Dorr MacLaury I told him what Mr. Howard

wanted and he said he had two cows for me. They would cost two hundred dollars apiece. That was a lot of money in those days for a grade cow. One of them was a perfect dairy type and I could see her merits at once, but the other cow absolutely startled me. She looked like an old ox, and she had nothing of the conformation I had been taught in school a dairy cow should have. When I protested, Dorr held up his hand. "Now, she's only a three-year-old, Murray, but if Mr. Howard takes care of her she'll surprise you. She has a great record as a two-year-old."

I shook my head dubiously. "Dorr, I've got a lot of faith in you and if you say she's all right I'll take your word for it, but—"

"But what?" MacLaury asked, eying me carefully.

"If that cow gives milk, I'd be willing to try and jump over the moon."

MacLaury grinned. "If she don't surprise you, you don't owe me anything. Is that fair enough?"

I agreed it was and took the cows home.

The purchase of those two cows had been well publicized. Mr. Howard was a prominent citizen, and it was well known that he was paying top prices. The day I delivered those two cows to him, dozens of people showed up to see them. I knew that everyone would think the white cow was worth the money we spent on her, but I worried about that odd-looking beast, Molly. The old cow dealers were out to see what I had bought, and there was a good deal of snickering and whispering when they saw her. Mr. Howard took me aside and said, "Murray, that white cow is all right, but why in the world did you ever bring that other one home?"

I swallowed hard and said, "Because Dorr MacLaury said she would surprise us." Howard looked at me oddly. "He said we wouldn't owe him anything if she didn't," I added lamely, and wondered why I had ever let MacLaury talk me into it.

Mr. Howard had a student of the agriculture college, a "shorthorn," working for him, and I made a deal with that boy to give those two animals extraordinary care. I wanted them cared for

as no two cows had ever been cared for before. I anxiously
waited to see what would happen.

The day finally came when Molly had a calf. The first few
days Molly didn't do too well, but then, after the fifth day, she
started to really pour it out. Where it came from is still a mystery
to me since she had almost no udder and none of the conformation all the experts said a cow ought to have. But she gave milk.
She gave more milk each day until finally she was giving a hundred pounds of milk a day. She kept that up for a hundred days
and broke every record for a grade cow in that territory. Dozens
of farmers came to see her milked and my reputation as a judge of
cows was maintained.

Once that news got about, the orders started to flood us, and it
little mattered what the old cow dealers had to say. Old Molly
just drowned them in milk.

One of the reasons the cows we bought had trouble giving
milk was that I had bought them on New York State farms, where
they had fed in fields of clover that grew up to their bellies, and
then had brought them to the stony, lightly grassed farms of
Massachusetts. In our country we didn't have enough land to raise
all the hay that was needed. Since cows do best on feed to which
they are accustomed, I got some feed that had been mixed by
Dorr MacLaury, with the help of feed experts at Cornell University, and put it in the middle of the car on which the cows
were shipped. Technically, we weren't allowed to do that under
the regulations governing railway freight, but my wife's cousin
was the station agent and he discreetly looked the other way. The
cows did so well on this feed that before long I started bringing
in carload lots of that special mixture and selling it to the farmers. I wanted them to buy it not to make a profit for the bank,
but to care for those cows on which the bank had loaned money.
And there I stepped on someone's toes and he said "ouch" in a
loud voice.

One day, Mr. Holland came up to my office, flushed and angry,
and said to me, "Well, we had a fight in the board today."

"What about?" I asked.

"About you," he added, looking at me carefully.

"Well, good Lord, what have I done?"

"That feed of yours is selling too well to suit Mr. Hall." E. C. Hall was one of the bank's largest stockholders, and he owned a wholesale grocery in town. I hadn't stopped to think that our sales of feed would cut into his business, but they undoubtedly had.

"What does Mr. Hall want me to do?"

"He doesn't want you to do anything. He wants me to fire you," Holland snapped.

I hesitated a moment, but before I could ask the question, Holland said, "I told him that you were doing what you were hired to do. I told him he could buy my stock or I would buy his, but I wasn't going to fire you for doing something that needed doing."

I accepted Mr. Holland's reassurance gratefully but still felt uneasy. Why was it that whenever I turned around I stepped on someone's toes? I sensed that this was but the beginning of my latest trouble. Now that there was opposition to me so close to home—in the bank itself—I had the feeling that I would be stopped just as I had been down in New London.

As always when I was troubled, I thought of old Pop Hart and I went up to see him again at Amherst. "My gosh, am I going to run into this sort of thing all the time? Have I got this to look forward to all of my life?"

Pop looked at me for a long moment. "Murray, just so long as you're doing something a little different from the way in which it's always been done you're going to find some sort of opposition. The best evidence you are doing something worth while is this *kind* of opposition. Now, you can go ahead doing something and getting into this kind of trouble or you can stop and just coast. But I don't think you're the kind that will stop. If that's your nature, then reconcile yourself to it. Don't get discouraged. This is the sort of competition that goes on all the time, and you've got to learn to handle it."

While Pop Hart's words made good sense and gave me courage, I don't think I could have gone on very long without the support of C. P. Holland.

Holland was a remarkable man in many ways. He was a big man in a little bank, and I always thought that if he had ever moved into a big bank he would have been a leading figure in American banking. Holland had courage and warmth and a strong sense of community responsibility in a time when a sense of community responsibility was rare in bankers. Shortly after I joined the bank, Holland and I attended a meeting of bankers who were interested in agricultural development. The topic of the meeting, worded in far more roundabout language, was whether it was safe to lend money to farmers. The question was important in those days because banks rarely loaned money to farmers, and when they did it was on a short-term basis. They gave mortgages which ran only a year, and farmers were reluctant to take them. Banks, skittish about farmers and the vagaries of farming, were apt to consider farmers poor risks.

During the course of the discussion, one banker rose to say, "I think it's good business to lend money to farmers. Our bank's been lending them money for twenty-six years and we've never lost a cent."

When Holland heard that, his eyes flashed and he came to his feet with the speed of a cat. "You're a damned poor banker, in my opinion!"

The man who had just spoken blinked in surprise and everyone turned to look at Holland. "What do you mean by that remark?" he asked, in a distinctly shocked and angry voice.

"If you've been lending farmers money for twenty-six years without losing a cent in the process, you haven't ever really taken a risk on a man!"

That man turned red with rage and I know he never forgot

Holland's remark. Eventually he found a way to make Holland pay. Some time later he was made bank commissioner of the state and when the banks got into trouble in the twenties, he remembered Holland, and the first bank he took out after was the little Brockton bank. Holland's bank eventually closed its doors, and I often tell myself that happened because one man had courage and another man bore a grudge against him for it.

Holland had the instincts of a teacher and a good father. He tried to help young fellows along, and I've seldom heard advice as good as that which Holland gave me. He was a stickler for personal appearance. "Murray," he once told me, "one of the first things to do is to take care of what you've got. You can shine your shoes even if there are holes in their soles. You can have pressed pants even if they're patched. You can have a clean shirt even though the cuffs are frayed. And when you're before the public you want to put on the best personal appearance you can."

His advice on business, I still consider the most pungent, the most complete, the most remarkable I've ever received. I repeated his advice once to a group of the faculty at the Harvard Business School, and one of the professors remarked that books have been written which don't say as much. I agree.

Holland's advice was this: (1) If you're going to do a big business you've got to do it through people. You can't do it all by yourself. If you try to do everything yourself, then you're limited to what one person can do and that isn't very much. (2) Help make policy. (3) Be where there's trouble. (4) Don't do anything yourself you can get somebody else to do. (5) When you see some little thing, however insignificant, and you don't like the looks of it, stop right there and go right to the bottom of it, because generally that'll show up some bigger things. In short, look for little red flags.

I've been trying to follow C. P. Holland's advice ever since he gave it to me.

3

THERE'S A STORY about a little fellow who lived in a tiny, isolated village in Czarist Russia. He was fascinated by numbers. He wasn't educated; he just seemed to have a head for numbers. One day he stumbled on a brilliant idea. He grew so excited that he ran about the village trying to tell people what he had discovered, but no one really understood what he was talking about. Then he heard that a famous mathematician was going to visit Russia and lecture at the university. The little man announced that he was going to see the distinguished visitor. He had discovered something so great he could not keep it to himself.

At the university he spied the distinguished mathematician standing in a corridor surrounded by members of the faculty. "Please, please, let me speak to the professor!" he cried. "I have something to tell him that will change the world!" At this point people became alarmed and they started to carry the little man off. The distinguished mathematician told them to wait. He would hear the fellow out. So the little man hurriedly began to explain his theory and the mathematician listened attentively, as did the other Russian professors. The little man finally finished, his face beaming with pride and joy, and waited to be congratulated.

"But isn't that merely calculus he's talking about?" one of the professors remarked with some disdain.

"What is calculus?" the villager asked.

"This great discovery of yours," the professor said haughtily, "was developed many years ago."

The distinguished mathematician regarded the bewildered little man with a kindly smile. "You are, sir, a great mathematician. You have reinvented calculus."

The story has always interested me because I learned years later how that little fellow felt. He had fought his way through to a mathematical development that had existed for years before him. I had to fight my way through to an economic development that had existed for years before I ever heard of it. I knew nothing about cooperatives, yet when I decided we ought to have a milk plant in Brockton, I began duplicating the long struggle which thousands of cooperatives had undergone. Of course I didn't have the excuse the little fellow had. I wasn't cut off from the civilized world. But the truth was, cooperatives were then little known in the United States (although they were an old story in Europe). They were so little known that even years later, when E. R. Bowen, executive secretary of the Cooperative League of the U.S.A., went to the library in the town where the League president had been educated and asked the librarian for what literature she had on consumer cooperatives, she gave him a stack of books on consumption, which used to be the old medical term for tuberculosis.

The Rochdale flannel weavers of England started the development of cooperatives. Those pioneers in that English city laid down the principles on which a cooperative ought to be run, the simple rules of: open membership; one man—one vote; limited interest on share capital (to discourage speculation); and patronage dividends (refunds of net earnings to patrons in proportion to their patronage). And yet when we were seeking to operate a milk plant cooperatively, we found no one to tell us how to run it so that it benefited everyone without giving any one man or combination of men a chance to control it for their own selfish use. We had to reinvent the cooperative in the same way that little mathematician of the story had to reinvent calculus.

I got sixty farmers to agree to build their own milk-processing plant. The bank agreed to finance the plant on the same basis it had financed the cows—one-third in cash and two-thirds out of the sale of the milk from the plant.

Horace Flagg, who was the attorney for the bank, was a Harvard graduate and he and I got together to see how we could organize the plant without letting anyone but the producers control it. I went up to Amherst to find out and Flagg went to Harvard, but neither of us got any satisfaction at either place—this despite the fact that the Rochdale principles were there all the time for us to use. We simply did not know they existed, and there was no one to tell us. We finally decided the way to organize the plant was to require that each farmer buy a share of stock in the milk company for every two eight-and-one-half quart cans of milk he produced. If he contributed more than seventeen quarts of milk he would have to buy more shares, and if he contributed less he would be required to sell his shares back to the corporation. But we still hadn't stumbled onto the principle of giving each shareholder just one vote, no matter how many shares he held.

The main milk distributor in Brockton was a man named Weston Manley. The dairy farmers disliked Manley more than anyone else in the territory. It was their claim that he never paid them enough for their milk.

Well, we had to know something about the costs of processing and distributing milk and Manley certainly wasn't going to tell us about it. Nor would any other milk distributor in the immediate vicinity.

Holland called me into his office and said, "You find out how much it really costs to distribute milk so we'll know how to finance this plant."

I traveled to Syracuse, New York, to remove myself from the hostile atmosphere of Massachusetts, but evidently the news traveled fast for I had no sooner settled myself in the hotel there than a man telephoned my room and introduced himself as Loton Horton, president of Sheffield Farms, a subsidiary of National Dairy Products Corporation. He said he wanted to speak to me.

I went downstairs and probably the first question he asked me was, "What are you up to, Mr. Lincoln?"

The question was asked so aggressively that I prepared myself to be as short-spoken as my questioner. "What do you mean?"

"I understand you're around here telling the farmers that they can save a lot of money if they set up their own milk plants. You know better than that. And if you don't, you ought to."

"Well, mister, that's none of your business. It's the farmers who have to decide it."

"You aren't going to make any money in it," he warned. "Take my advice and stop now."

I was so irritated with his manner that I left him there and then. To this day I don't know who told him who I was and why I was in Syracuse. I presume the word went out among the old-line milk processers that there was a young fellow talking about farmers processing and selling their own milk to the consumer, and they probably thought it a dangerous and wicked idea. I don't recall if I ever did learn anything in Syracuse but eventually, down in New Jersey, a little German-American milk dealer opened his books and showed me that it cost him about three cents a quart to collect, process, and distribute milk. On that basis farmers could receive nine cents a quart and the cost to the consumer would be twelve cents.

I returned to Brockton, put my figures before Mr. Holland, and the whole matter went up before our board of farmers and the bank. Weston Manley, the principal milk dealer in Brockton, was the archvillain in the milk drama that now started to shape up. His brother, a truly delightful man, was one of those who was working with me, and when the proposition came before the board, he said to me, "Murray, you're going up against one of the meanest men in the country. I tell you that honestly, even if he is my brother. I'll help you out as much as I can, but take fair warning: Watch out for him—don't trust him an inch."

I had that conversation in mind the day I went to visit Weston Manley to ask him if he would sell us his milk plant. His answer was short and simple, "Sure, if you'll pay sixty thousand dollars."

"Well, can we have an appraisal made of the property?"

"Sure, go ahead," he said with a look that was more sneer than smile. If he had had a long black mustache he would have twirled the ends.

We hired a couple of bright young fellows, one of whom was an M.I.T. graduate, to appraise the building, the bottling machinery, and other equipment. We got a sharp horse dealer to appraise the animals and the wagons. The whole appraisal came to twenty-nine thousand dollars. We decided to offer thirty thousand.

William N. Howard, whose cow Molly had saved my cow-buying project, was now chairman of our farmers' committee. He went with me to see Manley with the offer, and I guess we were both nervous and edgy. In my eyes thirty thousand dollars was an awful lot of money. When I made the offer, I watched Manley very closely, almost hoping he'd turn it down. Manley did pale slightly when he heard the figure. He swallowed. Then, to my astonishment, he nodded and said, "Well, I accept."

The corporation was formed quickly. Howard was made president and I was made secretary of the milk plant. Our first problem was to find a general manager to supervise the place. And the greatest shock I received was to discover that the farmers wanted Weston Manley to run the place.

"Good grief!" I exploded to them. "It wasn't more than a few weeks ago that you told me you detested that man worse than anything in the world."

"Yes, we did," the farmers told me, "but we figure if he was sharp enough to get all he could out of us, he'll get all he can out of others—but this time he'll be doing it for us."

What bothered me was the recollection of the remarks his brother had made. "Watch out for him—don't trust him an inch." But this was what those farmers wanted and no amount of argument or persuasion would change their minds. I told Mr. Howard that I thought they were making a mistake but they no more listened to him than they did to me and so we had to hire Weston Manley.

It became fairly obvious to me afterward why Manley had accepted an offer so low. It was his hope to wreck our corporation and then buy the whole shooting match back at less than the amount we'd paid him. He had gone into the scheme to show me up and to discourage farmers from ever getting such uppity notions again.

Shortly after Manley was hired, our drivers went out on strike and the newspaper in town, *The Brockton Enterprise,* blossomed out with the blackest, biggest headlines I'd ever seen, accusing me of conspiring with the farmers to raise the price of milk and so starve little babies. The newspaper and the Field Shoe Company were owned by Fred Field, who had a big farm of his own and was also a milk dealer and the president of a competing bank. He hadn't been quite happy about other things I'd done in the past but had kept quiet about his feelings until the strike came along. I was horrified by this public criticism. It was something I'd never met with before. I had had pieces written about me in the press and magazines when I was county agent and had run the pig club, and I couldn't have asked for fairer or more favorable public attention. Individuals grumbled, of course, but I had never been attacked in the public prints. Now, suddenly, I was a depraved monster out to starve babies to death by pricing milk out of the reach of their parents. It was a frightening experience. We got the strike settled and our wagons back delivering, but the newspaper articles had done their damage. Our milk business dropped down to one-third. To hide the bad state of our affairs, we filled up our wagons with empty cases.

While I was embroiled in the problems of the milk plant, my life and career were about to be influenced by an important public figure. Myron T. Herrick, who was twice ambassador to France and president of the Cleveland Society for Savings, had been requested by President Woodrow Wilson to gather data on rural life in Europe as a member of the Country Life Commission. As a result of the Commission's survey, Herrick wrote an article entitled "Pork and Beans" in which he referred to the work we were doing in the Plymouth County Trust Company. Mr. Holland wrote to Herrick thanking him for his kind words. Herrick replied, saying that the more he thought about helping farmers to help themselves the more he felt that his bank ought to be doing something similar in Ohio. Did Mr. Holland know anybody he could recommend to them?

Holland came to me one day and showed me the correspondence with Herrick. "Murray, you're doing fine work here and I think the milk plant is going to straighten itself out soon, and I'd hate to lose you—but in your own interest I think you ought to go out to Cleveland and look into this proposition. I'm going to write Herrick and recommend you."

This concern for others was typical of Holland, and I couldn't deny that I was interested in moving into a larger area.

In 1917 I left Brockton and went to Cleveland.

4

THE CLEVELAND SOCIETY FOR SAVINGS was an immense old bank, with deposits of seventy million dollars, headed by a man who was internationally famous, the confidant of Presidents. It was the largest savings bank between Chicago and Philadelphia, and it enjoyed the implicit trust of all the immigrants who had flocked to Cleveland and its outlying areas. It had a reputation for stability, earned during the years when bank panics had sent a great many other banks under. Its board of directors had seven millionaires on it. Its halls were lavishly finished in marble, and there was a quiet, austere, and powerful air everywhere in it. The board room was most impressive, with carved oak tables and silk tapestries for wall coverings. I was twenty-six years old and very much of a country cousin. When I was invited in to meet the directors I wore my best suit and tried to carry myself with proper decorum. If there was anything that place demanded, it was decorum.

The faces that greeted me in the board room were faces of men who were wealthy and powerful and accustomed to having what they wanted without much argument. I remember being especially impressed by one man, a handsome, dignified fellow with a neatly pressed blue suit, wearing a high stand-up collar and a blue tie. He had a magnificent mustache which was carefully combed. Not a hair was out of place. If ever I saw a human being in full and absolute control of every molecule of his being it was that man—who I later found out was Mr. John Dexter, the secretary-treasurer.

The president, Mr. Herrick, invited me to sit down and tell the board just what sort of work I'd been doing for the Plymouth County Trust Company in Brockton. I started from the beginning, with the pig club, and then went on to describe what we had done with feed and with cows. Their faces, at first, were hard and solemn. But as I went on I began to see a smile here and there and now and then I heard a chuckle. I took heart at that, assuming that it was a sign that I was succeeding. The smiles grew broader and the chuckles longer and deeper and fairly soon they were all, with one exception, enjoying themselves. Finally, Mr. Sam Scovil, who was the president of the Cleveland Electric Illuminating Company, laughed out loud and said, "Governor, I move we set up a cow and pig department." (Everybody who knew him apparently called Mr. Herrick "governor"; he'd been governor of Ohio from 1904 to 1906.) With that there was an outburst of laughter from everyone about the table—everyone with the exception of the tall, handsome, well-groomed, dignified secretary-treasurer, Mr. John Dexter. He fixed me with sober and somewhat cold eyes. I knew then that whatever I had accomplished with the rest of them, he had no particular use for me. In the midst of all this laughter and joking over the cow and pig department, the motion was adopted and I was hired as agricultural representative for the Cleveland Society for Savings.

Anne and I moved with our baby daughter to Cleveland. The job didn't pay very much and costs were going up. I had made a bad investment a year earlier and was paying off my debt on that. I don't want to convey the impression that I was much of an investor in those days. In fact, it was only one of the two investments I'd made up to this time. My first investment was a good one, and forty-five years later it is still paying good dividends. It was an investment in a wedding license. The bad investment, I'm sorry to say, came as a result of advice from a good banker.

One day about a year after I'd become an agent for the Plymouth County Trust Company, Mr. Holland called me up and told me that a group of bankers and businessmen in Brockton and Boston were going in on a new venture to recapitalize a company known as the Atlantic Coast Fisheries. They were the principal suppliers of fish for the Fulton Fish Market in New York and the Faneuil Hall Market in Boston. The original company had evidently done extremely well. A hundred-dollar investment in the company had paid $1250 in dividends and the current stock was worth $3750 a share. The new stock issue was to be sold at $100 a share and Mr. Holland told me that they were giving insiders a chance to buy fifty shares apiece. I told Mr. Holland that I'd love to get in on it but didn't have the wherewithal. He told me that the bank would be glad to lend it to me on my personal note.

I went home that night in high glee and told my new wife that we were going to be made for life now because every share of stock I could buy for $100 would soon be worth $5000 and the simplest arithmetic proved that this would amount to a quarter of a million dollars in no time at all. Anne thought it was a lot of money to borrow but agreed to go along since I was so confident. And so I signed a note for $5000 and got fifty shares. Well, the stock did pay off $1250 in the first few months, but I realize now that this money probably came out of capital and not out of earnings. When the war came on the Federal Government ordered the company to store all of its fish and took the fishing boats away to convert them into mine-sweepers. The company was sued for being in violation of the antitrust law and it looked for a time as though the president of the company, Mr. Monks, would wind up in jail. My investment went up in smoke and I think I spent the next ten years paying off my debt to the bank. Ever since then I've made it a rule to invest only in government bonds or in something I know about from experience. I can't say I ever knew much about fish or fishing.

In any event, when I was in Cleveland with Anne and our baby

I still was paying off my debt to the Plymouth County Trust Company and things didn't look good.

Shortly after I was hired, Myron T. Herrick departed on one of his frequent trips to France, and when I reported to work at the Society for Savings there was nothing for me to do. I wasn't given an office nor was I given a car. Nor was I asked to do anything. I didn't understand the attitude of the bank. Why was I hired if I wasn't going to be given a chance to do anything? There was no one I could really speak to. Mr. Herrick was away and Mr. John Dexter did not seem to be very interested in whether or not I got started. As a matter of fact, he did not think a cow and pig department was a very dignified adjunct to the staid old Society for Savings and was pretending very hard that I didn't exist.

Because I had nothing to do and was feeling uneasy about it, I made it my business to accompany the bank's appraiser when he drove out to farms. His name was Charles Musselman and he was just as immaculate a dresser as Mr. Dexter and went Mr. Dexter one better by wearing highly polished patent-leather shoes. He took great care of these shoes. They were something of a fetish with him.

In those days there were brick roads leading out of Cleveland to the county seats, just wide enough for one car at a time. In his appraisal duties, Musselman preferred not to get his beautiful patent-leather shoes muddy or dirty and it wasn't long before I noticed that if a farmer was on a hard-surface road he would get a fair appraisal but if he was on a mud road he wouldn't, and all because of Mr. Musselman's concern over his shiny shoes and his shiny automobile. That annoyed me, but since I was a junior employee I kept the annoyance to myself.

Musselman grew confidential with me one day and remarked, "You're lucky, young man. You've come into the bank on the right side of the ledger."

"What do you mean by that?" I asked.

"You've come in on the Governor's side."

"Good land!" I said, surprised. "Is there another side?"

"Of course there is," he said with a smile. "John Dexter's side. Don't you know those two fellows aren't getting along?"

That information made my heart sink a little. I went home to Anne and the baby that night ready to give up the job. Here I had come out to Ohio and it was the first farm country I had ever seen without stones in it—a sort of fertile paradise I hadn't thought existed outside of the Book of Revelation—and I was employed by one of the biggest banks in the country. So happy at this bright and beautiful new chance, I now found that I was in the middle of another dog-and-cat fight of the kind I had seen in New London and Brockton. And where people were fighting and struggling for power, I'd found I couldn't do anything worth while or lasting.

The Society for Savings had a charter which would have allowed it to operate on a cooperative plan, paying patronage dividends each six months in addition to the regular interest on savings. But trusteeships were always considered an honorary position and so the trustees were composed of the prominent gentlemen in the community who deposited their money in the commercial banks on Euclid Avenue and therefore didn't have much interest in enlarging the Society's field of activities. Mr. Herrick knew what he was up against on that board and his hiring me was one way of chipping away at the encrusted, conservative, do-nothing-but-sit-tight attitude of the board and John Dexter. But that information sifted down to me only a little at a time, and when Musselman hinted that there was an open breach between the men Dexter represented and Myron Herrick, my first instinct was not to rush forward to fight for the Holy Grail, but to groan inwardly over what I thought was, for me, rotten luck. That breach, however, turned out to be a lucky stroke for me.

When Herrick returned from France I went up to see him. His office was on the mezzanine and he reached it through a little private electric elevator from the main banking floor.

"Governor," I said to him, "they haven't given me an office."

Herrick looked at me in surprise. "What? We've got a seven-story office building here! Do you mean they can't find you an office?"

"I don't know if they can't. But they haven't. And they haven't given me a car."

"Well," Herrick said, "that's a hell of a note. Come on with me." He took me out to his anteroom and pointed to a desk and said, "You take that desk and go to work. Don't say anything to anybody." He pursed his lips. "Now, about a car. All these fellows around here drive Stearns-Knights. You go buy a new Stearns-Knight and send the bill to the bank and don't say anything to anybody."

I lacked the nerve or the gall to buy a new Stearns-Knight. I knew there was going to be resentment toward me for being in the president's office and didn't want to rub salt into any fresh wounds by driving a new car. The Stearns-Knight I bought was secondhand.

Herrick's office commanded a view of the whole bank from the mezzanine and he never closed the door between the anteroom and his office. The anteroom was enormous, beautifully furnished with carved oak furniture and silk tapestries. Within a short time I was given a secretary, Miss Jean Tuttle.

Because Herrick's door was never closed, I had ample opportunity to see and hear the visitors who came to the Society to talk to him. And many people of importance came to see Herrick. Among his visitors were Newton Baker, Marshal Foch, Cardinal Mercier—all of the great from far and near whom Herrick knew.

One of Herrick's great delights was to call me in when he had some dignitary visiting him and introduce me as "my cow and pig man." He would ask me to explain my job to the visitor and I suppose it always seemed funny because I never failed to make one of his visitors laugh. Old Cardinal Mercier said to me, "Well, young fellow, you're awfully fortunate to be able to be this close to such a great man." That opinion must have been shared by a lot of other people in the bank for it made them angry to think that I had gotten the jump on them.

I knew little about banking but I was greatly impressed with it, especially with its glamour and power and prestige, and I made up my mind to know more. I started to go to night school, taking up public speaking, banking law, and advertising. There were twenty-five or thirty other young fellows in my advertising class. Our instructor was Mr. Tim Thrift, who was developing the addressograph machine and working out some of the first direct-mail methods of advertising. My classmates asked me why the Society wasn't advertising, since we were all in agreement that it was such a powerful force in American life and advertising was just the thing for an institution or business that wanted to grow.

I asked John Dexter why the Society didn't advertise. Mr. Dexter favored me with the sort of look you'd hate to get for using the wrong fork at a formal dinner and said, "There is no need to advertise an institution which is known around the world. And in any case, it is undignified for a bank to advertise." Dignity was to Mr. Dexter what those patent-leather shoes were to Mr. Musselman, something to cherish and protect.

My classmates kept needling me about the Society's failure to advertise. One night, as we were traveling home on a trolley, one of the group, a smart young fellow named Eastman, asked me, "Why don't you make a market analysis of that bank?"

"What's that?" I asked.

"Well, you get a tabulating machine, pick out certain facts about your customers, and you'll get certain facts back about the kind of business you're doing, and so on."

When I went back to the bank, I spoke to John Dexter about the possibility of doing a market analysis of the bank's business. He seemed less than interested. When Herrick returned from one of his periodic trips I mentioned it to him.

"What do you want to do it for?"

"Well," I said, "we can't make many loans because of this

government freeze on credit and I'd kind of like to learn more about banking and this bank in particular."

Herrick thought for a moment and then asked, "What do you need?"

"I need a tabulating machine. I've never seen one. But I understand you punch up certain things on these cards and the machine sorts them out and gives you conclusions of one kind or another."

Herrick called in his male secretary. "Dick, Murray wants a tabulating machine. Do you know where to get one?"

His secretary smiled. "Well, you ought to know where to get one, Mr. Herrick. You own the Powers Tabulating Machine Company."

Herrick blinked with surprise. "I do? When did I get that?"

I was a little shocked at that moment to think that any one man could own or control so much that he would lose track of the extent of his holdings. Herrick wasn't trying to impress me. He was too important a man for that.

The tabulating machine, Miss Tuttle, and I found a place for ourselves in a dusty, unoccupied office on the top floor of the building, and we took a sample of ten thousand accounts distributed throughout the alphabet. We broke down the accounts on three bases—the age of the depositor, the place in which he or she lived, and the activity of the account.

John Dexter, who had made a career of ignoring me when my office was on the mezzanine, now came up to the top floor to see what I was doing. He asked me again and again, "What are you doing this for? What do you think you're going to get?"

My reply invariably was "I don't know." And I didn't.

When we had completed the analysis of ten thousand accounts we came up with some surprising information. The average age of our depositors was forty-eight. All the texts on banking said that the average age should be about twenty-eight if a bank expected to grow with the earning capacity of its depositors. Sixty percent of our business came from downtown Cleveland. We weren't getting any business at all from the new developments out in the suburbs like Cleveland Heights, Shaker Heights, or Lakewood. The "normal growth" of the bank that Mr. Dexter took such pride in wasn't growth at all. Our deposits, although substantial and increasing yearly, were increasing almost solely through the growth of dead interest, left to accumulate in accounts whose activity was almost nil.

Herrick's delight when I brought in the report was so real and so strong I thought he was going to kiss me. At the next board meeting he hammered the report home and an advertising agency was hired. The Society for Savings began to advertise for the first time in its long history, although Mr. Dexter never did agree that it was necessary or dignified.

Working for Myron Herrick was a great education for a young man, but education is made up of unpleasant facts as well as happy ones, and I learned something about the governor that made me wonder if men can accumulate wealth without injuring others.

Herrick had been dabbling in utility companies, buying up a bunch of small ones and trying to buy one good one like the Cleveland Electric Illuminating Company to sweeten up the lot. Sam Scovil, the board member who had made the motion to hire me, was president of the Cleveland Electric Illuminating Company, and I had heard Herrick trying to convince Scovil that he ought to throw in with him. Scovil, however, saw no point in joining his first-rate utility company with a lot of dogs and cats that Herrick had picked up cheaply.

One night when I was working late, Scovil came to see Herrick and he was dreadfully upset. They pitched their voices low at first and then they got in a loud, no-holds-barred argument. The substance of it was that Herrick had, without Scovil's knowledge, bought out the majority stock interest in the Cleveland Electric Illuminating Company and was planning to combine it with the little companies he had collected. I can still hear Scovil's voice, hurt, betrayed, crying out, "Myron, why did you do it to me?"

Herrick's voice was calm, self-assured. "Well, Sam, we're going to make more money than we ever dreamed of making."

Scovil said bitterly, "I don't give a damn about any more money. I want to be let alone to run my own business."

Herrick's final words were, "Sam, it's too late. I got it done."

Scovil left the office then, and as I watched him walk through the darkness of the main banking floor I thought to myself: If this is what a man can do with other people's money, then somehow people have got to control their own money if they're ever going to get anywhere. I never forgot that experience.

The war in Europe was getting hotter and when the county agent was drafted I was asked to look after the office until a new agent could be found. The agent in Cuyahoga County had an office in the old courthouse building just a couple of doors from the bank, and it was while I was working there on a program called "Dollars from Ditches" that I met Uncle George Cooley.

Like mine, his ancestors were New England Yankees, although Uncle George (he was about fifty-six when I met him and everybody called him Uncle) was born in Ohio, in Dover Township, Cuyahoga County. He had taught school, had studied architecture, and had spent several years as a builder and contractor of barns and homes. He was also a grape grower and a road builder. He built the first hard-surface road in Cuyahoga County and later went on to become a federal road inspector. In Louisiana he became the country's first state highway director. He returned to Ohio and to farming and in 1915 helped organize the Cuyahoga County Agricultural Association, which two years later became the county Farm Bureau.

Uncle George was a prominent farmer and farm leader in the area and a depositor at the Society, but I didn't really get to know him until the Dollars from Ditches program was started. In Uncle George's area there were many farmers who wanted to make maximum use of their land but couldn't unless the main drainage ditch that led into Lake Erie was cleaned out. The deepest part of that ditch was on Uncle George's farm and cleaning it out meant dumping an enormous amount of dirt on his farm. He didn't propose to allow anyone to do that. I can't say that his position was unreasonable, but it was vital that he give us his permission, since earlier attempts to clean out the smaller drainage ditches had been unsuccessful.

Uncle George and I had a number of discussions about the drainage ditches and about my theories of farmers helping themselves. I cited the example of the milk plant in Brockton (which, by the way, was now out of its difficulties and going along well). I also told him what my experience had been in the bank, watching men get rich by using other people's money.

Uncle George and I met time after time and we finally got the county authorities to agree to take away the dirt cleaned out of the drainage ditch. Uncle George then told them to go ahead and do the job properly.

Farmers were getting into all sorts of difficulties as the war came to an end. Prices for the things they bought were rising faster than the prices they got for their produce. Uncle George, who had been elected president of the Farm Bureau, was working toward a state federation of the various county Farm Bureaus, since the farmers' problems were getting larger and larger and it looked as though the only way they could be met would be through the efforts of consolidated groups.

On January 27, 1919, in the Botany and Zoology Building up at Ohio State University, the Ohio Farm Bureau Federation officially came into being with Uncle George Cooley as its president and Mr. W. H. Hanna of Wood County as its vice president.

There was a later meeting in Ithaca, New York, at Cornell University, for the purpose of consolidating the state Farm Bureaus into the American Farm Bureau Federation. Almost from its inception, the feeling among the leaders of the American Farm Bureau Federation was that the farmers had enemies and that they were, principally, the United States Chamber of Commerce, the National Association of Manufacturers, the American Bankers Association, and the American Federation of Labor. In fact, it looked as though the farmers had more enemies than friends. At the Chicago convention in the fall of 1919, the AFBF elected James R. Howard of Iowa as its first president. It was a surprise to Mr. Howard, who had expected, along with most of the delegates, that O. E. Bradfute of Ohio would be made president. I guess Bradfute's appearance was against him. He was portly, he wore well-cut conservative clothes, and he had the bearing of a city man. In the delegates' eyes he looked more like a Chamber of Commerce representative than a real farmer. As one delegate said, "Howard would look better between the corn rows than Bradfute."

Though it kept the AFL for its devil, in time the Farm Bureau lost this sort of nervous concern over the possibility of spies from the NAM and U.S. Chamber. In fact, I'm sorry to say that its national policies came to be almost indistinguishable from those of these two powerful organs of big business.

The year after World War I was a difficult one for the farmers, particularly those in Ohio. Price levels were falling off for the things the farmer produced but the cost of living remained high. From the city folks, the farmer got an unfair share of the blame for the high cost of living. Automobiles were coming out in great enough numbers to bring a demand for improved roads, and a big highway-building program was undertaken and financed in such manner that it hit rural real estate hard, and farmers were caught in the pinch of getting less for what they produced and paying more taxes. In short, the farmer was paying to build roads on which he couldn't ride because he couldn't afford a car.

Uncle George Cooley came into the bank one winter day in 1920 and asked me to attend a meeting that the Ohio Farm Bureau would soon be holding in Columbus. He wanted me to talk to the members about some of the things we had discussed. I agreed and on February 9, 1920, went down to Columbus.

A number of other people appeared before the Bureau's board

the same day, and I discovered that they were all applicants for the job of executive secretary. Clarence A. Henry, a farmer from Licking County, was an applicant. So was Chester A. Dyer, who later became legislative representative for the Grange and the Farm Bureau. So was M. C. Thomas, one of the Ohio county agents. So was Forrest G. Ketner, who became the head of the Livestock and Grain Departments of the Ohio Farm Bureau. And so—much to my surprise—was Murray D. Lincoln. I didn't realize it at the time, but that was the real reason Uncle George had asked me to go to Columbus.

After I'd returned to Cleveland, Uncle George came to see me and asked me if I would be interested in the job. I said I would be, and made a second trip to Columbus at his invitation. Uncle George told me then that the farmers had made up their minds to pay five thousand dollars to the man they hired. The other applicants, he said, were all holding out for seventy-five hundred.

"Do you want the job?" he asked.

"Sure," I said.

"Then take five thousand."

"I will, if they'll have me."

When the board learned I would take less than the other applicants, it looked at me more carefully. Lou Taber, a board member and master of the Ohio State Grange, took me off in a corner and made me promise that I wouldn't hurt the Grange in any way, shape, or fashion. When I promised I wouldn't, he said he would vote for me. Before I knew it, I had the job.

I went back to Cleveland and because Herrick was again on a visit to France, I cabled him my resignation. Anne and I returned to Columbus early in March of 1920, and on March 15, 1920, in Room 402 of the Southern Hotel, I began my job as executive secretary of the Ohio Farm Bureau Federation.

Part Two

5

To AMERICAN FARMERS in 1920–21, one of the hottest legislative issues was the Muscle Shoals question. Muscle Shoals was the new giant hydroelectric dam and nitrate plant built on the Tennessee River in Alabama under the National Defense Act in 1916 but not finished in time for use during World War I. Now the question was, what to do with it. Organized farmers wanted the government to operate Muscle Shoals as a source for manufacturing fertilizer ingredients. Arrayed against that proposal were electrical and chemical interests, the United States Steel Corporation, the Solvay Process Companies, the American Cyanamid Company, and a large number of the fertilizer interests that didn't want to see the price of fertilizer cracked. Organized farmers pitched into the battle. Perhaps for the first time in history farmers began to make their influence felt in Washington.

The final vote against the Muscle Shoals Act was taken in Congress without a roll call, reportedly to shield individual congressmen from criticism in their home territories. James Howard, president of the American Farm Bureau, polled each of the congressmen by mail, pointing out that the Bureau represented a million and a half farmers who felt that the Muscle Shoals proposal would increase nitrate supplies and decrease their costs. It was the feeling of the American Farm Bureau, Howard wrote, that the proposal was evidently defeated through the efforts of the large corporations which had selfish interests in maintaining fertilizer costs at their high levels. The final paragraph of the letter called for the congressman to record his vote with the Bureau's Washington representative, Mr. Gray Silver.

That letter caused a cyclone of howling over Capitol Hill. The screaming and the anguish just shook the stones of that lovely city from one end to the other, and there were demands that Silver and Howard be brought before a congressional committee. The result of the uproar was that farm blocs were created both in the House and the Senate. Nineteen senators, including Norris of Nebraska, La Follette of Wisconsin, and Gooding of South Dakota, joined the farm bloc in the Senate. In the House, L. J. Dickinson of Iowa led the bloc of thirty congressmen from both parties. Both blocs pledged themselves to stand without regard for party lines when it came to agricultural legislation.

Creation of the farm bloc in both houses of Congress gave the farmer political powers he hadn't had in decades. The big trouble, of course, was that there was a confusion of economic problems with political problems, and the passion for legislative work got so great that farmers began to feel that there was no economic problem they couldn't lick with some sort of political means. On the other hand, they got the feeling that all of their economic problems stemmed from the wicked political maneuverings of big business.

My interests lay in a different direction. I wanted to see the Farm Bureau used to persuade farmers to create economic organizations through which they could acquire the power to solve their own problems.

I don't recall the first time I said these words but whenever it was I believed them with a conviction that I feel to this day:

People have within their own hands the tools to fashion their own destiny.

I do not pretend that it's easy to get people to fashion and use these tools. It never was and never will be. But it can be done. It has been done again and again.

While the American Farm Bureau was badgering congressmen to get the Government to supply the farmer with cheaper fertilizers, in the Ohio Farm Bureau we set out to see what we could do ourselves in that direction.

What we wanted to do was find a manufacturer who would sell us fertilizer of a quality that met the highest standards of the Ohio Extension Service. Then we wanted to pool orders from members of the various county farm bureaus, buy the fertilizer in carload lots, and that way get a discount on the price. But even before we were able to work out the details of that plan fertilizer was to figure dramatically and significantly in our organization history, without any real intention on my part. It came about this way:

To help out on buying and marketing, the Franklin County Farm Bureau employed a man who was called a commercial agent. This man had a brother who was a Ford automobile distributor. One morning the agent came into my office and said that his brother had just come back from Detroit.

"Henry Ford is going to cut the price of his automobiles," he said.

I whistled. "When?"

"Soon. In the reasonably near future. I don't know what this means to you, but if it means anything you can use it if you don't tell anybody I told you."

It meant probably more than he knew. This was 1921 and we farmers were still caught in a price squeeze. Although our products were bringing less and less on the market, the price of everything we had to buy had been going higher and higher. Now it looked like the beginning of a break.

We'd been having preliminary meetings all over the state, setting up county farm bureaus, so I sent out a telegram to each one of the new organizations suggesting that they tell farmers in their counties to defer purchases of fertilizer and farm machinery. Almost immediately, the National Fertilizer Association called a special meeting of its directors in Columbus. As I recall it, Mr. J. T. Welch, president of the Welch Chemical Company, was an executive of the fertilizer association and he asked me to come to the Hotel Deshler and appear before the board, which I did. He wanted to know by what right I'd advised farmers to hold off buying fertilizer for a while.

"By the right of the Great Jehovah and the Continental Congress," I said, though why it occurred to me to paraphrase Ethan Allen I don't know.

That irked him and he showed it. "Now just a minute, young man. This is serious business."

"I am serious," I said. "I've been told the price of Ford cars is going to come down. And when that happens other things are going to have to come down too, including fertilizer. I think farmers ought to know about it."

Welch just bristled at that. "We don't think you have any right as a government agent to be telling farmers what to buy or what not to buy, or when to do either," he said.

"Oops! Who told you I was a government agent?"

"Aren't you?"

"No, sir."

"Who does employ you then?"

"A bunch of independent farmers."

Well, the meeting collapsed right there. I told them just what Farm Bureau was and made it clear that, although I worked closely with the state university, I was not on any government's payroll. They asked me no more questions and I bowed out. And sure enough, not long afterward, the price of fertilizer came down.

Giving our members that advice when we did brought Farm

Bureau some needed respect, and it galvanized Ohio farmers into action as much as anything else we undertook. Fertilizer was a good thing to start with. For one thing, it and feed were the two largest single cash purchases made by farmers; for another, it was something farmers had had experience with before, and because there was so much shabby manipulation of its price it offered the greatest opportunity to save money. When the Farm Bureau got into the fertilizer business, farmers were being sold something like seventy-eight different analyses of fertilizer. The Extension Service of Ohio State University told us that there were twelve different fertilizer combinations that would suit every crop and soil condition in Ohio. Farmers, in the main, were using a very low-analysis fertilizer like 2-8-2 (2 percent nitrogen, 8 percent phosphorus, and 2 percent potash) when the scientific people at Ohio State told us they ought to be using a high-analysis fertilizer. Farmers were also buying their fertilizer by brand name, without any regard for its particular chemical composition. We went to the farmers and said, "Now, look here, this is the fertilizer you ought to be using. Forget all the brand names like Swift's and Armour's and the like. The Farm Bureau will give you a fertilizer just as good or better than what they are selling you and it'll be cheaper—maybe three to five dollars cheaper a ton." A lot of farmers were skeptical, but there were those who were members of the Farm Bureau and trusted us and placed their orders with us. The first pool of fertilizer orders for the fall of 1921 was for twelve thousand tons.

Of course the word as to what we were doing soon got around to the manufacturers, and our first problem arose in finding someone to sell us fertilizer. Various companies within the state put us off with one reason or another. They had their own salesmen to think about and I suppose they were worried that we might not be able to live up to our contracts.

A local salesman approached one of our members and tried to sell him his company's fertilizer. The method he used to demonstrate the superiority of his product over the sort of stuff the

63

Farm Bureau would be selling was to show the farmer two pieces of rock. One was a piece of pure Florida phosphate rock, soft and crumbly and used in the best fertilizers. The other was purely and simply a piece of granite. "Now, look here," he said to the farmer, "this is the sort of stuff we put into our fertilizer," and he held up the piece of Florida phosphate. "But that Farm Bureau fertilizer—well, here's what they're using." And he then produced the granite.

I know this happened because one of our members wrote and told me about it. Among my duties as secretary of the Ohio Farm Bureau was the preparation of a weekly newsletter which was circulated among the county leaders. I circulated that story in one of our letters and named names. The president of the company in question telephoned me long distance and called me a liar. But I soon convinced him that I had the facts and he said he would put a stop to that kind of salesmanship. And to give him credit—he did.

Forrest Ketner, one of the unsuccessful candidates for the job I held, was the first man I employed. Ketner had been county agent in Delaware County. One of the first jobs we gave him was to find a company that would sell us fertilizer. He went east all the way to Baltimore before he got a tip. Somebody there told him to get in touch with a certain company in Atlanta, Georgia. He did, and one day he called me from Atlanta to say we had a supplier who would fill our orders. I remember the day distinctly because I had never before received a telephone call from so great a distance.

The company started to ship carloads of fertilizer to us, but for some reason they weren't delivered. The planting season for wheat was on us, and of course the farmers who had given us their orders were anxious to receive the goods. Letters and telephone calls didn't seem to produce any results, so we finally asked Chet Dyer, who was then serving as legislative agent for both the Grange and the Farm Bureau, to start east with his pocket full of stogies. At each railroad terminal he'd stop and inquire about any cars of fertilizer consigned to the Ohio Farm Bureau. It wasn't until he got to Harrisburg, Pennsylvania, that he found that most of our cars from the southern fertilizer company had been shunted onto what railroad people call a breakdown track, a spur reserved for cars that break down in service. All ours were there all right, but on each car someone had pasted a little sticker that said, "Scab fertilizer. Kill it."

We never found out who was responsible for this, but obviously someone had approached the employees of the railroad to get them to do it. Once we found the cars, they were started rolling and the fertilizer was delivered.

In those days the manufacturing processes weren't what they are today and because we had shipped our material from some distance, when the weather was warm, by the time the fertilizer reached our various member-farmers it had hardened or "set up," as the phrase is used in the fertilizer business. Many a farmer who had trusted the Farm Bureau took his shipment behind the barn and with a sledge hammer pounded it into a consistency that would allow it to pass through his grain drill. The reason he did it behind the barn was that he didn't want any neighbors who weren't members of the Bureau to see how badly he had been treated. But we saved three to five dollars a ton for a total of some fifty thousand dollars on our first pool of orders. The pools grew larger with each season and the savings held up, although the opposition from the fertilizer companies grew more intense.

While our fertilizer campaign was on, we were, of course, having meetings all over the state. In those meetings there began to develop the outline of a rather ambitious program. It was suggested that we set up machinery to market livestock, grain, poultry and eggs, and dairy products. There was already a wool pool in Columbus, established by wool growers. It was probably the most successful wool pool in the country, and Ohio farmers were convinced that if cooperative marketing worked for wool it would work equally well on other products. I, too, was interested in establishing marketing co-ops, but I felt that farmers had even more to gain by buying together; after all, they spent great sums every year for fertilizer, feed, and machinery, and I knew that a purchasing company could save as many dollars, or more, than a marketing company might earn for them. But few farmers would hear me out. Time and again they would tell me, "Sure, I'd like to pay less for feed or fertilizer or seed. But the important thing is, just get me more money for my grain and livestock and dairy products." It seemed almost impossible to show the farmer that he was a consumer as well as a producer, and that if he could reduce the prices on the things he needed he would have less need to increase the prices of what he sold. Some of them began to change their minds after our success with fertilizer, but support for a really effective statewide purchasing organization was a long time in coming.

We worked closely with Ohio State University in those days. Before the Extension Service could get a county agent established it had to organize a county farm group, and so the staff there was helping us organize county Farm Bureaus. It was very valuable assistance.

Professor Harry C. Ramsower was the head of the OSU Extension Service at the time. He was, and is, a grand gentleman. He was concerned that we were going too fast and particularly concerned about our undertaking business enterprises.

One day he suggested to me that I ought to take one project, such as livestock marketing, and center all our attention upon it and find out whether or not it would work to give the grower a higher price. I balked at that. For one thing, I argued, the farmer did more than just sell; he was also a consumer. In addition, if we put all our eggs in one basket and upset that basket, we'd be ruined. We might fail at livestock marketing, or at any one enterprise in which we put all our effort, either because we did not know enough about it or because of outside circumstances over which we had no control. Far better, I thought, for us to go into a whole series of projects on the theory that if one didn't work another might, when the success of one would wipe out the failure of the other.

There already were organizations in the state doing separate jobs. One was a dairymen's association sponsored by Oscar Erf, a professor in the Dairy Department of Ohio State. There was a small livestock association. There was a grain-elevator association which had been promoting the organization of farmer-owned grain elevators. The Grange was particularly active in promoting group buying.

I set myself to work trying to put these various groups together into one organization. We were getting all sorts of advice from people. One fertilizer dealer, a friend of mine, came to me and said, "Now, look, you can't do anything on fertilizer. We're doing as good a job as can be done. You ought to spend your time setting up marketing agencies for the farmers, especially livestock." And shortly after I saw him, a livestock dealer from West Jefferson came in to see me and told me confidentially, with the air of a Dutch uncle, "Now, see here, I don't want you to make a fool of yourself. There's no use trying to do anything with livestock. Growers are getting the best prices available right now. We're doing all we can. But if you do want to make a lot of money for the farmers, why don't you look into fertilizer and things like that?"

Of course it was the old story of people with tender toes telling us to go somewhere else and step on someone else's toes. But I wanted to get a lot of things done at once. I was convinced that if we wrapped up all our activities, marketing and purchasing, we could have an organization powerful enough to make its needs and desires felt everywhere and not just in isolated cases.

For some time the Ohio State Grange had maintained a purchasing department to assist local Granges in buying certain of their members' needs. The purchasing agent at that time was W. G. Vandenbark. Charlie Latchaw was the secretary and organization head of the State Farmers Elevator Association. But

67

this association was not doing much in mobilizing orders for supplies, nor in selling its members' grain. So it was proposed that the SFEA and the Ohio State Grange join with the Farm Bureau in setting up a company to purchase farm supplies. And that's how the Farmers Commercial Service Company came to be set up. Each organization had equal representation on the board, each put in a small amount of capital, and we hired a Fred Green to run it.

But it didn't last long. The other organizations were perfectly willing to sit on the board and help make decisions but they either wouldn't or couldn't put up any additional money. Our business was increasing and we had to have capital.

This experience gave me my first lesson in the primary grade of organization politics. The lesson had two parts. First, it showed the need for aggressive leadership in an organization and taught me that people keep moving whether organizations do or not. Second, it pointed up the difficulty of getting organization heads to work together. Something happens to a person when he becomes a manager or an executive. I've been one all my life so I ought to know what I'm talking about. The person's purpose in life seems to change when he becomes an executive. But more about this later.

Things came to such a pass that I finally went before the Farm Bureau board and said: "Let's do it ourselves—buy the others out and take all the risks." The board agreed. So we bought the others out and on the same day—January 9, 1923—we liquidated the Farmers Commercial Service Company and set up the Ohio Farm Bureau Service Company. David M. Odaffer became the president, Harry G. Beale the secretary-treasurer, I became the general manager, and G. E. Lasher was made field manager. The company had an authorized working capital of twenty-five thousand dollars and was owned by the Farm Bureau Federation.

We set up a purchasing department and marketing departments for livestock, poultry and eggs, fruits and vegetables, wool, and dairy products. We hired people to head each department.

To help them along we had the Federation staff do their legislative work and their auditing, as well as most of their field work over the state.

One of the first things our new service company did was to concentrate on developing our feed business. Farmers in those days generally were having a hard time getting decent feed. Most of the stuff that was being sold as feed was little more than ground-up leavings off the grain elevator floors—pure rubbish. What we did, in cooperation with farm groups in our neighboring states, was to ask the twelve eastern land-grant colleges to lend us their feed experts. We brought them together, gave them a name (The College Feed Conference Board), and asked them to work out for us the formulas for feed that would give farmers the highest yield—that is, to tell us what combinations of ingredients would make one feed that would produce the most pounds of pork, another that would produce the most pounds of beef, another the most pounds of milk, another the most dozen eggs, and so on. Importantly, we also wanted to know how these feeds could be produced the most economically. We weren't interested in making a profit, we told them, because we saw ourselves not as feed dealers but as the farmers who would be using those feeds.

Those experts knew just about everything known at the time about animal nutrition and they leapt at the chance to put their ideas to work. The results were really outstanding. It was, for instance, the first time "barreled sunlight" was put into chick feed. Barreled sunlight, of course, was cod-liver oil, which had been found to be very good for small chickens. Actually it marked the beginning of the whole business of introducing vitamins in prepared food, whether for animal or human consumption.

What turned out to be almost as important as the formulas themselves was the fact that on each bag of feed we sold we put an analysis of the ingredients that were in that bag. Furthermore, we guaranteed that the feed was constituted as described. We called it Open Formula Feed. For the first time the farmer could be sure of what he was buying. We didn't make any friends among the old commercial feed dealers, I can tell you, but it was one of the greatest things that ever happened to the average American farmer.

Farmers, though, aren't always immediately willing to pay for quality. This we found out when we began selling seed through our county co-ops. We offered a superior seed of known origin, purity, and germination, but because it was top-quality seed it sold for three or four dollars more per bushel than the commercially produced brand. Now a bushel of seed will seed eight acres of farm land and even though it costs four dollars more, it would cost the average farmer just 50¢ more per acre to seed with the Farm Bureau's certified seed. And 50¢ an acre is a small enough price to pay for a seed that's been especially adapted for your climate and soil, is pure, and guaranteed to have a high percentage of germination. But farmers, like everyone else, have a streak of suspicious stubbornness in them and our co-op managers kept wailing that they couldn't sell the certified seed.

What we had to do, finally, was to buy the commercially produced seed, price it a dollar or two lower than the going rate, put it on display but tell the farmer, "Now here, if you want the kind of stuff you've been buying, here it is at a dollar or two cheaper than what you can get it at any other place. But, you ought to be buying this other certified seed because in the long run it's cheaper." Once we had demonstrated that we could get them their old stuff cheaper they began listening and buying the certified seed—proving, I suppose, that some kind of truth never hurts anyone as long as it's made clear.

Although we had some surprising successes, our service company operations were anything but peaceful. Trouble really began when we put two representatives of each commodity on the board. The factionalism then became so pointed and so naked that it would have been funny if I had managed to keep my sense of humor about it. I particularly remember the two representatives of the dairy marketing group. They came to our board meetings and shortly after the meeting was called to order, they regularly fell asleep and dozed until either the appropriation for their division came up for consideration or it was time to go to eat. One of the two always woke up in time to make the motion that we eat. It happened that way so frequently that we used to kid them about it. But it wasn't really funny. Those men didn't seem to care about the Ohio Farm Bureau as a whole. They were interested only in their small corner of it.

Although the marketing groups always needed subsidizing, the little purchasing department always made a profit. We generally used it to support the over-all education and promotion program. At the time I was unable to put this fact in its proper perspective. As sellers of what we produced we weren't doing well, but as buyers of what we needed we seemed to do well. Of course what was involved was that tremendous fact which Beatrice Webb discussed in her book *The Discovery of the Consumer*. She said that the flannel weavers of Rochdale, who had pooled their purchases in order to get ahead in money so that they could become self-employed producers, discovered their power as consumers. We had yet to discover ours.

The economic status of the farmer began to decline throughout the twenties—he suffered his depression before the collapse of Wall Street—and the income from Farm Bureau dues, which had been set at ten dollars a member, was going down each year. Before each annual meeting, there would be a titanic struggle by each department head to get more money out of Farm Bureau. As secretary I had to take the brunt of these fights. Department heads, together with the representatives of each commodity, would come to me in turn with a demand and a threat. "Look," they would say, "if you don't give us the money we ask for our department, the livestock men of the state are going to withdraw from the Farm Bureau." The dairy people had the same complaint and the same demand and wound up with a similar threat: "All the dairymen will withdraw from the Farm Bureau." There were so many threats and demands at one meeting that I finally blew up. "Listen, you guys, if you don't help get some money in here, or stop taking it out, or start conducting your business in such a manner as to attract more members into the Farm Bureau, there ain't going to be nothing to withdraw from," I said. A whale of a fight followed, and although I didn't realize it at the time, I'd lit the fuse for the explosion that rocked Farm Bureau three years later. But I'm ahead of my story.

In trying to serve the farmer, we determined that he wasn't getting a fair break in automobile insurance rates. The rates were geared to the number and kinds of accidents and claims of urban drivers and really bore no relationship to the experience of rural car owners. We found out that the State Farm Mutual Automobile Insurance Company in Illinois was selling insurance to farmers at farm rates, and so our first step was to try to get them to sell auto insurance to Ohio farmers. State Farm was willing but Bill Safford, Ohio's insurance commissioner, wasn't. He refused to grant it a license because at that time the company didn't meet all the state's requirements for an insurance operation from out of state. My next step, then, was to appoint a committee to look into the feasibility of Ohio farmers setting up their own mutual insurance company. I had about decided in my own mind that it was something we ought to do and was going to recommend it to the board. The moment that news got out, one of our board members took a day off from his farm in western Ohio and came to Columbus to advise me against it.

"Oh, Murray, don't make such a recommendation," he said. "What do we farmers know about running an insurance business? You'll just ruin yourself and the Farm Bureau." He was so earnest and upset about it that I never forgot it. He was the secretary of a little farmers' mutual fire company that later on got into trouble. When I learned about his experience, I realized that even as he was trying to talk us out of going into insurance he was probably thinking of his own troubles. For years after that I got a lot of fun showing him our financial statements.

The moment the decision came to start the Farm Bureau

Mutual Automobile Insurance Company in 1926, one of the first
questions that arose was whether we would insure anyone but
Farm Bureau members. There were a few people who looked
skeptical at the suggestion. They were convinced we couldn't
consider insuring anyone but our own members. I argued against
it. The very principle of insurance involved spreading risk over as
many people as possible, I pointed out. While we would be willing to restrict ourselves to farmers, we couldn't cut ourselves
completely out by sticking to those farmers who were members
of the Farm Bureau. I recall arguing heatedly at one meeting,
"Farmers only constitute twenty percent of the population and no
farm organization—the Grange or anyone else—has enrolled
more than twenty percent of all the farmers. Twenty percent of
twenty percent is four percent. What you're asking us to do is to
go out and compete with all these other insurance companies but
only call on four percent of the population and spread your risks
over them and get lower rates for them than the insurance companies that can call on one hundred percent of the people." We
won that argument, but not on the basis of reason. We just managed to outtalk them.

We were most inexperienced at the whole business of insurance. But fortunately, from the very beginning, we had the help
of Illinois' State Farm auto insurance company. They showed us
how to set up our operating procedures and also helped us in
drawing up policy forms. The first year we paid them a percentage
of every coverage we wrote. Sometime later, though, we settled
the contract with a flat payment and took off on our own.

But even more valuable to us, we discovered, were those devoted farmer-members who acted as a missionary force. What
we did not realize until quite a bit later was that we had one of
the finest forces of insurance agents that has ever been collected
on the face of the earth and that this was so for several reasons.
For one thing, these devoted members of the Farm Bureau got
our first policies written without any cost to us. They wrote two
thousand new policies in a new company and they didn't ask for

a dime in agents' commissions. That was because they didn't function as agents. The insurance company was *their* company and they were happy to do it for a company they owned and managed. Another reason they were so good, and this didn't show up until we compared our loss ratios with the industry in general, was that they were not simply insuring everyone they could convince—they were insuring only those farmers they knew to be good risks. Technically, these are called select risks. That is to say, if an insurance company can insure only those drivers who never have accidents, premiums will amount to almost nothing since no claims will be filed, no money will be paid out, and the only costs in running such a company will be administrative costs —what you have to pay the clerks, the executives, and the janitor. We sent out our members to solicit insurance from their neighbors. If you were a Farm Bureau member you started out one rainy day when you couldn't work in your fields and you stopped at those places where you knew the man was a good risk. If there was a neighbor you knew who was a fast or a careless driver, or a cantankerous type who yelled for money every time he collected another scratch, scrape, or dent, you avoided him. We didn't tell our members to do that. It was something they automatically did for themselves. As a result, during the first two years of our operation, we had a quality of risks that neither we nor any other company has been able to duplicate since from regular paid-time agents.

We didn't know what the cost of insurance would be. We knew that the commercial rate of the old-line companies for a Ford or Chevrolet was fifty-five dollars, and we were hoping to get under that, if we could.

We took the old-line rate as our target and told the farmer: "Now, this is how it works. First, you pay fifteen dollars for a membership fee. You just pay that once and you're a member for life and that gives you the privilege of insuring one car so long as you live and have one. Then you give us twenty dollars and that's called a premium deposit. Out of it we pay the expenses and losses, and you're insured for six months. At the end of that time we'll bill you for whatever your share of the expenses and losses actually were. If you want to cancel with us then, we'll deduct your share from the premium deposit and refund the balance. If you want to stay, you can pay up, leave your twenty dollars in, and you'll be insured for another six months."

At the end of the first six months, we discovered that the cost of doing business was so low that we called for a premium of $9.18 on a Chevrolet or Ford. At the end of the year it was again about $9.18. That meant that we had come down below the old-line insurance companies' rate of $55. We were down to $53.36. But the next year was more dramatic, because in the second year there was no $15 membership fee to pay and no need to lay out another $20 for a premium deposit, which meant that the farmer could insure his Chevrolet or Ford for $18.36 instead of $55. Well, we just went to town after that.

One of the curious things about the premium deposit was that many of our first policyholders didn't believe they would ever get it back on request. Somewhat to our surprise, we found that some policyholders, even after they'd paid their six-months' premium, wrote in and asked for their twenty dollars back. We sent them their checks just as we'd promised. Then, once they'd satisfied themselves that we meant what we said, danged if they didn't send us another premium deposit so they could still be insured by us. In fact, most of them simply returned their refund checks, endorsed back to the Farm Bureau Insurance Company. It was a natural suspicion. We were a new young company and there had been a great deal of talk by agents from competitive insurance companies that we would never last. Well, we did last. By 1951 we were the second largest mutual auto insurer in the country even though we were represented in only twelve states and the District of Columbia. Our low rates, naturally, had much to do with this growth. For a good many years we were able to sell auto insurance at rates as much as forty percent under those of most of our competition. Today, with our name changed to Nationwide, our policy is still to sell good insurance at low cost, only now we handle more than a hundred different kinds of coverages—life and fire as well as casualty. We're also expanding fast into new states. Our vice president-operations, Howard Hutchinson, tells me that by the time this gets into print we'll be in 23 states and the District of Columbia, with close to three million policyholders. And it really thrills me to think that all this started when a bunch of Ohio farmers came together to serve their own needs and started talking to their neighbors.

We have come so far so quickly in this account of the Farm Bureau that I'd like to back up a bit and touch on certain significant details I've let go by.

I can't think of any greater bore than the man who grows up without learning anything from the life he's lived and tries to convince you that he was just as smart at twenty-six as he is at sixty-six. Now I'm not saying there *aren't* men who haven't learned anything from the moment they started to speak until the moment they start to mumble. There are. Plenty of them. I hope I am not one of them. I hope that I do not give the impression that I knew every moment of my life where I was going and what I was doing. I didn't. I don't now. I've groped for things, taken them by the wrong end, hammered them when I should have stroked them, stroked them when I should have walloped them, set fire to things I should have doused with cold water. In the early 1920s with the Farm Bureau I had a dozen itches in different places and I lost my temper at the wrong times. I resigned periodically, sometimes because I was disgusted, sometimes because I wanted to be coaxed back, sometimes to make a point, and sometimes just to break a deadlock. I'm grateful that the board of the Ohio Farm Bureau never accepted any of my resignations.

When I joined the Farm Bureau I recommended that we go into the banking business and the utility business. I had been steered onto the utility business by an old utility man who, as an employee of Ohio Bell Telephone, had set up many of the toll lines in the state. He had come to me one day with a fascinating idea.

"If you really want to make some money for the Farm Bureau, here's your chance," he told me. It seemed that earlier in the history of telephone communications in Ohio farmers had established a large number of mutual telephone companies to serve themselves and their neighbors. There were some three hundred companies all told, and they had come into conflict with Ohio Bell, whose network was spreading over the state. The hitch was, Ohio Bell couldn't buy any of those mutual telephone companies directly. Years before, in order to get some sort of permissive law passed, it had entered into an unwritten agreement to that effect with the farm majority that controlled the Ohio legislature. "But," the old utility man went on, "there's no question that in the future these companies are going to have to be tied together into the Ohio Bell system to cover the state effectively. Now a lot of these companies are on the rocks financially, simply because their subscribers won't pay fair rates for service or because the people running them aren't able to maintain them. If you're as smart as I think you are, you'll get that board of yours to organize a utility company, go out and buy up the stocks of these little companies, and then turn around and sell them to Ohio Bell Telephone and make about two million dollars." Well, that got me all excited and I went to Uncle George and tried to persuade him that this proposal ought to be presented to the board. As a result, we got into the only argument we ever had in our many years of association. It was probably the only time Uncle George ever flatly laid down the law to me.

"Young man," he said severely, "you pay attention to feed and fertilizer and forget these crazy ideas of getting farmers together to build their own banks and utility companies."

I finally gave in, although we did, later on, have an Agricultural Farm Credit company with one of the lowest loss ratios in the country. And as for the telephone companies, there are still some one hundred and twenty independents in Ohio, a fact that few people know. Ohio Bell tried to organize itself in the middle of the state so that any companies wanting to cross the state would have to hook into them. But some farmers figured out what they were up to and there's still an area in southeastern Ohio where Bell Telephone has never been able to enter. The possibility of combining those companies into one large cooperative still exists but we've never got around to it and probably won't now. Nevertheless, ten years after we missed out on the telephone companies, Farm Bureau did get into the utility business through the REA.

There is no denying that one of the reasons I was interested in the utility companies in Ohio was that I was still under the spell of that master financier at the Society for Savings, Myron T. Herrick. I had visions of our being able to accumulate vast sums of money as Herrick had done, for I was convinced that only with a good deal of money could opportunities be seized and used to their best advantage. I suppose my interest in money as a tool scared a good number of honest farmers. I know that when it was proposed that we have an insurance company, there were dark rumors that I would probably run off with the assets—not so bad a charge as the one laid against me in Brockton, that I was starving babies, but bad enough. A number of farmers mistrusted me for my banking background. Bankers as a group were assumed to be traditional enemies of farmers, chiefly because bankers did little for farmers and were generally considered allied with the business community against the rural community. Of course I had had my experience with Mr. Holland and the Plymouth County Trust Company and knew that generalizations about bankers were about as false as most generalizations about groups of people are apt to be, including generalizations about businessmen. One of the most enlightened businessmen I ever knew was Mr. A. J. Brosseau, president of the Mack Truck Company.

I met Mr. Brosseau sometime in the early twenties, just as the Farm Bureau was warming up for its first real battle in the Ohio legislature. We felt strongly that farmers were being taxed unfairly to help finance a road-building program then under way between cities, and to prove it we had a survey made of the kinds of people who were traveling the existing through roads. What the survey showed was that only 17 percent of the traffic on these roads was from local people, while 83 percent was from those traveling from one city to another. Yet the farmer, because the road tax was based upon the amount of abutting property, was paying 66 percent of the total cost. With the aid of the Bureau of Public Roads we drafted legislation calling for a gasoline tax to pay the cost of road construction. The moment the proposed legislation was announced, all the automobile clubs throughout Ohio, particularly in Cleveland, Toledo, Cincinnati, and Columbus, pledged undying opposition. At the height of the uproar, Mr. Brosseau came into my office, introduced himself, and told me he wanted to help us get our bill passed. I was highly skeptical and frankly told him so.

"If all these auto clubs are against it, I don't see why a truck manufacturer like you ought to help us."

"My reasons are simple, Mr. Lincoln," he told me. "I make trucks. Trucks have to have good roads. I think there's a great development for trucking in this country if we can get good roads. I know these costs are unfairly assessed on the farmer. I know that what we've got to do in order to keep good roads coming on is to get a more equitable system of taxation. That's why I want to help you." He was a man of his word and with his help we managed to get the bill passed. We became good friends during the next several months and, of course, he learned of what we were doing in the Farm Bureau and was greatly impressed.

One evening he said reflectively, "Murray, some day the things that you people have been doing may help save this form of government."

"What do you mean by that?" I asked, startled by his words.

"There are inequities in our society," he said. "We people in industry have had control of a good many things for a long time and we won't give them up without a struggle. Labor unions are not really as stable or responsible as they ought to be to assume the economic leadership of this country as yet. Farmers, on the other hand, work with the soil and with nature and they're a combination of labor and business. I think they're going to be the first group to begin to see these inequities and do something constructive about them—and so save our form of government."

I didn't understand why he felt farmers had to correct what was wrong with our society, but he sensed that the process of putting people together to solve their own problems and serve their own needs would someday prove valuable to the preservation of democratic society. I myself did not see it that clearly and only years later was I able to appreciate Brosseau's astuteness. The professional farm leaders would have said he was an enemy of the farmer. I know he wasn't. I've known many big business-men and they are not enemies of the farmer. Nor is the city dweller an enemy of the farmer. But in the twenties that sort of factional nonsense was rife among farmers. Among some agricultural leaders it was almost a mania. I believed some of those things too. I believed them because I had been raised to believe them. I worked with men who believed them—men I liked, men I admired. It took a good deal of experience and thinking for me to shake prejudices like those. I have been shaking prejudices of one sort or another for many years. I'm still shaking them, and I hope I never stop.

6

Much of the trouble that we had in the early days of the Farm Bureau could be laid to the refusal of our affiliated groups to take the risks and responsibilities of running cooperative enterprises along with the privileges. By way of illustrating what I mean let me tell you a little family story that took place during the first week of my marriage.

When I was organizing the milk plant in Brockton I was out all day and sometimes most of the night. I took off two weeks to get married and the moment Anne and I came home, I rushed right back into the business of trying to put the milk plant on its feet. Anne said she had had the feeling before our marriage that this was the kind of life she was going to live. She had thought that if she married a farmer she'd see him all the time, because farmers hardly ever leave home. But I turned out to be something only a little less mobile than an energetic gypsy. In the first week of our marriage we were settling ourselves in with what little new furniture we had at my grandmother's house. A problem arose over the placement of an antique secretary. I said it looked better on one side of the room and Anne thought it looked better on the other. The first thing we knew we were having an argument. I don't argue any more with Anne because, after all, we've been married almost forty-five years, but I didn't know any better in the first week of our marriage. Finally, in exasperation, Anne said, "Now, look here, young man, you're preaching cooperation to your farmers. Why don't you practice what you preach? Cooperate with me and do it my way."

That, of course, is the danger of any cooperative. Cooperatives are human organizations and human organizations are subject to human frailties and there are always going to be people in cooperatives who will want to be the "co" part while they let others do the "operating." Another danger in the cooperative is that its members, when they become successful, are apt to forget the original purposes for which they organized. A good example of that is what happened to the milk plant in Brockton after I left it.

The plant was in sad shape when I left it in 1917 to go to work for Myron Herrick. The farmers hired a young Irish lad to run it and gave him two thousand dollars a year as a salary. In addition, they made him sign a note for ten thousand dollars' worth of stock and told him they would pay him a bonus equal to the dividends, if any, that might be earned on that amount of stock. He did pretty well the first year and they raised him to three thousand dollars. The second or third year he made so much money for them that they declared a 100 percent stock dividend, which meant he got a salary of thirteen thousand dollars. The moment the members realized he was getting that much they demanded he take a cut. Mr. Holland went to the farmers and told them off. "Look here," he said. "You would have paid this man anything the first year if he could have pulled you out of a hole. Now that he has pulled you out, I think you've got a lot of nerve to kick over what he's earned for himself and for you. You better stay with him." They finally did. But this seems to be characteristic of the farmer. While I consider farmers on the average honest, respectable, hard-working human beings, they aren't, as a rule, generous with hired hands. They won't raise the hand's wages unless he kicks or threatens to quit. This is certainly one of the troubles with farmer cooperatives. They just will not pay the technical and executive hired hands what those hands would get in comparable positions in private industry. They want first-rate leadership at cut-rate prices and, on the whole, they have been lucky that they have gotten it as often as they have. Also, among cooperatives—particularly among successful farm cooperatives—there's a tendency for the members to become individually or collectively selfish about their institutions. Once the Brockton milk plant was successful enough to declare a 100 percent stock dividend, the members closed up the company as tight as a drum and refused to take in other farmers. Rather than purchase more milk locally, they turned for their supplies to northern Vermont and Canada. They were, of course, piling up all the money they could for themselves by shutting out men they should have welcomed into their midst. They turned what could have been a true cooperative into an old-line stock-interest corporation devoted to the making of profits and nothing more.

I do not mean that a cooperative should not make money. It must if it is ever going to expand and enter other fields of interest. But money-making is not its main purpose. The cooperative is designed to care for the needs of those who use it. It is designed to expand its usefulness to the people who own and operate it. It is designed, by its rules, to keep any one man or any small group of men from controlling it. Now, the old-line private-profit organizations are the simplest instruments for the wealthy to control. You can buy control of them, as Myron Herrick bought control of the Cleveland Electric Illuminating Company. It is, essentially, an undemocratic process, because it means that one man, because of his wealth, casts a weighted vote.

The simplest analogy of the dangers of a weighted vote is this: What would you think of a government where a man, coming to the polls to vote, would be given more than one vote because he had more money than the man who stood in line behind him? Sounds bizarre, doesn't it? Suppose he were given one vote for every thousand dollars he had in the bank, in real property, in bonds, and so on. It gets even weirder considered in that light. But that is precisely the situation in stock corporations. Most of the stock in our business corporations is owned by a relatively small number of wealthy men. According to a study published by the Department of Economics of Harvard University, in 1953 the top wealth-holders of the country—accounting for little more than 1 percent of the population—owned nearly 90 percent of the corporate bonds held by all persons, virtually all of the state and local government bonds, and at least 80 percent of the corporate stock.

As the modern corporation developed in our country, the Federal Government found it necessary to impose a number of restraints in an effort to enforce the principles of fair play and competition and to protect the public against unscrupulous economic practices. When corporations growl about governmental interferences these days, it is merely a whisper compared to the anguished screaming that used to be heard the length and breadth of the land. Although we tend to forget it, the fact is that the Federal Government had to enact and enforce the Sherman and Clayton Anti-Trust Acts to keep the big corporations from stifling or swallowing up every small business that started. The fact is, the Government had to enact a Pure Food and Drug Act and set up a Bureau of Standards to protect people from adulterated, unhealthy, or poisonous foods and drugs, and from short weight, short measure, and other forms of cheating in the market place.

Free enterprise, in other words, had to be protected from the giants who shouted "Free enterprise!" in order to bludgeon free enterprise among others. As a small example of the sort of resentment monopolistic business feels against free enterprise and aggressive competition, I'd like to tell a little story of what happened when we began selling insurance outside Ohio.

Two years after we had started our auto insurance company we were doing so well that farmers in neighboring states started petitioning their own Farm Bureaus to establish a like service. Where the Bureaus didn't feel up to the job, they came to us and asked us to sell them insurance. By 1928 we were selling insurance in West Virginia, Maryland, Delaware, North Carolina, and Vermont. Now, in small Vermont it was quite easy for any citizen to get in to see the governor. A few years after we started selling insurance in Vermont, there was a regular parade of old-line agents for big auto insurance companies coming in to pester Governor George Aiken. "Governor, you've got to do something about this Farm Bureau insurance," the typical agent would say. "I represent a good company, one of the largest in the country, and these Ohio people are selling 40 percent or more below our rates. There's something wrong." Now there was nothing wrong and they knew it. But they were just trying to get the governor to find something wrong with us because we were competing too effectively. These cries for help against the inhuman competition of a small Ohio insurance company got so irritating to Governor Aiken that he finally told his secretary, in effect: "You tell the next insurance agent who comes in here to complain about Farm Bureau that I'm not going to spend any time listening to him unless (1) he can prove that the company is unsound or (2) that they don't settle claims or (3) that they're guilty of something improper. If they can't do any of those things, then I won't spend any time listening." And a more sensible answer to complaints about business competition I haven't heard in a long time.

So often when people have found themselves victims of economic injustice or trickery, they have turned instinctively to their governments for protection, as we did in obtaining antitrust, food and drug, and agricultural legislation. But this turning to government for the solution of all our problems can be dangerous. It can lead, sooner or later, in one way or another, to statism— either communism or fascism or socialism.

The method that does not lead to any of these "isms," and does not make the individual completely dependent upon his government is the cooperative way. The cooperative way is for people to combine their resources, under proper leadership of their own selection and within the framework of a free economy, to serve their common needs. If you, as a consumer, were a member of a food cooperative—a supermarket, let us say—you would have one vote (but only one) in determining policy. You would get patronage refunds in proportion to the amount you spent in your cooperative. In the case of the Greenbelt cooperative in the Washington, D.C., area, this has meant for many years that your annual refund would be the equivalent of one week's supply of meat and groceries. In determining policy for that cooperative, the member-owners, who are also the buyers, would be much more apt to cast their votes in the public interest than they would if there were stockholders interested primarily in profits. What this means is that the cooperative management, including its democratically elected board of directors, is much more likely to look at problems of pricing, quality, advertising, and merchandising from the consumer viewpoint than is the management of a corporation controlled by a comparatively few wealthy stockholders.

Cooperatives, for example, pioneered in "open formula" feed for farmers. They have led in letting consumers know what's "in the can" by putting government quality grades on the label with factual information about the peaches or pears or beans inside. When the coloring added to Florida oranges came under investigation, a cooperative in Superior, Wisconsin, was first to stop the sale of such color-added fruit. In the Upper Midwest, the cooperative service stations dotting the rural areas are given credit for keeping the price of gasoline down.

The primary purpose of a cooperative, in other words, is to serve the needs of the people who are at the same time owners and customers of that cooperative. In theory, it would be unthinkable for a co-op knowingly to sell adulterated goods, to use short weight, short measure, or to attempt any other tricks of the trade. You don't, in other words, knowingly try to cheat yourself.

When I speak of the cooperative way and of cooperatives throughout this book, I am not speaking of something mysterious, or something that is a political belief, or something that is exclusively for farmers. More than thirteen million families in the

United States are member-owners of consumer cooperatives of one kind or another. It is a movement which is in the forefront of the coming Consumer Economy.

I am speaking, instead, of something that can prevent the average man from being smothered between Big Business and Big Government. I am speaking of a means whereby the average man can have some control of his own destiny. I am speaking of a means whereby the control of economic institutions can be returned to individuals. An old German professor once gave me some good advice about economic control. *"Herr* Lincoln," he said, "your cooperatives in America must get control of the money they need with which to operate. If they don't, your cooperatives someday may find themselves in a bottle, with somebody else holding the stopper." I've never forgotten that advice.

I believe that cooperatives, properly directed, can help save the world from the self-destruction toward which it seems to be headed. If I did not believe that, I would not be writing this book. I would not be wasting my time doing what I have been doing for more than forty-five years. I do not expect you to believe that now —right this minute. But before you've finished this book I believe you will understand what I am talking about. You may not agree with me, but you will understand why I believe as I do. And I am of the opinion that understanding takes us halfway toward agreement.

Life is an educational process, if you will get out of your back yard and let it educate you. In 1923 I had an opportunity to travel to Europe to look into the nitrate fixation process that the Germans claimed to have perfected. Nitrates, of course, are the base of farm fertilizer, and fertilizer was one of the hottest subjects of controversy between organized farmers and their legislators. Now, here was a process for obtaining nitrates from the very air we breathed. If the claim was true, and there were quite a few who didn't believe it was, it might be a very important thing for the American farmer. To find out, the American Farm Bureau Federation formed a committee to visit Germany. The first I knew that I was to be on that committee was a noontime telephone call from its chairman, Gray Silver, in Washington, asking where the deuce I was. It seemed I was expected to leave for Europe the following day. I got packed and ready to go in four hours and we sailed on the *Bremen*.

As part of our trip we visited cooperatives in both Germany and Denmark. I was especially intrigued by the life insurance companies the German farmers had organized. It was my own theory in those days that the farm family could take better care of itself if the head of the family died than an urban family could in the same circumstances. Farming was a family proposition, after all, whereas the urban family depended upon a single breadwinner. If the farmer could have enough life insurance to cover the family's indebtedness upon the death of the husband, that would be a great comfort for the widow and the surviving children. The Germans had formed associations of little farmers, associations of middle-sized farmers, and one for the big farmers. In addition to their life insurance companies they had their credit unions.

But it was when we got to Denmark and I saw their big marketing co-ops that I got the full impact of what a force cooperatives could be. I spoke no Danish nor any German and shared the typical Midwesterner's disdain for foreigners. I thought to myself, "If these dumb clucks can run cooperatives, we certainly ought to be able to." I learned later that because a man doesn't speak English it is no sign that he hasn't got any brains. I had met the sharpest, astutest, most sophisticated farmers in the world in those cooperatives but had no way of knowing it because they appeared simple, and I was too ignorant to know their language and too prejudiced to know that I was ignorant.

Myron Herrick, who was now American Ambassador to France, learned that our committee was stopping in Paris. He invited us out to a château owned by Philippe Bunau-Varilla, the French engineer who had been a prominent figure in the building of the Panama Canal. After a delightful dinner in this lovely château, we all sat on the leather-padded railing in front of the fireplace and talked. Later Herrick and I had a quiet moment together and he asked me how I was getting along. "Pretty good, Governor." I hesitated a moment but decided to bring up a matter that had bothered me for some time. "I was very disappointed at not hearing from you after I sent you that telegram of resignation."

Herrick looked at me. "Well now, Murray, I'll tell you. I think I told you once that you were the only young man at the bank I would want to see as president of that bank. You could have been president if you had continued to do well and were willing to wait twenty-five years."

"I didn't want to wait twenty-five years, Governor."

Herrick smiled. "When, after I had told you what your prospects were, you wired that you were leaving to go with a group of unorganized farmers—well, I thought you'd lost your mind or your good judgment. To be frank, I was rather irritated. But now I want to tell you something. If I can ever help you, let me know—because I think you've made the most important decision of your life and I think you've decided it the right way."

The most interesting part of that evening arose when Herrick and our host fell to reminiscing over the days when Bunau-Varilla had come to the United States, filled with the dream of digging a canal across the Isthmus of Panama. Herrick had taken him to see Teddy Roosevelt, and my eyes popped when I was told that Bunau-Varilla, Herrick, and Roosevelt had conspired to create a revolution in Panama so that Panama might break away from Colombia to give the United States the right to build the canal. The only time I have ever seen this story alluded to in print was at the time of the Nicaraguan difficulties during the twenties. Garrett Garet, writing in *The Saturday Evening Post,* said that the desire for a Nicaraguan canal would lead to another coup such as the one planned by Bunau-Varilla, Herrick, and Teddy Roosevelt in Panama. The fact that foreign governments manipulated the internal affairs of other nations for the convenience or profit of businessmen was something I had known for a long time, but I had never suspected that our own country was capable of such a thing. If America had her Age of Innocence I was still living in it.

Of course in the twenties you could never have convinced a great many people in Ohio that Murray D. Lincoln had ever drawn an innocent breath in his life. To Lou Taber I was a "traitor to agriculture"; to some businessmen in Columbus I looked like a Bolshevik out to ruin American capitalism and their particular branch of it by early next week; to some farmers I looked like an undercover agent from the American Bankers Association. Those charges were brought against me when I was a dyed-in-the-wool, bedrock Republican. You can imagine what they started to call me in the thirties when I shifted my feelings toward the Democrats. In the 1950s I changed my registration from Republican to Democratic and got called different names. I guess the times have tempered somewhat. Either that or I've been connected with so many successful projects and been proven more right than wrong so often that the people who used to criticize me have quieted down. Anyway, the names I get called nowadays are more respectable.

Dr. Ramsower, head of Extension at Ohio State University, was the man who had cautioned me to go into one thing at a time. Now, while the Extension Service had performed invaluable services for the farmer, it sometimes opposed our going into business. It opposed our going into business because every time we did some businessmen on whose toes we'd stepped would yell, "We help get your appropriations from the State House. What do you mean by encouraging those farmers to put us out of business?" Well, it was true. The businessmen of the community had helped Ohio State get its appropriations from the legislature. And our going into business did cut into their sales—although not as deeply or as often as their protests implied.

The opposition from the Extension Service angered me and one day I told Ramsower, "Look, one day you've got to make up your mind. Either you're going to be for the farmer or the businessman." In a sense, it was unfair of me to put pressure on him. He was caught in a squeeze. If he stood up for the farmer, the businessman, who is always vocal, let out a yowl to be heard back and forth across the state. The farmer, on the other hand, would just silently pat the Extension Service on the back.

I wasn't the only one who thought that the solution to the farm problem lay in business. The Hoover administration also got the same idea but, characteristically enough, it got hold of the idea from the wrong end. Out of the deep Republican faith in business, and particularly in big business, the Republicans decided to put farming on a businesslike basis and created the Federal Farm Board. Naturally they put a big businessman in charge of it, Alexander Legge, who had been president of the International Harvester Company. The kernel of the Farm Board's solution to the farm problem was to organize farmers into imitations of business trusts so that they might set artificially high prices for their products and so take the profit out of the hides of the consumers.

My first run-in with Mr. Legge and his methods came when the Farm Board began to cast sheep's eyes at our uniquely successful Ohio Wool Pool. Jap Walker, who was on our staff at the Farm Bureau as one of the commodity secretaries, was secretary of the Ohio Wool Pool. The Farm Board had organized a National Wool Pool and of course the Board wanted the Ohio Wool Pool to join it. There was, unfortunately, one small hitch. The National Pool had a marketing charge of about three cents a pound. The Ohio Pool was doing very nicely with a charge of two and a half cents a pound.

In the course of events a meeting was set up between Mr. Legge and me. After that a committee composed of Lee Palmer, Jap Walker, Ray Ascham, and Walter Sollars sat down to discuss the matter in detail with Mr. Legge in Washington.

It wasn't long before I found myself arguing with Mr. Legge that three cents a pound was out of line with the experience we had had in Ohio. It seemed to me that the National Wool Pool ought to go into other sections of the country where no marketing groups existed and put them together toward the end of reducing that three-cent charge by half a penny. Until he did so, I saw no sense or justice in asking Ohio farmers to pay three cents when it was quite plain that two and a half cents was enough.

My argument incensed Mr. Legge to the point where he finally charged me to go back and change my ways or I'd be out of business in three years. I suppose he felt that we were treading on his vast business experience with big ignorant feet. Legge then started out on his own to control the wool market in Ohio. The National Wool Pool hired a man, gave him a bank account, and set up a warehouse somewhere in Licking County. So far as we know they never managed to get further than collecting one or two carloads. Meanwhile, our own pool kept growing. It's still operating successfully today. Later on the Ohio Wool Association did join the National Pool, but the Farm Board was abandoned as another bust of the Republican years.

Business, however, was the key to my feeling about the function of the Farm Bureau. The more businesses we got into, the happier I felt. But not everyone was happy, nor was everyone convinced we ought to be going in the same direction. Forrest G. Ketner, the first man I hired, turned out to be one of them. As I have related, Ketner had been one of the unsuccessful candidates for the job of executive secretary which *I'd* gotten, and this may explain why from the start there had been a tension between us that neither of us seemed able to overcome. Our livestock marketing venture, which he managed, was relatively successful and before long he was trying to pull away. Farm prices had started their steady decline and the dues coming into the Farm Bureau had fallen off, year by year. The majority of our board felt that the commodity cooperative associations, such as livestock and grain and so on, should stay under the control of the board, but fellows like Ketner wanted to be on their own. They started a campaign to increase the size of the board, feeling that if they could bring in enough new members who thought as they did, they could break what they considered my control of the Farm Bureau. At that time some 90 percent of our effort and 90 percent of our funds were going into the commodity marketing associations.

Mr. Edward Rector, one of our directors from Pickaway County, sided with Ketner and the livestock people, and Rector and the livestock group had the support of some of the people at Ohio State University's Extension Service. The livestock people also had the sympathy of the Farm Bureau president, Lee Palmer, but he didn't show it openly. The disagreements over control grew sharper and sharper until December, 1929, when the showdown came at the Neil House in Columbus, at a convention designed to revamp the constitution of the Farm Bureau. Ketner, Rector, and the livestock people had a number of proposals to make and we had counterproposals to make. Their main ones were to increase the size of the board with their own candidates and to free the marketing associations from control of the Farm Bureau board. It was a heated argument on a cold day, and we had a close vote on a number of propositions. On the most critical one of all—freedom from control for the marketing associations—they won.

When they won it, I felt as though we'd been dealt a mortal blow. Evidently they felt the same way. Our office manager, Cleve Nelson, happened to be walking down a corridor of the Neil House when he overheard Rector gloating to another board member. "Well, we got the sonofabitch this time. All he's got left is insurance and the service company and they won't amount to anything." When Nelson reported that to me I got angry. At the same time I felt, underneath, that perhaps they were right. But I wasn't willing to admit it. I kept thinking about those stolen horses. If my horses hadn't been stolen, I might have wound up as day laborer on the highways of Massachusetts. Well, someone had stolen the horses again and now I'd have to turn in another direction.

The following Monday I called the staff together.

"Well, all right. This is all we've got left but let's give insurance and the service company the darndest whirl we know how."

We did our best, but the country was going downhill pretty fast. Our dues income was declining and farmers didn't have the money to purchase supplies. They had everything they could do just to hold on to their farms. Now the depression, which hit the whole country in the thirties, was just an extension of the depression that had started for farmers as far back as 1922. As Andy, of that famous radio team, once said, "We had a slump in our depression." That slump came in 1932. I don't think the Ohio Farm Bureau could have gone as far as fast as it did in those years if farmers hadn't felt the economic pressure compelling them to act together. My deepest fear today is that until we do run into another great depression we won't be able to get people to work together to do the things they ought to do about the control of their own economic machinery. And if it has to get that bad, then I'm afraid the result will be nothing less than a change in the form of government under which we live. That prospect concerns me very much. To prevent it, I think we've simply got to pay more attention to the educational process. I think maybe this is the only thing we can do to prevent such a change.

Education was much on my mind in the late twenties, since I felt it was the only way to keep the Farm Bureau working and held together. Aaron Sapiro, an attorney who had acted as counsel for some of the California cooperatives, was convinced that the watertight contract and the controlled market were the way to the farmers' salvation. Under his persuasion the Kentucky Tobacco Growers Association had formed a tobacco pool with a three-year watertight contract. It was my own feeling that those tobacco cooperatives were doomed to failure because what they did was to buy out the tobacco warehousemen at good prices and then put the same people who had owned the warehouses in charge of the cooperatives. I never thought that they really had their hearts in what they were doing. The memory of what Weston

Manley had tried to do to our milk plant was still vivid in my mind.

Not only that. I was pretty sure that if Kentucky farmers acted like Ohio farmers they'd never go along with the idea of three-year watertight contracts. Years before, we'd tried signing our farmers to contracts for dues on a three-year basis. The dues then were ten dollars a year. When some farmers refused to pay in the second year we made the mistake of suing them. We found out fast that farmers didn't like lawsuits any better than they liked watertight contracts. The protest had been so strong that we had no alternative but to abandon this method of marketing.

And sure enough, Lee Palmer was at some meeting where he heard that the Kentucky tobacco pool was going to fold up because not enough of the farmers had signed up for the second term of three years of marketing through the pool. There he met Miss Verna Elsinger, of Cincinnati, who had been the tobacco pool's educational director. What she had to tell our president was most enlightening. She had found that wherever the educational department had been able to work with the tobacco farmer and his family, and wherever it had managed to explain the principles that made the pool necessary and desirable, the pool had no trouble signing farmers up for a second three-year term. But, because the majority of the counties had no educational department, the majority of the farmers refused to sign up, and so tobacco was passing out of the cooperative picture. Lee Palmer thought her ideas good enough to recommend that we hire her as our educational director. And so we did.

Although we didn't recognize their importance until much later, these were the two most significant changes in the Farm Bureau in the late twenties. The break with the commodity marketing groups freed us to concentrate our time, money, and energies on insurance and purchasing. It resolved the conflict that had about torn the Farm Bureau apart and which, I believe, would have wrecked it if it had gone on much longer. The de-

95

cision to begin an educational program led us finally to the establishment of advisory councils. And today I consider the sixteen hundred advisory councils set up by the Ohio Farm Bureau the most significant contribution ever made by a farm group to the salvation of our country and of the world.

But the process of my own education was really just beginning.

7

I WAS, from birth, a conservative Republican. I grew up and worked in an atmosphere where to be anything else was almost immoral. One day I vowed I would never vote Republican again as long as I lived. I remember that day very well.

During the Hoover administration I was appointed to a committee that sought to have the President introduce legislation to keep farmers from being foreclosed on their farms. Farmers, as I've mentioned, were in the midst of the depression long before the stock market crash of '29. A committee under the auspices of the American Farm Bureau went down to the White House. We were ushered into the Cabinet Room. Because I was the junior committee member, I moved to the rear of the room, allowing my more distinguished colleagues the places near the front. To my alarm and surprise, President Hoover entered and sat down beside me. I almost jumped from my seat from surprise and stage fright. Hoover was told why we had come to see him, although he had been briefed beforehand, and he then made a short speech, the substance of which was that he believed that the Federal Farm Board and the various measures the government had already taken were enough. The speech upset us, and me in particular. At the end Hoover presented Congressman Franklin Fort of New Jersey to discuss the matter further with us. Fort was introduced as a friend of agriculture, a farmer himself who understood and sympathized with farmers and their problems. Under our questions it developed that there was only one farm in Fort's congressional district and that belonged to a wealthy greenhouse owner. A number of points were raised with the congressman. I said that if the farmer had some kind of credit arrangement he would be able to keep his farm. But Fort said that the Administration was now doing all it could. It could do nothing more. The inexorable laws of economics would have to prevail. I went out of that room furious.

Some years later I met Cyrus Eaton, the Cleveland financier, who told me that he too had left the Republican party after a meeting with President Hoover. For a while he'd been one of several businessmen whom Hoover used to call in occasionally for advice. During one of their conferences, at a time when the depression appeared to be worsening, he asked Hoover if something couldn't be done to guarantee the deposits of people who had small savings accounts. Hoover got the impression that Eaton was talking about banks and not their depositors. A call was put through to one of the major banking houses in New York and Eaton heard the speaker at the other end of the phone tell Hoover, "If the banks can't stand up, let them go under." Eaton protested that it wasn't the banks he was worried about but the depositors whose savings would be lost. This was a matter that seemed to be of little concern to either Hoover or his advisers and Eaton told me he left Hoover's office swearing, like myself, never again to vote Republican.

I've broken my vow a few times since. But there's no doubt that this episode is what caused me to break away from the dinosaur branch of the Republican party. Actually I'd been drifting for some time without realizing it. What in particular had begun to bother me was the ruthlessness of large corporations. Even I, a political innocent, couldn't escape noticing that these corporations, almost without exception, were run by Republicans. Was this what the Republican party stood for? Would it always stand for the big fellow and against the little one? Would it always stand for the privileged and against the needy? After that meeting at the White House, I thought I knew the answers.

Others had recognized this drift toward liberalism in me, or suspected me of it, even before I did myself. It infuriated some of them, especially during the days of the New Deal. Verna Elsinger, whose untimely death in 1933 ended what could have been a long and brilliant career, was the first to spot it, I believe. She said to me once, "You're a liberal and you don't know it. You're doing the best job of advocating and struggling for something you don't know anything about of anyone I've ever seen."

"What do you mean?" I asked her.

"You're groping to establish consumer cooperation and you don't know the difference between consumer cooperation and producer cooperation."

"No, I don't," I admitted. "What difference is there?"

It was at this point that she gave me a copy of Beatrice Webb's slender classic, *The Discovery of the Consumer*. As I read it and began to understand it I caught on fire. It seemed to me the greatest single bit of economic literature I had ever stumbled across. It was Mrs. Webb's theory that there were two great classes of societies based upon association. One consisted of associations of producers, people who had the same occupations or professions; the other consisted of associations of consumers. While associations of producers were almost as old as the history of mankind, going back to guilds, societies, castes, and the like, associations of consumers were only about a century old. Of this distinction, Mrs. Webb wrote: "I believe this distinction between the kinds of organization—between Associations of Producers on the one hand and Associations of Consumers on the other—to be no idle fancy, but perhaps the most pregnant and important piece of classification in the whole range of sociology." The fact that they existed at all was not understood until in an effort to improve their lot, some poor flannel weavers of Rochdale, England, organized themselves as consumers and set up their own grocery stores.

Mrs. Webb's description of their struggle is worth quoting. She wrote: *"These unlettered flannel weavers had unwittingly dis-*

covered, in the course of years, by the method of trial and error, that the most essential element in the creation of value in the economic sense is neither labour nor capital, but the correspondence of the application of labour with some actually felt specific desire."

That statement struck me as probably the most electrifying I had ever seen in print. What did it mean in simple, practical terms? It meant that neither the manufacturer nor the worker in a plant or factory, nor the farmer, could create anything worth having unless there were people who wanted what they made. Let us suppose a group of capitalists gathered together and invested a vast sum of money to build a plant, to buy machines, to hire technicians and laborers and clerks and managers—the whole complex system of modern manufacturing—and let us say that this vast assemblage of money and skill and brains and muscle and machines produced individually wrapped containers of pure fresh air. And let us suppose that the workers, dissatisfied with their wages, went to the capitalists and said that they wanted more money. Conceivably the argument might seesaw back and forth between the capitalists and the workers until finally it reached a philosophical stage, and these questions were asked: Which of us has created a thing of value? Have the workers created it by the skill of their hands, by the devotion to their labors, by the attention to their jobs? Or have the capitalists, by providing the machinery, the plant, the materials, and the workers' wages, created this thing of value? The answer, of course, would be resolved when an attempt was made to market the perfectly wrapped packages of pure air. No one would want to buy them. What had been created had no value. *Value* did not exist until there were consumers who wanted to buy what had been made. The power, then, of creating value lay in the hands of the consumers and not of the producers.

Let's turn again to Beatrice Webb and her account of this accidental discovery by those English weavers who, in 1844, organized the Rochdale Society of Equitable Pioneers: "They stumbled along slowly and painfully, and I doubt whether they themselves ever realised exactly where they were getting to. They began to sell groceries to themselves, partly to free themselves from the toils of 'truck,' but also with the idea of accumulating a capital fund from which they might realise their ideal of self-employment in flannel weaving. . . . In order to attract purchasers to their store, they pressed each new customer to become a member of their society, and, as such, entitled to share in its management and in its accumulating capital. In order to secure continuous membership, they invented the device of 'dividend on purchase,' whereby the margin between the cost of the article and the retail selling price was returned to the purchaser himself as a sort of deferred rebate or discount on his purchases—a sum of money which each purchasing member found automatically put to his credit in the books of the society until this credit amounted to the £1 qualifying share. . . . In those early days there was no thought of profit-sharing with the employees, for the very good reason it seemed that there were no 'profits' to divide, the so-called 'dividend on purchase' being merely a device for returning to the consumer the whole of what proved to have been charged in excess of the cost of retailing, and of carrying on and developing the common services rendered by the society to its members."

The political implications of what the Rochdale flannel weavers did were especially fascinating for me. "One peculiar, and possibly unforeseen, result was that *it established the Co-Operative Movement on the broad foundation of human democracy,* in which each member, whatever his holding, has one vote and one vote only. But it was a democracy of the customers of the store, and thus of the consumers (not the producers) of the commodities and services concerned—a democracy which was by its very nature bound to be . . . perpetually open to newcomers, without limitation of class or sex, for the simple reason that the larger the number of customers the greater the financial prosperity." I cannot convey the excitement these sentences of Mrs. Webb's touched off in me. When we first started our insurance company it never dawned on me that we would ever insure anyone but farmers. But once we started insuring farmers other than Farm Bureau members we found that we simply could not keep out the barber in the small town, the grocer, the gas-station attendant, the shopkeeper, or any other type of small businessman. Finally, as our company grew, we had to throw out the window the concept of restricting our insurance only to farmers. All along we had been moving slowly but surely into the broad-based democratic mainstream into which the Rochdale flannel weavers moved.

As I pondered the words of Beatrice Webb a thousand questions that had troubled me seemed magically answered. Why had we failed in marketing but succeeded in purchasing? Because we had powers as consumers and no real powers as producers. When would we succeed as we should? When we farmers started to link up with the greatest power in the United States, the urban consumer. Which among the farm groups was doing that? None of them. Take the Grange, for example. What was it? A great old institution. It was made up of farmers and it met a real need. The farmer had few social contacts. He didn't use his car much, he had no television, phones were few and far between, he often had no radio, and until we started rural electrification in Ohio he didn't have an electric light to read his bills by at night. The Grange brought him in touch with his neighbors. It gave him a sense of belonging. It sponsored ox roasts and ice-cream socials. It even had a secret ritual patterned after that of the Masons. It did a little marketing, a little purchasing. It had an educational program. It had a youth program. The women were members as well as the men. It was a family affair and it should have been the most natural thing in the world for it to go ahead and forge a link with its members' kin in the cities. Why didn't it?

I began to ask that question of the Grange and eventually one of the grand masters told me. "We just went to sleep at the switch." Clearly the Grange wasn't going to do this, wasn't going to link up with city people to make a giant cooperative that would eventually have an influence on every basic economic enterprise in the United States. Well, what organization would? Not the American Farm Bureau Federation. Sidney Rubinow, a little fellow who put out a newspaper for the AFBF, was one of the few people who understood that the farmers and the urban consumers had to come together. But the inescapable truth was that the American Farm Bureau was determined to keep itself strictly a farm organization. It was determined to maintain that artificial and deep schism between the farmer and the city dweller. It was determined to remain an association of producers. When the New Deal came in, I was on the board of the American Farm Bureau, the only state Farm Bureau executive secretary on that board. The rest of them were presidents of their respective state Farm Bureaus. They resented me deeply as a hired hand in the parlor. They thought I had no right to be on the board.

When the New Deal started killing little pigs and plowing grain under, creating an artificial scarcity to push up the prices of food, I kicked like a steer. "This idea of creating scarcities to create artificially high prices is social and economic suicide," I told my fellow board members. "What we ought to do is to find out how to get people to have enough money to buy what we produce." They wouldn't listen to me because the New Deal's Triple-A programs played directly into their hands as narrow-minded, self-centered producers.

The American Farm Bureau had listened to the dream music of legislation. Legislation was going to solve everything. All the farmer had to do was to let Uncle Sam fix everything for him. I wanted to see if the farmer couldn't do more for himself by lessening his costs, bettering his markets, and saving money by purchasing and marketing cooperatively. If, I argued, we'd done all we could in those areas and then decided we wanted to turn to the Government for additional help, I would have no objection. But we had not, I thought, done all we could in those areas of self-help.

I brought that up in the American Farm Bureau meetings for a number of years and got licked consistently. I remember going to Arthur Packard, who was president of the Vermont Farm Bureau and saying, "Arthur, don't you believe in what I'm saying here?"

He said, "Yes, I do."

"Then," I said, "why don't you second the motions I make? If no one seconds my motions they don't have to enter them in the minutes. And I'd like to get them into the books so we can refer to them later on." I wasn't sure I was right, but I did feel enough right on my side to want to see whether or not time would prove out what I had to say in those meetings.

Arthur's reply was simple and very frank. "Murray, I fundamentally believe in what you're saying, but I can't argue it. I can't debate it. I don't know enough about it to debate it. If I second your motion I'd have to get up and defend it. I'd make a fool of myself, and because I don't want to do that I do nothing."

I remember returning to our Ohio board with the word that I was not going to stand for re-election to the board of the American Farm Bureau. They were going up the wrong road, as I saw it, and I didn't want to spend any more time with them. Some of our people thought my attitude was just terrible. They felt, I'm sure, that I was acting ungratefully. In their opinion being on the board of the American Farm Bureau was something highly desirable, a great honor no less. Honor or not, I'd worn out my welcome.

The hostility among the board members of the American Farm Bureau varied. Earl Smith, who was president of the Illinois Agricultural Association (the equivalent of the Farm Bureau), had very successful farmers' cooperatives in operation in Illinois. And yet he was the most able advocate of the legislative program. I asked him once, "You're always talking legislation, but you've got good cooperatives. Why don't you talk about them for a while?" He never did give me a satisfactory answer.

Ed O'Neal's case was a different sort. Ed O'Neal was president of the American Farm Bureau and although I think he fundamentally believed in cooperatives, he always achieved more public prominence and glory appearing before legislative committees than he ever did in running a business. I know that the fertilizer purchasing association he set up when he was president of the Alabama Farm Bureau never did well. It was one of those sore points he didn't like brought up. Well, perhaps his reason for pushing for a legislative program had something to do with Ed O'Neal's image of himself as a farm leader. He cut a better figure in committees of Congress than he did in working cooperatives.

I want to point out that I am not against legislation simply because it is legislation. I did feel, and argued, that if we tried to solve the farmers' problems through legislation, then laws could be used to take something away from us in exactly the same way they could be used to give us something. Farmers were, and still are numerically, a decreasingly important part of the over-all population, and people who live in cities are more interested in cheap food than they are in the success of the dwindling group that continues to farm.

The debate over the New Deal farm program, or the AAA program as it came to be known, split the state of Ohio right down the middle. Western Ohio, which is largely grain-growing and made up of fairly large farms (which are necessary to grain crops), was for the AAA program, whereas eastern Ohio, which was devoted principally to dairy farming and small farms, was against it. That split ran right through our twenty-six Ohio Farm Bureau board members. Thirteen of them were for the AAA program, thirteen against it. Perry Green, who was president at the time, and I were in the middle. Everyone knew my feelings, so Perry and I had to be ultracautious.

We invited Ed O'Neal to one of our annual meetings when the debate was at its height and we had an attendance of four or five thousand. As I should have expected, he made his speech largely around support of the AAA program, the program that I called "a scarcity program." When he sat down, I threw away my own prepared remarks, took a deep breath, and went out after him as hard as I could. The effect on that audience was electric.

I went down to the men's room afterward and there found one farmer from Washington Court House so incensed over my tackling Ed O'Neal that I thought he was going to hit me. Well, if the sentiment was that strong, I wanted to know more about it.

I went home that night and said to Mrs. Lincoln, "Put your hat on, young lady, we're going to the country." For twenty-two days and twenty-two nights we toured the districts of Ohio. We met with the directors of each Farm Bureau local in the afternoon; in the evening we held open meetings for everyone.

Almost at the first meeting I noticed that there were men who ably presented the AAA program. They didn't have Art Packard's problem of being unable to state the case clearly and persuasively. They knew what they were talking about and weren't bashful. I presented my case and told them that we were there to find out what the farmers wanted to do. But these able advocates puzzled me. I asked some people to tell me who they were and I was told that they were employees of the AAA—paid representatives of the bureaucracy that had been built up around the Agricultural Adjustment Act.

At the next meeting we held, the AAA had its paid advocates and they were primed to start flowing at the first push on the pump handle. But I had caught on by this time, and when one of them got up and started to speak, I stopped him. "Now, what's your source of income?" I asked.

"I'm a farmer," this fellow replied.

"Did you earn more money on the farm last year than you did from some other source?"

And when I asked that the crowd began to laugh and chuckle and nudge one another. The man standing began to redden slightly and stammered, "Well, no, I earned more money otherwise."

"Oh, then you're on the AAA payroll," I remarked. He finally admitted it. Of course I hadn't exposed him at all. Everyone there knew who he was. But it was a sort of a point scored in my favor that I was able to find out that he was more of a bureaucrat than he was a farmer.

At every meeting thereafter I'd start out with those questions and identify the AAA agents. The opposition simmered down a little but by the time the last meeting was held in Geauga County, in the midst of a tremendous snowstorm, I knew we were licked.

Anne and I returned home at four o'clock in the morning and I had to face the fact that the twenty-two days and twenty-two nights had taught me only that the farmers wanted the AAA program. I made the switch in my own mind. "Well, all right," I said, "if that's what they want, we've got to go through with it."

I then went to Dr. George Warren of Cornell University, a man with whom farmers had consulted a good deal about their economic problems, and I said, "Doc, this AAA program isn't going to work."

"Nope," he agreed.

"And it's going to cost a lot of money," I warned.

"Yep." He nodded.

"And we're going to build a bureaucracy that'll be difficult to get rid of," I added gloomily.

"Yes, Murray, but we've got to go through with it."

"Why?" I asked.

"Just to prove that it won't work."

Just to prove that it won't work. The Agricultural Adjustment Act was passed May 12, 1933, as an emergency measure. Portions of the act were declared unconstitutional by the Supreme Court in 1936. But the AAA went on with its major program, which was price-support. I am writing twenty-six years later, in 1959, and today, *billions* of dollars later, we're almost at the point where we're willing to confess that it won't work. It was a long and expensive lesson, running through three different presidential administrations.

But one of the things in it that certainly worked, and which interested me, was that core of persuaders who were able to present the AAA program. When I was accepted back in the fraternity of farm leaders, after admitting that we had to try the AAA program, I went down to Washington and one of the first questions I asked some of the top men in the Agriculture Department was: "How did you train a bunch of these average farmers to be so effective in presenting the AAA program?" They said they got the lawyers and the legislative experts together to write down the basic, essential facts of the program and the reasons they were necessary. Then they took their principal facts and arguments to two schoolteachers and said, "Now, how do we say this in language that fourth- or fifth-grade students can understand?" And once this was done they turned over the material to their field agents. And so I learned an essential truth about education. While it's necessary to have the facts down, it's even more necessary that they be stated in the simplest, clearest language you can use.

Just as I was on the wrong side of the fence with my opposition to the AAA program, so I was on the wrong side when I sought to find some way of tying farmer and urban groups together. My readings had convinced me that here was where the farmer's true salvation lay.

Casting about for some organization that thought as I did, I heard of the Cooperative League of the U.S.A. It sounded like what I was looking for, but at first I wasn't sure. It had been founded in 1916 by Dr. James P. Warbasse, a scholarly gentleman who had been a successful surgeon. A rich man, Warbasse had organized the League to try out some of his theories of consumer cooperation. Having struggled through some of his writings before I met him, I considered him too theoretical. The impression continued after I met him. He was a fine, sincere man and a crackerjack when it came to expounding theory, but he didn't seem to know how to proceed beyond theory.

But in the early thirties the League acquired as its executive secretary a man of more practical bent, a businessman named E. R. Bowen. For years Bowen had been in charge of sales for the Avery Company in Peoria, Illinois. The company had failed in the twenties and again in the thirties. After the second failure, Bowen began to think there was something fundamentally wrong with our economic system. As he later told me, he was worried because "we're building machinery to produce food, and twice circumstances outside our control have put our company to sleep. What's wrong? Why does it have to happen?" He began to read earnestly, and through his readings he discovered a reference to consumer cooperatives, and that led him to talk with some of the League members in Illinois. He kept asking questions and, knowing Bowen, I'm sure they were the sort of questions the average cooperator couldn't fully answer. Finally, one of them said he ought to go see Paul Douglas, who was then teaching economics at the University of Chicago. So Bowen went to see Douglas, told him of his experience in the machinery business, and said, "I want to get into the consumer cooperative movement."

"Thank God," Paul Douglas told him. "That's where you belong."

"But there's one thing I don't fully understand," Bowen said. "Can you help me clear up the relationship between the organized producer and consumer?"

Douglas laughed sympathetically and then proceeded to write out a list of books on consumer cooperation, beginning with Beatrice Webb's *The Cooperative Movement in Great Britain*.

Bowen, of course, practically ate them up, he read them so carefully. And shortly after that, Douglas introduced him to Dr. Warbasse, who was so taken with him that he offered Bowen a job as the League's general secretary. At that time the League was in desperate financial straits and badly in need of some new blood. It took a dedicated man to accept that job, believe me, but Bowen took it, confident that he'd caught on to something and determined to do everything he could to put the League on its feet. First thing, he started traveling around and looking for likely new members, and that's how one day he showed up in my office.

It was on a Saturday, as I remember. I found him already there when I got down that morning. He showed me his card.

"I don't want to talk to you," I said.

He looked taken aback. "I've been selling for a long time," he said, "and this is the first time anybody ever turned me down before I started talking. You don't even know who I am."

"You're secretary of the Cooperative League, aren't you?"

"Yes."

"Well, I've read some of your literature. We don't want anything to do with an outfit that believes consumers ought to own all the farms in this country."

"I don't believe that either," he said. "I don't believe consumers should own the farms."

"You mean you're the paid secretary of this organization and you don't believe all that's in your organization's literature?"

"Look, Mr. Lincoln," he began to explain, "what you've read is one man's opinion, and the opinions of some people who agree with him. But the Cooperative League is a democratic organization, and there's room for lots of opinions."

I gestured him into a chair. "Sit down and let's talk."

We talked for two hours. He told of his quarter-century of experiences in the ups and downs of manufacturing and distributing farm power machinery and why he had finally decided to enter the consumer cooperative movement. He said that the Cooperative League was dedicated to the principle that consumer cooperative groups held the economic key to prosperity and to peace. My own feeling was that he was right. When he got up to leave, I shook his hand and said, "We ought to be in your organization."

I started at once talking to our board and the staff about the Cooperative League. That caused an enormous explosion. They reared back and declared they wanted to have nothing to do with these harebrained city people. Lou Taber met me one night on a train platform in Columbus and said, "Murray, you're a traitor to agriculture! You're trying to get these city people together and all they're going to do is to organize to try and get food cheaper from the farmer."

"Well, what's the farmer doing?" I retorted. "He's getting together to get his fertilizer cheaper, as cheap as he can, without any regard to what wages the fertilizer people are going to have to pay to meet those prices."

Lou Taber railed on and on, but the gist of it was that I was betraying the farmer and a good deal of other such nonsense. Well, Lou was asleep at the switch with the rest of the Grange and I guess when he flailed out at me like that he was simply having a nightmare.

It didn't help matters much for the board to discover that the principal members of the Cooperative League were somewhat idealistic men and women who looked upon cooperatives with starry eyes and displayed little willingness to work. Except for a few European groups around the Lake states who'd brought their cooperative ideas from Finland and the Scandinavian countries, the membership was centered mainly in the big cities along the eastern seaboard. And, there was no denying it, the movement was shot full of theory. I remember the first time I visited a cooperative cafeteria in New York City. It was during the depression, at a time when there was no idea too wild to listen to or talk about, so long as it showed some promise of putting the props back under the economy. It seemed that this cafeteria, which was located on Union Square, was a regular meeting place for left wing extremists of the labor movement. I had a friend with me and neither of us had ever seen human beings like these. They were all talking and shouting at once, all of them very serious and intent. I remember, too, that most of them seemed to have long hair, beards, and flowing ties. My friend apparently didn't feel safe there, for I don't think he was altogether kidding when he said, "My God, Murray, did you bring a gun?" I was quite relieved later to learn that this so-called co-op cafeteria was considered something of an outlaw type by my friends in New York, that in fact it had no connection at all with the genuinely cooperative cafeterias run by Mary Arnold and her Consumers Cooperative Services.

But at the time I accepted what I saw there as merely another aspect of a movement that ran in many layers and represented the legitimate feelings and hopes of all kinds of people. So I hammered away at the board for us to join the League and I would probably have been thrown out on my ear a dozen times if the late Perry Green had not somehow felt that I was sincere, even if he didn't agree with me. Perry had become president of the Farm Bureau in 1933. At every meeting I brought up the Cooperative League and what I thought it could mean to farmers. I must have infected people with my excitement even if I didn't convince them. In a few cases I convinced them and excited them without really making them understand. Ray Ascham, an engineer who had given up his profession to manage his wife's farm, attended one of our meetings and listened spellbound to my vivid claims for the Cooperative League and what our membership in the League would mean for the United States and the world at large. When the meeting was over he shook my hand vigorously, his eyes alight, and said, "Murray, I don't know what you're talking about, but it's great!"

Finally, in 1934, the Farm Bureau, after a good deal of groaning and moaning and head-shaking and grinding of teeth, voted to join the Cooperative League.

8

During the depression of the thirties, we of the Farm Bureau hung on for all we were worth. Our dues had dropped from ten dollars to five and then to two and much of the time we were collecting no dues at all. Things got very tense, although we never missed a payroll. I think we survived because we were engaged in purchasing and service. People had to have insurance for their cars and farmers had to buy feed and seed and fertilizer, even if the prices of what they sold were very low.

Despite my conviction that we were able to make their hard times easier, farmers resisted joining the Farm Bureau. This bothered me. If what we had was as good as we thought it was, why did we still have to go out and drive the roads to get the farmer to join? I finally decided that we had to find some educational system that would convince farmers they ought to join with their friends and neighbors for their own common good. But how to do it? Everywhere I went, at every institution where I spoke, I asked the same question of people: What kind of a system must you have to educate people for action in their own interest? My question just seemed to go over the heads of many. But asking it led me to do a lot of studying and probing and eventually it brought me to the place where, much to my surprise, people were addressing me as something of an authority on adult education. Years later, in fact, it brought me an appointment to President Harry Truman's Commission on Higher Education.

Actually, my interest started from a disappointment. I'd

thought that once we'd proven to the farmer that we could get results, legislatively as well as economically, he'd pay his dues with delight, or at least with a minimum of pressure. But it just wasn't happening that way. If the farmer knew the Farm Bureau was working in his interests, why on earth did he have to be prodded to support it?

I remember asking one professor, "How do you get people educated to act in their own interest?"

"Mr. Lincoln," he said, "some people have been after the answer to that for two thousand years and they haven't found it. There is no specific answer. But it helps to keep asking the question."

Then, early in 1934, E. R. Bowen heard about a Catholic university in Antigonish, Nova Scotia, where the extension department was having remarkable success educating people to act to set up cooperatives. He invited the head of the extension service, Father M. M. Coady, down to talk at the League's biennial congress. Father Coady took the audience by storm. After that, Bowen was determined that some of us should get up to St. Francis Xavier University, where all the excitement was taking place, and see firsthand what Father Coady, Father J. J. Tompkins, and the other teacher-priests were doing. The occasion came in the summer of 1935, when Bowen got an announcement of the university's annual agricultural and industrial conference. Fishermen who had been organized into fishing cooperatives, farmers who had been organized into farm cooperatives, and some union groups that had banded together into cooperatives to build their own homes, all would be there. Bowen decided to attend and wrote to ask if I wouldn't like to go with him.

Because I had always wanted to explore Nova Scotia, Mrs. Lincoln and I preferred to drive up there. Roads then weren't what they are now and several times I was sorely tempted to give it up and turn back. I persevered, though, and I'm grateful to this day that I did.

Bowen had also invited another American to observe the conference with him, a young minister named Carl Hutchinson who was working among the rural churches in Indiana. The rural churches around Chicago and throughout the neighboring regions were in trouble because of the decline in farm income. To make matters worse, a bitter milk strike was in progress. The Chicago Theological Seminary, at which Carl was a graduate student, was disturbed by the effects the strike was having on rural congregations and the consequent loss in church income. They appointed Carl to investigate the strike and the problems that lay behind it. Carl spoke to the milk-wagon drivers, to the milk distributors, to the farmers, and to the customers, hoping to learn what steps might be taken to settle the strike, but he didn't come up with any satisfactory answer. The seminary, wishing to pursue the matter further, told Carl to move himself and his family down into the farm country and to live with farmers to see what solutions might suggest themselves. It was there that he got interested in cooperatives as a means of solving farmers' economic problems. He went to Antigonish, as I did, hoping to be instructed.

Our presence at the conference caused something of an explosion among the young priests and their bishop. How explosive an element we were we didn't learn until later. The other visitors included a young girl reporter from *The New York Times* and a man from the Church of England. While they were both interested in what was happening at the college, they were afraid actually to attend the meetings. I think they feared that the college was a hotbed of subversive activity or that the priests had organized Communist cells. But though they stayed strictly away from the college grounds, they would approach us the moment we'd returned from the college to the town and pump us about everything that had happened during the day. No amount of persuasion would make them leave the town to see and hear for themselves.

I was unable to make head or tail of what was going on. The second day we were there the priests invited us to use one of their cottages. The ocean was nearby and it was amusing to watch these young men rush down to the beach, take off their frocks, and plunge into what I considered ice-cold water, where they frisked and frolicked like polar bears. They would rush out of the water, filled with all the energy and vitality of a fresh football team, put their frocks back on, and sit down to talk. They were the hardiest-looking crowd of young people I'd ever seen.

Coady was an especially impressive man. If there was a pious platitude in his make-up, I never heard it. Nor were there any in the other young priests. During the evenings they would remove their collars, and their discussion was so free and frank and uninhibited that I was astonished. They spared nothing in their discussion, including their own church. I had never heard such free discussion from anyone, let alone a group of Roman Catholic priests.

One night they called on Bowen, Hutchinson, and me to speak. We each got up in turn and told something of what had brought us to Antigonish. I told them of what we were trying to do down in Ohio with the Farm Bureau and what progress we had made in organizing farmers to help themselves. Our speeches evidently made a great impression on the bishop, because the following morning he made a brief address to all of us. I was sitting in the audience, surrounded by a group of about six young priests, and at one point the bishop remarked, "Well, this is very interesting. We're glad to have our American friends up here. Perhaps we haven't looked at this work here the way we should have in the past."

Now while I didn't consider that remark especially exciting, the young priests around me could hardly restrain themselves. They punched one another and beamed, and I heard one of them chortling under his breath, "The old man is finally catching on! The old man is getting on the band wagon!"

Later on, I learned the whole story. This is what had happened:

When the depression struck Antigonish, the fishermen there suffered, as did the shopkeepers and laborers and farmers in the area. Father Coady and Father Tompkins decided that something had to be done. One thing they did was establish credit unions so that the people could keep their homes, buy food, and so on. They then got the people to organize themselves to ship their lobster catch directly to Boston instead of selling it, individually, to the local representative of a large corporation. Once they had done that, they found they were getting eleven to twelve dollars more a crate for their catch. They had, in effect, cut out the middleman's profit. News of something as dramatic as that rushed through the country with the speed of a prairie fire. Before long there were cooperatives among the fishermen, the farmers, the workers, and virtually any group that could find a common economic interest.

Word of what had been going on in Antigonish reached higher ecclesiastical authorities who evidently didn't approve. The bishop who had permitted Fathers Tompkins and Coady to organize these cooperatives was removed. When the new bishop arrived he relieved Father Tompkins of his scholastic duties and assigned him to a parish at a place called Canso, considered one of the poorest parishes in Nova Scotia. This action so angered the priests on the college staff that they threatened to resign, especially when the bishop told them they would have to stop trying to help people economically. The people in the community got wind of what was up and threatened to boycott their own churches. In a Catholic community that must have seemed like drastic action. Now, finally, the new bishop was on the scene at the conference and could see for himself how strongly the people of Antigonish felt about their co-ops. The presence of three sympathetic Americans apparently shook him even more. He began to think twice about his attitude. And when he mentioned that he might have to reconsider, those young priests, naturally enough, were jubilant. The tide had turned in their favor.

What I discovered at Antigonish electrified me. These Nova Scotia farmers and fishermen not only knew they were benefiting from their cooperatives, they knew how and why, and they were willing to fight for them. I knew now the answer to my question:

how to get people to act for themselves. The conference I attended was the third or fourth such conference and prior to each of them, the priests had organized *small home-study groups in which people studied ways of solving their own problems.*

I returned to Ohio just bursting with ideas. I rushed to our board with the recommendation that we set up study groups. The first thing I found out was that no one wanted to do any studying. I supposed it seemed too passive, too bookish, too unrelated to the things that mattered. Someone then came up with the idea of calling them advisory councils. They would be organized to talk over problems of one sort or another and would advise the various counties on Farm Bureau policy. The counties, in turn, would advise the state organization. My feeling was that they would follow any advice they gave us if we took action on it and handed it back to them.

Some members of the staff remained skeptical. Someone said to me, maybe maliciously, although I'm not sure: "Supposing we get these people together and they decide they don't want a Farm Bureau at all. Then what?" I guess he hoped that would sour me on the whole idea, but it just stimulated me to a wild hope. "Then maybe we'll get an answer to a million-dollar question. If we can find out why people *don't* want a Farm Bureau, maybe we can find out what to do so they will want it!"

One of the first questions thrown at me by a member of the board was: "Well now, you're not going to let them talk about anything at these meetings but Farm Bureau, are you?"

I never could quite understand why that came up. It was one of our women members who raised the question. Perhaps she asked it because, like most of us, she was so sold on the Farm Bureau it seemed a waste of time to talk about anything else at such a meeting.

"These are independent citizens," I kept saying. "We have no right to tell them what to talk about. Let's just get them to talk about their problems. Let them talk about the problems of the world. In those discussions they're bound to come to the assumption that they need to work together in an organization. And when they're looking about for an organization to work in, I hope they choose the Farm Bureau. Because if they don't choose the Farm Bureau then there's something wrong with us. And if there's something wrong with us, I want to know what it is. It seems to me that we shouldn't have to do all that pounding of roads every year to get our old members to sign up again. I'm not speaking of new members. I mean the old ones." I must have convinced the board, or outtalked them, because they approved the recommendation and the orders went out to set up advisory councils.

Herb Smoots, who was then the head of our field force, got up before a meeting of the field men and told them: "Now this advisory council business is just one of Lincoln's crazy ideas and we've got enough to do without worrying about it. So just don't pay any attention to it." One of the field men, Lewis Warbington, listened to Smoots and bridled. As he told me later, he said to himself, "Lincoln is Herb's boss. And Herb is my boss. And if my boss can ignore his boss, I can ignore my boss." Lewis Warbington went down to his home county, got forty-two families together, and set up the first advisory council.

Over in Licking County we had no Farm Bureau. We had started one but it had failed. Sometime after the board had adopted our recommendation on advisory councils, we sent one of our men over to Licking County and just as a matter of cold turkey got some people together. And lo and behold, one of the first groups we got together decided it didn't want the Farm Bureau. That played right into the hands of our people who thought the whole idea was bad. They came in with some glee to report the sad decision of the group. I said, "Okay. Now, let's go back and find out why they don't want it. Because maybe then we can find out what to do in order to make them want it."

Well, the answer was simple. They had originally come together as a farm bureau. They had started some commercial work, setting up a little purchasing department. They had put in

119

a little money. The board of directors had immediately taken all the money back in credit for themselves. The manager had run off with what little was left, and those poor people had decided, on a perfectly legitimate basis, that they didn't want the kind of farm bureau they had had back in 1922 and '23. I can't say I blamed them.

From the moment the first advisory council was formed, they started to pop up like mushrooms everywhere.

I had been so impressed with Carl Hutchinson that I hired him to help us out with the councils. The idea was to get farm folks together to discuss what was the trouble with the world in general and the world of farming in particular, and see if there was anything they could do to help themselves. The leaders at Antigonish had found that if groups got too large people wouldn't talk, or would let the burden of talking fall on the shoulders of people who liked to talk anyway. Our theory was that the groups should be no larger than twelve families—a convenient number to seat around a circle in one room. We also wanted them to meet in a neighbor's home rather than a hall. Such surroundings would lead to informality and ease that you couldn't get in a hall, and informality and ease would lead to more spirited discussion. Now, all these things meant a good deal and all of them helped to make the farm advisory councils successful.

When we were first trying to decide what the councils ought to talk about, Carl grew worried. "We've got to be sure we know all the answers if we're going to tell independent people what to talk about," he said. But from our discussion came the better idea of letting them talk about anything that interested them, and I believe this freedom was what saved them. However, we had to make sure that the councils would talk about *something,* so we prepared discussion kits on some problem or another, presenting the pros and cons and suggesting suitable questions. The kit was a sort of emergency ration for the discussion leader to distribute if his group fell upon lean moments. At the beginning the groups tended to stick to these kits, answering the questions put to them. Those answers came back to us. We analyzed them and circulated the findings to other groups to stimulate further discussion. Once they got the idea that they were free to discuss whatever they liked, some of them went off in all directions at once. They discussed such improbable things as how many hooks ought to go on a fishing line, the best way to trap rabbits, and so on. But in the main they took a fairly solid course.

Some years later, when we submitted the question of buying an oil refinery to our advisory councils, those that agreed we should were the ones that stood ready to back their advice to us with cash. I suppose this was the first time the councils ever impressed our operating personnel with the fact that the advisory council concept was practical and not just one of Lincoln's crazy new ideas.

The subject of oil, gasoline, and energy in general is one so important to me that I will be discussing it throughout this book. I consider oil the single most important commodity in the world and its ownership and distribution one of the most crucially important matters that people everywhere can possible consider. You can talk all you please about sputniks, explorers, rockets-to-the-moon, ICBM's and whatnot, but without lubricants these things will not work. Without oil, they will rust into junk, and so will any defense system that relies upon them.

It was in 1935 that we decided to get into petroleum, or at least explore the possibilities. We had had a reasonable success with fertilizer, feed, and insurance. When someone suggested petroleum as the next step, Silas Vance and D. M. Cash were sent out to make a survey as to costs. When they came back, they reported solemnly, "There's no money in the oil business."

I shook my head and smiled. "Boys, you sure missed something to come up with that, because John D. Rockefeller has done all right." Well, they started to show us the prices charged by the refinery to the bulk people and what it cost the bulk people to transport and what it cost the man who drove up to the gas station, and on the basis of those figures it looked as though there was no money in selling oil or gas.

I started buttonholing people to find out why we couldn't find the profit the Rockefellers had. One day, a smart little chap named Joe Horchow, who was selling machinery to some plants in the Columbus area, walked into my office and said, "Murray, I couldn't help overhearing one of your conversations about oil. I know a number of oil people. Let me look around and talk to them about your predicament."

"Well, Joe, that would be fine."

"But if I'm going to do anything for you I want to be able to tell them what sort of business you're in. Tell me about the Farm Bureau."

"All right," I said. "Let's say you're a farmer and we're the Farm Bureau. You pay us ten dollars a year, which is something like the membership fee you might pay to the Chamber of Commerce. We try to protect you legislatively by getting a reduction on licenses charged to farm trucks as opposed to commercial trucks, keeping your taxes down, and so on. Then we set up a company to take your livestock and market that for you, and your milk and market that, and your poultry and eggs and your grain and your wool. Then we've got a company to buy your fertilizer and feed. Then we've got a company to lend you money. Then we've set up three insurance companies—one to insure your car, one to insure your life, and one to insure your property against fire."

Joe was squirming a little in his seat. "Now, wait, wait," he said, holding up his hand. "Let's see if I've got this right. I pay you ten dollars a year and you spend all that in education, legislation, and so on?"

"Yes," I added, "just as the Chamber of Commerce does for you business people."

"Then," he went on, "you take my livestock and sell it for me and make a little money on it?"

"Yes."

"And my grain, and make a little money on it?"

"Right."

"And you sell my poultry and eggs and you're making money on them?" I nodded. "You buy my feed and fertilizer and make a little money on that?" I nodded. "And you lend me money and make a little on that?"

"Right," I said.

"There's just one question I want to ask you," Joe said. "What the hell do I pay you ten dollars for? If you did that much business with *me,* I'd pay *you* ten dollars."

After Joe left, I started brooding on the good sense that had been suddenly and violently dumped into my lap. Here we had been pulling ten dollars out of these farmers at a time when every dollar was crucial to them. If we needed money to continue our activities why didn't we just take a few pennies off the net from fertilizer and feed and the rest and run the Farm Bureau on that? It wasn't long before we began to do just that and found that we had more net money than we were ever able to get out of the dues. But the odd thing about membership in the Farm Bureau was that we could not so easily drop it. We kept up our drives for membership, not because the dues meant so much to us, but because they were an educational supplement. As we drew a hundred people together in each county to indoctrinate them in the cooperative concept, and the benefits to be derived from that system, we found each time that we'd created a hundred disciples to go out and spread the gospel. Each time a man had to convince a skeptical neighbor he was convincing himself all the more. Then, too, it came to be an honor for a member of the county Farm Bureau to be chosen to solicit new members. The process gave us a base of loyal members that would see the Farm Bureau through the lean years as well as the fat.

We were still interested in going into the oil business, so after some further investigation we tentatively started to build three gasoline stations. Harvey Hull of the Indiana Farm Bureau, which was already in the oil business and doing well, encouraged us. He told us to build three bulk stations and told us further that if they did not pay for themselves the Indiana Bureau would pay us for them. The first one we got built did so well we never needed to call on his generosity. I should pause here to say that there have been wonderful examples of Farm Bureaus cooperating with one another across state lines; this is a part of the whole farmer-cooperative movement that should never be forgotten. We in Ohio helped the Missouri farmers set up their insurance company, and that sort of friendly, helping hand went in a chain fashion across the country.

Our bulk stations began to sell all the gasoline we could get and it wasn't long before the little refinery over in Warren, Pennsylvania, where we had been buying our gas, couldn't keep up with our demands. We started to run out of gas just as we were doing well, and now no one seemed to be willing to sell us any. The local refineries, of course, wanted to freeze us out of the business and had decided to let us run dry.

I went up to Chicago to look for gas and while there called on an acquaintance named Caspar Grimm. He was one of the few people I knew in Chicago, aside from those who worked for the American Farm Bureau. I dropped up to see him at his office on North Michigan Avenue. He knew of my enthusiasm for horses and told me that I ought to go upstairs to meet a man he knew who had some real horses. Caspar took me in and introduced me to Henry Knight.

Henry Knight was then one of the highest-paid salesmen in the country. His specialty was trucks. He had sold so many trucks for General Motors that they gave him a title of vice president and made him their national account man. I discovered later that he had lived in Columbus, having arrived there a few years before I did. In those days he was selling Pierce-Arrows. Since I was hardly in the market for a Pierce-Arrow, I had not had occasion to call upon him, nor he on me.

Mr. Knight and I chatted about his horses for a while. I admired the horse portraits that lined the walls of his office and presently he asked what brought me to Chicago.

"I want to buy some gasoline," I remarked.

He looked at me sharply. In 1935 the stocks of gasoline were so high that some refineries were throwing them in as a bonus for sales of lubricants.

"Well, why don't you buy it?" he asked.

"Nobody will sell it to us."

"You mean to say nobody around here will sell it to you?"

"Well, they won't sell it to us."

Henry Knight studied me. I sensed that this was something new to him. Henry was accustomed to people buying what they wanted and didn't understand why people couldn't have what they could afford. "Why won't they sell it to you?" he asked.

"I guess it's because we're a cooperative."

"What's that?"

"Oh, it's a company like any other but it's owned by the farmers who use it."

"What's the matter with that?" Henry asked.

"I don't think anything, but apparently these fellows do."

Henry thought for a moment and then he said, "Could I ask you a question that might seem impertinent?"

"Yep," I said and waited.

"Do you pay your bills?" he asked in a voice that was as apologetic as he could make it.

"Yes, you can call up the bank. We pay all our bills." That stopped Henry cold. It just tickled me to see him wrestling with the problem. Here were some men who wanted to buy something that was glutting the market and they had the money and no one wanted to sell it to them because they were a cooperative, whatever the deuce that was. Of course while Henry was an old-line, old-fashioned capitalist, he had his own integrity as a man and as a salesman.

"Well, pull on your hat," Henry finally said, "and come with me." I followed Henry over to the offices of the Pure Oil Company. There he took me up to see Neil Watson, the vice president in charge of sales. Henry said, "Mr. Lincoln, tell Mr. Watson your story."

I began telling Mr. Watson what I wanted, but I could soon see I was getting nowhere.

"No, Henry," Mr. Watson said, "we don't want that business."

"What do you mean, you don't want that business?" Henry said, indignant and puzzled.

"Look, Henry," Mr. Watson said, "if this guy succeeds—and I'm not sure he's going to—but if he succeeds, the Pure Oil Company won't need any vice president in charge of sales."

I sat next to Henry Knight and I could see the color of his face and neck change to a deep, raging red. "Neil, I've got twenty-two thousand shares of your damn stock. I paid twenty for it and it's now down to two or three dollars a share. You claim that you can't pay dividends because people aren't buying gasoline. Here's a bunch of farmers who haven't got any production and nobody's treating them right. You and I have got to eat and these farmers are producing the stuff we eat. They need gasoline. And you mean to tell me you won't sell to them?"

"No, I'm not going to, Henry."

Henry Knight clamped his teeth shut and then rose. "Come on, Mr. Lincoln," he said, "let's get out of here."

Henry Knight then took me to see R. W. McIlvain, the vice president in charge of production. "Mr. Lincoln," Henry said, "if you're not too disgusted, will you tell the same story again to Mac?" I repeated my story. McIlvain, an elderly man, rose to his feet, shaking his fist.

"I knew it! I knew it! All these years Neil has been hounding me to make money on the production end while he's lost it on sales. Here you come begging for the stuff and no one's treated you right. I'll see what I can do."

I appeared before the executive committee of the Pure Oil Company three times while McIlvain and Watson hammered at one another. Henry Knight came with me and finally the decision went against us. McIlvain apologized to me. "I'm sorry we've taken up all of your time, Mr. Lincoln. The day'll come when they'll appreciate that perhaps you've given us one of the greatest opportunities that's ever walked into this place from the outside. But right now they can't see it and I can't get them to. I'm sorry."

Henry went out of there so hot that he could have cooked steam. "Well, I'll get you the gasoline," he said. "I don't know where. But I'll get it."

Henry was so wrought up about the treatment we had received at the hands of Pure Oil that we talked one night about getting together some of his wealthy friends and buying up about a million shares of the company's stock, which was then way down. The project never came off but it would have been a real tenstrike if it had.

As a result of all this, Henry Knight became a good friend of mine and of the Farm Bureau in general. Still, I knew quite a few people who didn't trust him, who called him "the guy with the big diamond" and thought he was interested in only two things—selling us trucks and pulling the wool over my eyes.

We managed to find a little gasoline in several places, but we were looking for a refinery. We finally found one for sale in Meraux, Louisiana. Shortly after we bought it we realized that we had made an error. We had invested three hundred thousand dollars in it, and that seemed like an awful lot of money. I went to Henry and told him what had happened. "Brother," I told him, "I'm in a stew. We bought that thing and now it looks like a lemon."

"Well, now," Henry said, "don't worry if you buy one horse that isn't any good. Don't cry, just buy some more horses and bury the one that isn't any good."

Henry got in touch with some people and it wasn't long till we found that he had a refinery for us in Louisville. He had a banker buy the refinery from its owner, General Fred Miles, and we bought it on a payment plan, two hundred and fifty thousand dollars down on a property that was worth about two and a half million. Our market was so well developed that we absorbed the whole product from that refinery. And we managed to make the equivalent of the purchase price out of the refinery in four years. What amused General Miles was that we were using his money to buy it. What astonished us was that we were able to pay for it in so short a time.

We discovered, of course, where the profit in gasoline lay. The point our men Si Vance and D. M. Cash had missed was that the big oil companies traded gasoline. For instance, we sold so many gallons of gas out of Louisville to, let's say, Company "A," and took an equal number of gallons of gas out of Company "A's" refinery at Toledo; we'd give so many gallons to Company "B" and take an equal number out of "B's" refinery in Cleveland. This trading went on everywhere and it made good sense as well as good business. It saved an immense amount of money in transportation charges. There was no sense in hauling gasoline from Louisville to Toledo and paying the railroads to haul it. We were amused to learn that all gasoline was essentially alike, in spite of the high-powered advertising of brand differences. Some firms simply colored their gasoline. The trucker who hauled it added the coloring matter just as a housewife mixes in vegetable coloring to make pretty-colored cream-cheese sandwiches for her party. The man who dumped the gasoline dropped a red dye into one brand, blue into another. Many people found this story of gasoline trading hard to believe and whenever I told it there was a lot of slack-jawed shock or downright anger. I remember once telling it to a group of Ohio State undergraduates who were members of a young people's club at the Indianola Methodist Church. One bright lad got up and said, "Mr. Lincoln, I'm sorry, but my dad runs an oil business in Pittsburgh, and if that was going on, I'd know it."

"Well, son," I said, "I've got to confess that I've actually never seen the thing happen, but our own oilmen tell me that's what goes on."

Later that week I received a telephone call from the minister of the church where I'd spoken. He told me that the controversy had become so hot and heavy after I left that a group of the youngsters had decided to find out if my claim was true or not. They had gone out and waited in an old jalopy on East Broad Street. About midnight an unmarked double tank truck had driven up and dumped a load of gas at one station, then gone around the corner and dumped another load of the same gas at the station of a competing company.

"They wanted me to tell you that they were sorry they didn't believe you," the minister said.

Part Three

CHAPTER

9

IN THE EARLY 1930s few farmers in Ohio had electricity. Only one farmer in five had electric line service, for which he paid, on an average, about nine cents a kilowatt. And at that rate, of course, he used very little electricity. He had a single drop light in the center of the main room and he turned it on in the morning when it was too dark to see, turned it off the moment it got light outdoors, and turned it on for a brief period during the evening before he went to bed. The utility people weren't interested in supplying the farmer with electric power. As one of their representatives told me, "Farmers will never use enough electricity to warrant our building power lines. That's why we haven't built them."

Considering how little electricity the farmer used in those days, the argument seemed to have some validity. No one foresaw the electric washing machines, the electric pumps, the electric incubators and dryers that were soon to come. Today, on my own farm in Gahanna, Ohio, our electric bill runs to sixty-eight dollars a month, because we use so much electrical equipment. But in the thirties, even if a farmer found that he wanted a power line to his house, there were all sorts of connection charges that utility companies put on, simply to raise the cost of supplying the farmer. The charges varied according to how aggressive and smart you were. If you were a smart farmer you might not pay anything at all to have the line brought from the road to your house. If you were easygoing about it, they'd charge you whatever they thought they could without causing you to scream in pain. The highest charge I ever knew a farmer to pay for such a connection was seven hundred dollars. Of course it was nothing less than a charitable contribution to the utility company.

Now, power of any sort interested me, and when, sometime in 1935, I saw that one of the first New Deal alphabet agencies was the Rural Electrification Administration, I went down to Washington to meet Mr. Morris L. Cooke, the administrator. Shown into his office, I told him that we of the Farm Bureau wanted to avail ourselves of the benefit of this legislation and set up our own utility plants.

"What do you know about the utility business?" Mr. Cooke asked.

"Not a thing," I admitted cheerfully. "I was trained in dairying and animal husbandry."

Mr. Cooke suppressed a smile and said indulgently, as one might explain something to a child, "Well, now, we expect about 90 percent of the rural electrification to be done by the presently existing private utilities and about 10 percent by public-owned utilities and cooperatives. As you may know, it is a highly technical job and I doubt whether you or your people are equipped to handle it."

"I'll turn those figures around on you if you'll let us try it," I said.

Mr. Cooke's demeanor changed. "Young man, you're crazy."

"Okay," I replied. "But just give us the opportunity."

Mr. Cooke struggled a little and then sighed. "Well, I suppose I must because the law states that I must. But I'll be frank. I don't have much hope for you."

I rushed back to Columbus and recommended to the board

that we go into the public-utility business. The board approved and we called together our field force and told them that we wanted to set up REA cooperatives. We set up thirty throughout Ohio so quickly that no other state caught up with us. Of the first five and a half million dollars the REA loaned to cooperatives, some five million went into Ohio. We got the program well under way in seven months, although every step of it was a fight. Farmers were just itching to have electricity, and to have it from their own cooperative was a dream come true. We rushed into the business half-blind, not knowing what it was going to cost us, but knowing that it was something that ought to be done and something that we ought to be doing for ourselves.

When we announced that we were setting up our first project in Shelby County, the general manager of the Dayton Power and Light Company rushed over to Columbus to complain.

"Why are you starting in our territory?" he said unhappily. "We've got 25 percent of our farms electrified, while the rest of the state has only 18 percent."

"Yes, but 25 percent means that the other 75 percent are without power and light," I replied. We concealed the real reason we had for starting in Shelby County, which was that Piqua, a close-by town in adjacent Miami County, had a publicly owned utility from which we could buy power. We feared that no one would sell us power, just as we had been refused gasoline.

I put Carl Frye in charge of the Shelby County project. I had been in school with Carl back in Amherst. He had preceded me to Ohio and was one of the first people Anne and I saw when we moved to Cleveland. Carl was an architect; he knew nothing about public utilities. But none of the rest of us did either. I hired him because I had the feeling that on some kinds of jobs—something big and brand-new—the chances for success were better if the man in charge (presuming, of course, that he was basically competent) didn't know anything about it. He wouldn't be tackling the job with any hidebound, preconceived notions. And getting a co-op utility started struck me as a job requiring this kind of

133

fresh mind. As it turned out, our greatest handicaps were caused by the engineers sent us by the REA. They had all, at one time or another, worked for private power companies and they didn't think cooperatives could make a utility work. They were so convinced of it, in fact, that they wouldn't really help us, and we had to do a good deal of traveling to Washington to work over their heads or get them removed. Farmers were excited about electricity and they were willing to fight for it. Of course we didn't know then that the Roosevelt administration had set up the agency more to provide employment in industries making wire and poles and electrical equipment than to do anything for the farmer. But that didn't enter into our thinking. We saw a chance for the farmer to have light and power and we were hungry for it. The two things that worried a farmer the most were a mortgage and the chance of a fire. The only effective way of fighting a farm fire is with an electrically operated water pump. That comes only with power, and now power seemed to be within our grasp.

The private utility companies, of course, started out at once to torpedo our efforts. At that time they virtually controlled the Public Utilities Commission and they figured that if they could get a bill passed that would bring us under the Public Utilities Act, and thus subject us to state regulation, they'd be able to cripple us even before we got started. Henry Ballard, our attorney, and others from the Farm Bureau board appeared before a committee in the Ohio legislature that was considering this bill. Our argument was simply this: We, as cooperatives, are owned and managed by our users and hence needed no governmental supervision. Somehow this argument absolutely floored them. It was one they hadn't taken into account and one they simply didn't understand. The utility companies, nevertheless, pressed the bill in the Ohio legislature, in the newspapers, on the radio, by every means they could.

One of the chief proponents of the legislation was a member of the utilities committee in the Ohio House. He was from a rural county and he should have been on our side. Inexplicably, he was using all his influence to have the bill pushed through against us.

Henry Ballard was living at the Athletic Club in Columbus, and during the height of the utility companies' campaign he and I had breakfast conferences there during which we exchanged notes as to how matters were going in our respective ends of the fight. I was out in the counties holding meetings, while Henry was following the legislature. One morning I noticed the utilities committee member having breakfast with a man named Wilson who represented the utility lobby in the Ohio legislature. From where I sat, it looked like a peculiarly one-sided conversation, with Wilson doing all the talking.

I nudged Henry and nodded my head. "Do you see what's going on there?"

"Yep," Henry said.

"I'll bet that's where our trouble is."

The next time I had breakfast with Henry, there was this committee member with Wilson, the power lobbyist, just as thick as bees over a honey pot. I nudged Henry. "Look at that. There they are together again."

The third time I had breakfast with Henry, there they were again. "Henry," I said, "that's the third time that's happened that you and I have seen it."

The auditor of the Athletic Club, a mild little man, happened to be at our table. He glanced over in the direction I was pointing. "Oh, yes, that goes on right along," he remarked casually. "In fact," he added, "Mr. Wilson pays all his bills here at the club."

Henry and I looked at the auditor in surprise. "He does?"

"Oh, yes, I get those bills every month and Mr. Wilson sends a check to cover them."

I gave Henry a triumphant grin, sprang to my feet, and said, *"Thank you!"*

The auditor looked anxiously at me, suddenly realizing that he had let the cat out of the bag. "Oh now, Mr. Lincoln, you won't tell on me."

"You didn't tell me this in confidence, you just spit it out," I said. "I'll try to protect you as best I can, but we're in a battle right now and I may have to use this bit of information."

Now, none of the newspapers in the state felt kindly toward what we were doing. I presume that they just naturally sided with the private utility companies because the utilities represented the solid business element of the state. There was a local reporter by the name of Bill Newton. He had felt sympathetic toward us even though his paper did not, and he helped us out whenever he could by dropping us bits of information we could use. I called him up and asked him to come and see me. When we were closeted together I told him the story of the utilities committee member and the obliging power lobbyist.

"How can I use this thing and get away with it?" I asked him.

"Well," he said, "you just let me quote you to the effect that you think you know the reason for his support of that pending bill. And you believe that reason to be undue and improper influence by the utility lobby."

I said, "Okay, go ahead."

I left town that afternoon to go to Payne, Ohio, to speak to a farm meeting about the REA program. Mrs. Lincoln came along with me.

If you've ever addressed a group of farmers you know that when they come in to a meeting they fill up the last rows first, as reluctant as a bunch of kids at school. Often they will prefer to stand in the rear of the room rather than occupy the front benches or seats.

While I was speaking, one young fellow came right down to the front and took the very first seat. When he did that I sensed that there was something wrong.

The moment I finished he got up and plucked my sleeve. "Mr. Lincoln, come on outside." I followed him out. When we were out of earshot of the committee and the others, he said, "Your office has been calling you. Mr. Henry Ballard and Uncle George Cooley want to talk to you." I went to a telephone and called Columbus. Henry Ballard and Uncle George told me: "Get out of the state. The sergeant at arms of the Senate has been instructed to arrest you and bring you before a committee to substantiate the charges you made against that utilities committee member in the afternoon paper."

I suddenly got a cold feeling at the pit of my stomach and sent that young man in to get Mrs. Lincoln. When he returned I told him what I had to do.

He said, "I'll show you out of town and head you toward the Fort Wayne road, which is about ten miles from here. I know a short cut." Without so much as a good-by to the committee or the farmers I had come to address, we rushed into my car, a new Buick, and bounced off on that little country road for the crossroad.

It was a hot night and it had been dry for weeks so there was plenty of dust. Just as I hit the crossroad, with the young man sitting beside me and Mrs. Lincoln in the back, a car swung in behind us. I decided it must be the sergeant at arms on my trail. I shoved the accelerator down to the floorboard. As we roared along that primitive road at sixty miles an hour the dust boiled up behind us like a cloud. The other car kept hanging on. I just couldn't shake him and I began to have visions of myself languishing in jail. I pushed on the accelerator a little harder.

As we neared the Fort Wayne road leading to the Indiana state line, I had to slow down to let my guide out. He hopped out and I made a sharp right turn onto the road and ripped down on my accelerator, peering in my mirror for my pursuers. I was absolutely stunned to see the car that had been following me make a sharp left turn and race off in the opposite direction. Why he had hung on my tail for ten miles, eating all that dust, is still a mystery.

We arrived in Fort Wayne around midnight and put up at a hotel. I had a restless night. Anne told me that in my sleep I kept calling for Henry Ballard to get me out of jail.

The following day we spent visiting horse farms around Fort Wayne. When we returned to our hotel room late in the afternoon there was a call for me. I called back and heard the welcome news that I was to come on home. It seemed that our newspaper friend, Bill Newton, had gone to see the utilities committee member, and when he heard what we had on him, he called off the battle.

This was by no means the end of the private utilities' attempts to hamstring us. Part of the reason they didn't want us to generate our own electricity and distribute it was that they were afraid of letting us in on what had become a complete structure of prices, costs, and rates which had no relation to actual prices and costs.

Carl Frye came to me one day and said that the company in Shelby County was now organized and ready to buy transformers.

"What are those?" I asked. Morris Cooke would doubtless have shaken his head in despair if he had heard my question. Carl explained that transformers were hung on poles and that they reduced the current flow from the high-tension lines to the house lines. He went on to say that only four companies in the United States made them. We needed a fairly large order, perhaps a thousand or more, and word went out that we wanted bids on them.

I was then on the advisory board of a bank in Columbus and one of my fellow board members was an electric parts distributor. He was locally prominent and personally was a grand guy. He come in to see me one day and said that he'd like to have that order for transformers.

"Okay," I said, "get out your pencil and sharpen it."

He looked puzzled. "What do you mean?"

"Well," I said, "you have to remember that we're just a bunch of farmers and we're trying to get the cost of electricity down for our members. You've got to give us the best price you can."

"I can't cut price," he said, still looking at me as if he didn't understand what I was talking about.

"What do you mean?" I asked. "If you want the order you're going to have to give me the best price of anyone around."

He shook his head. "You don't understand. The prices on all these things are agreed to by all the companies that make them."

I looked at him steadily. "I didn't know that. How does it go on?"

"Well, it's fairly simple. We can't cut the price because the companies have all put some money into a pot and if anybody cuts price on any of this stuff, he can't take another contract until the fellow he has undercut has a contract of equal size. Then, as a penalty, the price-cutter loses what money he's put into the pot."

"Does the Justice Department know about this?" I asked.

He looked a little pained. "No, and I wouldn't want them to. If they did, and you told them, you wouldn't ever get any transformers and I'd probably have to give up the business my father started because I trusted you in the first place."

"Well, all right," I said, to pacify him. "But we're still just a bunch of farmers and we want to get as much of a saving as we can on what we buy."

"I can't cut the price," he said gloomily.

"Then we'll just go somewhere else."

"You won't get them anywhere else," he protested.

"Well, then, maybe I've *got* to go to the Justice Department."

He hesitated for a moment and then said, "Let me see what I can do."

He left and came back a short time later and said unhappily, "Murray, I just can't do anything. We simply can't cut these prices."

"That's a hell of a note," I said. "Here we are in a depression. The farmers' prices have been cut, the price of everything he sells has been cut away." I used every argument I could think of but I couldn't sway him. He remained adamant. What was worse, he would no longer discuss his real problems. He indicated that he had already said too much. I suppose I had scared him badly when I said I might have to go to the Justice Department.

I went to the president of the bank we both advised. "Will you tell this fellow that he can talk to me in confidence? That I won't betray him?"

"What are you up to?" the president asked.

"Never mind," I told him, "I've got something to do and he has to help me."

In a day or two the president had spoken to the distributor and he showed up again in my office.

"Do you want this business?" I asked him.

"Oh, gosh, yes, I do want it."

"Get your pencil out," I said.

"I told you that I wouldn't cut price," he reminded me.

"And I told you we wouldn't buy unless you did. Now tell me, off the record, what sort of a price you'd give me on a hundred-thousand-dollar order if you could do as you liked. That is, if you were free to do it."

"I'd give you 26 percent off," he said.

I shot right up in my seat. "My gosh, man!" I shouted. "Why, that's saving over twice the salary I'm getting to run this whole shooting match. That twenty-six thousand represents a whale of a lot of money to poor farmers. Why can't you give us that saving? I can't tell you what it would mean!"

"I can't, Murray," he said stubbornly. "I just can't."

"Will you tell me what the real problem is? In confidence?"

He shook his head. He couldn't and wouldn't.

I had almost despaired of hearing from him again when he showed up in my office one day after phoning to tell me that he wanted to talk business. "Now, here is the problem," he said. "The utility act in Ohio allows the private utilities a fair return on all the costs of their investment, including their maintenance charges. And they're permitted to base their rates on a percentage of that return that's usually construed to be between six and seven percent."

"Okay," I said, nodding.

"Now," he went on, "this formula which the Utility Commission approves comes out to about two thousand dollars a mile as a fair investment. If we gave the discount you wanted and you were able to construct a mile of line for eight hundred the Utility Commission would be in a box trying to explain the difference."

"Good grief," I said, "is that what we can build them for? Just eight hundred a mile?"

He turned a little pale and began to stammer. "N-n-no, no, I just used that figure as an illustration. That's way out of line." But I knew from his face and his manner that he had given me the true figure.

"Since that's the case," I said, "let me see what we can do."

Later, in discussing our problem with Carl Frye, I said, "I think we've got the tip-off." We wound up, finally, building a mile of line for $863 which was a far cry indeed from the $2000 a mile that the private companies had made the Utility Commision accept as a fair price.

How did we do it without upsetting the apple cart? We set up a separate corporation, paid the full price, and then took a rebate. Then, after everybody had forgotten the whole thing, we sent the money back to the cooperatives and dissolved the corporation. In that manner the private companies maintained their price, we got our transformers, took the rebate, and everyone was happy. I suppose to some readers all the backing and filling, the coaxing and denying, will seem childish. But the fact of the matter was that the contractors in Ohio refused to build our lines. They were afraid that if they did they would lose their chance of ever building for the private utilities. A certain young contractor was the only one with enough courage or business acumen or sense of community responsibility to do business with us. I'd like to give him credit by telling you that his name was Paul Gilmore.

The practice of price-fixing materials used by utility companies to establish artificially high costs wasn't confined merely to Ohio or to electrical components. My understanding was that it extended throughout the industry, and I suppose it touched everything the companies used, from paper clips to telephone poles. Morris Cooke told me that one day he was on a train coming up from Louisiana, and in the club car a lumberman who had too many drinks confided that he was on his way to New York for the annual setting of the price of poles.

"I wish I could sell all my timber to those fellows up there," the lumberman said with a chuckle.

Cooke wanted to know why.

"Because I go up there and they tell me what to charge them."

I suppose there is a question of morality involved in what the private utilities were doing then, but they would have been the last to admit it. In fact I am sure that in their own judgment they were doing only what they had to do in order to protect their investment. But I don't believe that a cash investment in a business gives a man a right to try to influence legislatures, to act collusively, to be protected from failure through mismanagement, imprudence, or greed. I don't believe a cash investment in a business gives a man a right to do anything but get a fair return on his investment. To my mind the story of the private power utilities in the United States has been an ugly one. I realize that there are many good people who will disagree with me on this, but in view of my experience I can hardly think otherwise. In my opinion the attitude of many private utilities to this day is so pious and the façade of public service so smooth and unwrinkled, one sometimes gets the impression that they are making no money at all. I contend that they make plenty. They wouldn't stay in business if they didn't. If they found themselves failing they would promptly turn the job over to public ownership. There is money in power and proof that there is comes from the continuous and bitter campaigns some private power companies wage against any other method of operating. When a utility gets to represent a majority interest in an area it should be publicly owned or cooperatively owned. After the cooperative electric companies began operating in Ohio, we managed to cut the cost of electricity directly in half, from nine cents a kilowatt to four and a half. Those excessive connecting charges went out of the window all over the state the moment the cooperatives announced they would not levy them. I often wonder how that poor devil of a farmer who paid seven hundred dollars for a line to his house felt when that happened. When we were done in Ohio, 98 percent of all farm homes were electrified.

However, the private utilities still had a trick or two up their sleeves. While we managed to squash the bill that would have brought us under the Public Utilities Act, the power interests succeeded in passing legislation that prohibited us from crossing established utility lines. Of course, they then raced to put up poles everywhere they could to block us. This led to some interesting situations. In one area in downstate Ohio, our lines were going to pass for a short distance on a road between the lines of the two established utilities. When they became aware that we intended linking up two counties they joined forces to cut us off. In their haste they neglected to obtain consents on right of way from the farmers in the area. And the farmers happened to be members of our cooperative. We had a little newspaper going out and while the whole rural electrification fight was going on we sent out bulletins. The farmers were steamed up for a fight.

When the poles went up, the farmers got together and chopped them down. The utility people came back and put them up again and again the farmers chopped them down. It got to be a sort of game. One day I got a call from a sheriff in that area. "Look, Mr. Lincoln, these guys have made up their minds that they're not going to let them put up any more poles. They're going to be out there with pitchforks to drive that construction gang off. Someone's liable to get hurt." I telephoned the county committee and told them that while we deeply appreciated their loyalty and their support we didn't want to see anyone get hurt. In the end we went to court and got out an injunction against the utility people.

We had started operation of our first company and it was a bright day for us when the power came on in Shelby County.

Our second company was scheduled to start operation in the neighboring county, Champaign, because we wanted to hook up to that same publicly owned utility for our power supply.

The Farm Bureau in Champaign was scheduled to have a meeting in Urbana to discuss its participation. There had been opposition within the board of that county Farm Bureau and I was worried about it. It was pretty important that we build our companies in sequence, joining one county to another. Our men had had two or three meetings with the local board of that county Farm Bureau and now there was to be a membership meeting at which a vote would be taken.

Some sixth sense told me I ought to be at that meeting. Carl Frye and Herb Smoots went with me. When we got to Urbana I told Carl to go down to the office of the Farm Bureau and see what was stirring. Herb Smoots and I went on up to the hotel. As we entered the lobby I saw two members of the local board huddled up with two power-company officials from Dayton. These were the same two board members who had strongly opposed participation in the utility cooperative. My sixth sense had been right. I marched up to them and said, "Hi, you're going to be at the meeting tonight, aren't you?" They looked kind of sheepish and said they would be. I went on to the meeting and made a little speech and kept my eyes glued on that pair throughout the evening. I didn't think they'd have the gall to vote against entering the cooperative electrical net after I had seen them parleying with the power lobbyists. Had they voted no, I would have told them off in front of their friends and neighbors, and I guess they knew I would. As it turned out, they cast their votes for participation and so Champaign County came peacefully into the fold.

We were running up quite a bill, about a hundred thousand dollars, advanced to county cooperatives for the engineering work, and our staff began to nag at me about the money we'd invested. Two of the staff, I suppose, were just financially cautious. They saw us paying out a lot of money. Other members of the staff disliked our association with the New Deal in any guise.

The Government had, of course, guaranteed that we would get back what we paid out and 5 percent additional for planning and engineering and administrative costs. John Carmody, who had taken Cooke's place as head of the REA, reassured me, "Now, Murray, you'll get all your money. Just keep at it. Don't raise any questions, just keep on doing it as you have. You're doing fine."

But the temper of the staff and that of some members of the board wasn't favorable. There were cries that we were going to be hoodwinked, that we would lose our money. Frankly, I didn't care if we did lose what money we had invested. It seemed to me that what we had done was a great boon to the farmer and the money would be well spent. I hadn't thought of it in terms of a cash investment from which we were going to get a cash return. We had helped thousands of farmers to electrify their homes and their machines for making their livelihood. To me, this was return enough. We had, of course, lowered utility rates not simply for the farmer but for everyone else. We had demonstrated what simple people, working together without special technical skills, could accomplish for themselves. We had, in short, demonstrated what the cooperative way could do for people and I thought it worth every dime we had spent. The Government had not yet paid off the monies we had spent because the engineering was not completed. Members of the staff kept yapping that it never would pay off—that we ought to quit now and not pour good money after bad. The question of when we were going to stop arose at every discussion of the budget. There was so much acrimonious wrangling and bitterness that I finally gave up and said, "Okay, we'll quit."

We did and lost, after a final count, about forty thousand dollars. If we had stayed on another six months we would have recouped that and made something more. Indiana stayed in, and not only got its money back but made some sort of a profit.

One of the odd human sidelights that came out of the Farm Bureau's participation in the REA occurred after we had actively withdrawn. One of the local REA cooperatives was trying to buy the Ohio Midland Light and Power Company, a small utility with headquarters near Columbus, to add to its territory. There were two bids put in for the purchase of the company. One was from the local REA cooperative, the other came from a mysterious figure in Chicago. We were tipped off that the Chicago party represented a major utility in Ohio. Despite the fact that the local cooperative's bid was the higher one, the Ohio Midland Light and Power found itself tied up in court and it appeared that the local cooperative's bid would lose out.

We had meanwhile bought the Eureka Maryland Insurance Company, and had just transferred all its stocks and bonds to our office in Columbus. Lee Taylor sat there counting them and checking them and, lo and behold, we discovered that we owned some one hundred thousand dollars' worth of stock in the parent company of the Ohio Midland Light and Power. That put a totally different complexion on the matter.

Then the strangest thing happened. We received an anonymous telegram from Philadelphia informing us that on some trumped-up technicality both bids were going to be thrown out and the whole thing opened up for re-bidding. This would give the Chicago party, or whomever he represented, the chance to raise his bid, and we were told that if that local co-op really wanted to buy Ohio Midland Light and Power it had better be prepared to raise its bid too. In other words, Ohio Midland's directors meant to move heaven and earth before agreeing to sell out to a cooperative.

I wired the parent company, informing them that we were stockholders to the tune of a hundred thousand dollars. I told them that if the higher bid by the cooperative was not immediately accepted by Ohio Midland Light and Power we would enter a suit against the parent company. Officers from the parent company informed us that the bid would be accepted and that we need not sue.

Who was our mysterious informant? We don't know. Not to

this day. Why did he send us that wire? We don't know that either. Why should anyone in Philadelphia care what happened to a bunch of farmers in Ohio? I don't know. I prefer to believe that someone who was on the inside of something crooked couldn't stomach it and had to yell, "Look out!" Whoever it was, if he or she reads these words—our thanks.

I wish we had stayed in the utility business, but we didn't. Well, all right, there are other things to do in the world that are just as important and perhaps even more so. However, I believe that the rural electric cooperatives established by the Ohio Farm Bureau Federation are among the most dramatic demonstrations of the power of the cooperative concept that this country has ever seen, and I am proud to say that I had a share in their conception, beginnings, and early days.

10

Shortly after I'd been elected to the board of the Co-operative League, in 1934, I got into an argument with dear old Dr. Warbasse. The board had voted to do something which required twelve hundred dollars and the treasurer reported that there was no such money in the League's account. I said, "Well, Dr. Warbasse, if I'd been with an institution for twenty years and it didn't have twelve hundred dollars in the bank to do something the board wanted me to do, I'd say there was something wrong with me or the institution or both."

There *was* something wrong, and it didn't take long for me to learn what it was. Except for those Finns up in scattered stores in and around Duluth who knew what they were doing and were willing to work hard for it, the groups within the League were pretty ineffectual. Then too, a good many of the people in the city co-ops were as leery of us as our farmers were leery of them. I suppose they were afraid that we would take the leadership away from them because we were bigger, richer (or at least richer than they were), and more vigorous.

After I'd been on the board for about a year, though, an old Finnish member, Bill Liimatainen, came up to me and said, "You're all right."

"What do you mean, I'm 'all right'?" I asked.

"You're all right," he repeated, nodding his head.

"Well, that must mean that at one time you didn't think I was all right."

He smiled. "No," he said, "we were just afraid of you fellows from the Farm Bureau. We really didn't believe that you believed in consumer cooperation. But you're all right. You've got it." I don't know whether that feeling of trust pervaded the League but I was proud to hear it from that man, at least.

In the thirties, two national purchasing organizations were set up, each for the same purpose—to enable wholesale cooperatives to reap the benefits of economy-size buying. Regional oil cooperatives, some serving both urban and rural people, formed National Cooperatives, Inc. State farm bureau cooperatives of Michigan, Indiana, Ohio, and Pennsylvania, and other regional cooperatives which served only farmers—the Grange League Federation of Ithaca, New York, and the Southern States Cooperative of Richmond, Virginia—formed United Cooperatives, Inc.

We were members of both National and United, but that was about all the two organizations had in common. United would have nothing to do with National because National did business with city people and United not only refused to do business with city people, it refused to do business with farmers who did business with city people.

It didn't make any sense, but the animosity was there just the same and it worked against our common interests. I recall once that the sales manager of one of the big Akron tire companies approached me at a meeting and said, "Aren't you people co-operative?"

"Yes," I answered.

"Well, why in the world don't you two organizations get together to buy all your tires from one source? Some of you buy them from me and some from Dunlop. If you'll pool your orders you'll get a lower price."

The answer, of course, was a simple one, even if it wasn't a pleasant one. I had to explain the jealousy of the managements involved and the stubborn refusal of United Cooperatives to have anything to do with any cooperative organization "tainted" by the presence of city persons in its membership. What that sales

149

manager asked was a question of ordinary common sense. The reason why my answer made no real sense was because sense had nothing to do with the dispute. Emotions lay at the bottom of all these antagonisms and hostilities.

I was not fully aware of how deep these emotions and hostilities lay. If I had been, I might not have made the speech I made on June sixteenth, 1936, before the twelfth annual session of the American Institute of Cooperation at Atlanta, Georgia. Looking back now, from a vantage point of some twenty-three years, I consider it the single most significant address I have ever delivered. And yet it was a total flop. It was called "The Producer and Consumer Cooperative Relationships in America." The title alone was a kind of red flag in front of a bull because the principal attendants of that session were producer cooperatives. Their chief interest was in agriculture, and not in the consumer's end of it either. Not by a long shot.

You will recall that I had discovered Beatrice Webb's little book, and that I had gone through the long fight over the AAA program. It now seemed to me that I was beginning to have an understanding of why farm groups hadn't been more successful. To some degree I thought it was their frustration in trying to do things for themselves that led them to turn to the Government during the crisis of the depression. I felt that if they could become more effective in the area of helping themselves they might be weaned away from government support programs. One of the ideas I'd come across was that the consumer interest came nearest to being the main interest of people in general. Well, if you can't lick 'em, join 'em, is a strategy that still makes good sense. Producer cooperatives had always tried to find some way of licking the consumer. What was wrong there, I saw plainer and plainer, was that producer cooperatives would *never* lick the consumer, but stood a fair chance of disappearing in the fight. It seemed to me that producer cooperatives would never truly be successful unless and until they accepted consumers as equal partners.

One of the most important groups at the American Institute's session was the National Council of Cooperatives, an educational and informational organization of marketing and purchasing cooperatives that had been especially effective in influencing farm legislation. Ed Babcock was later to become president of that organization and Ed Babcock and I had a curious temporary alliance, but I do not want to get ahead of my story.

My speech at Atlanta was fairly long and I will spare you the details. What I said, in substance, was this: We are born consumers. We become producers in order to live and consume. The true value of what we produce is ultimately determined by the consumer and not the producer. The people at Antigonish have said that people must regain the power to serve their own wants by owning and operating the machinery by which their wants are served. There are three ways open to us for regaining that ownership. One is by asserting ourselves as citizens through political action. Another is by acting together as producers. And the third is by mobilizing our resources as consumers. Which of these is best?

Political action cannot pioneer. Resting as it does upon the consent of all (or the majority, anyway) of the people, political action is an effective procedure only after the feasibility of an idea has been demonstrated and the people are of one mind. Cooperation as producers stresses the selfish interest of one group as against another and promotes the same self-seeking competition among groups of producers that defeats its own end in private enterprise. Cooperation as consumers is a vital element of economic control. The free decision of the consumer to buy in any market he chooses constitutes a power that neither direct political action nor direct producer action can rival. In short, the consumer is the most important single individual in any economy. And the farmer is a consumer as well as a producer.

When I finished my speech, the secretary of the National Council of Cooperatives declared that if the farmer was a consumer then he (the secretary) was a jackass. And as I've said so many times since, that proved that he was.

The leaders of the Council of Cooperatives were so upset and angered by my speech that one of the first things they did was change their name to the National Council of *Farmer* Cooperatives in order to separate themselves from any consumer cooperative liaison that E. R. Bowen or I might dream up to entangle them. I was thrown out of the official farm circles from that moment on. I became a marked man.

But there was one ironic sidelight. Despite the nature of my speech, Ed Babcock rose at this meeting to say that he was about to become president of the National Council of Farmer Cooperatives, that he understood I was due to be the next president of the Cooperative League, and that between us we were going to cooperatize America. Why he did that I'll never know.

Ed Babcock had been a county-agent leader. At the time I met him he was an organizer for the Grange League Federation in New York. He and GLF had some reservations about the AAA program. In fact, the whole eastern part of the United States had some reservations about the program since they were the ones who had to buy the grain and cotton and other commodities which were being price-supported by the AAA. So Ed Babcock and I had some grounds for agreement on this point at least. He had dramatically demonstrated his agreement with me when he described us as the cooperators of America. And yet the National Council of Farmer Cooperatives was one of the bitterest and most implacable opponents of farmer-consumer cooperation.

Mr. Babcock asked me to visit him the next time I was up his way. So not long after, when my wife and I were returning from a visit East, we stopped in Ithaca and went out to have lunch with him. Mrs. Babcock wasn't present, so Anne cooked the meal. After we were through, Ed asked her if she wouldn't like to go outside and look about the place or go upstairs and take her rest. We'd had a good night's rest already and Anne said no, she'd rather stay and listen to us talk.

So Ed and I sat down and talked. We talked about the Grange.

We talked about the Farm Bureau. We talked about him and we talked about me. We talked about Lou Taber and Ed O'Neal and all the other farm leaders. And in that kind of deep wisdom which often follows a good meal in pleasant surroundings, we decided that these other fellows weren't going to get the job done. Toward the end of our conversation, Ed said something I've never forgotten. He said, "Murray, you've been studying this whole question of consumer and producer cooperatives and I think you've got it. You're ahead of most of us and I just want to be a worker in your vineyard."

My wife and I then left to drive back to Columbus. As we drove through the hills of Ithaca, I said, "Did you hear what I heard?"

Anne said, "Yes, and I don't understand all this opposition you've been telling me about."

I tried to envision Ed Babcock as a worker in my vineyard and somehow the picture didn't look right. "Something's going on here," I said, "but I certainly don't understand it."

One of the things we had discussed in that long post-luncheon talk was a piece of legislation having to do with agriculture. I have forgotten now what it was. But Ed and I agreed that if we were going to make a joint venture of turning America into a cooperative vineyard we would have to consult the White House about this particular matter. It was a basic first step.

Shortly after we got home, I got a telegram from Ed summoning me, along with all the other farm leaders, to Washington for a consultation. I called Ed and asked him if he had checked the matter with the White House and he said he had. If that was so, I said, I would come along. I didn't want to attend a meeting unless this preliminary had been taken care of.

My previous agreement with Ed Babcock had so elated me that I happened to mention it to David Niles, Franklin Delano Roosevelt's administrative assistant. The news so impressed Dave Niles that he said, "Well, let's go in and tell that to the boss."

"Whom do you mean?" I asked.

"Roosevelt," he said with a smile.

I was shown into the President's office. He was sitting at his big desk signing papers and I told him the story of the agreement I now had with Ed Babcock. Roosevelt, with his usual gusto, smiled and nodded and said, "Fine, fine. Well now, that's good. That's very good."

After we'd left his office, Dave said, "Did you notice the boss's fingers?"

"No," I admitted. "I was too excited just being in there talking with him."

"Well," Dave said, "he had them crossed."

"What does that mean?"

"He was telling me 'Look out!' Not that he was questioning your truthfulness. But he was questioning whether or not the circumstances were as you thought they were."

That warning was in my mind when I attended the meeting in Washington. Ed Babcock was chairman. The first fellow he brought in was Ed O'Neal of the American Farm Bureau. Because I knew Ed O'Neal was diametrically opposed to everything I believed in and advocated, I slipped out of the meeting and went back to see Dave Niles.

"Did Ed Babcock check with you about this matter?" I asked.

"Hell, no," Dave said.

I returned to the meeting and took a chair on the aisle to give Babcock plenty of opportunity to see me during his trips in and out—to give him the chance to stop and say, "I made a mistake," or something like that. But he never did.

What came out of the meeting so disturbed and alarmed me that I went back a second time to the White House. I told Dave Niles, "I've either been double-crossed or I've misunderstood or something."

He grinned and said, "Do you remember the day you told this story to the President and he crossed his fingers?"

"Yep."

"Well," he said, "we're not surprised, Murray."

"I am," I said unhappily.

"We know politics in New York and while we were very happy that you thought you had an agreement with Mr. Babcock, I'd like to tell you one thing that tipped us off. Nobody believing as you do could be chairman of the Board of Trustees of Cornell University, and Mr. Ed Babcock is chairman of the Board of Trustees of Cornell University."

I packed my bag and went home without talking to Ed Babcock. I have seen him just one time since. Some years later I was on the second floor of Brooks Brothers in New York. It was early in the morning and the only other customer on that floor was Ed Babcock. I deliberately approached him, meaning to give him a chance to explain whatever it was that had caused him to reverse himself. Instead, he just said "Hello" and walked away. "Hello," I said, and that was the last word I ever spoke to him.

This controversy over farmers joining with consumers was bound to reach home. When we'd joined the Cooperative League there had been an explosion at the Ohio Farm Bureau, but the most serious part of that explosion took place underground. Hostilities were started that I didn't understand or even see much of. Some of our staff people—particularly Lee Taylor and Gene Hensel, who was a nephew of Henry Ballard and a member of his law firm, and whom we called our house attorney—were violently opposed to me and my ideas. But not openly.

I used to dread the day when the question of renewing our membership in the Cooperative League came up because of the opposition I'd meet. I knew some members of the board were opposed to it. But I had not realized that the staff was also deeply involved in that opposition.

One day Gene Hensel came to me and made the suggestion that he go on retainer rather than continue on salary. He wanted to work this way, he said, because he eventually wanted to start his own office. He wanted to know if I'd sign two one-year contracts with him to pay him as much of a retainer as he had previously received as salary. I said, "Sure."

The minute he got my signature on those two contracts, he said, "Murray, all I want is your confidence."

I looked up, rather startled, and said, "Have you done anything to warrant your losing my confidence?"

"All I want is your confidence," he repeated, and he left my office.

Now when a man says a thing like that all he does is arouse ominous feelings in the man whose confidence he wants. And I was no exception. I went across the corridor to Perry Green's office.

"Perry," I asked, "is there something going on around here that I don't know about? It looks to me as though somebody's conscience is beginning to trouble him and I haven't the slightest idea what's up."

Gene Hensel's plea for my confidence was my first intimation of the power struggle that was eventually to break out within the Farm Bureau. Of course I knew that some members of our staff resented what we were doing. This was clearly illustrated by an incident reported to me a little later.

Gene Hensel and other members of the staff represented us at different insurance meetings throughout the country. On one occasion they traveled by train to California for a life convention or some such meeting. One night as they were crossing the continent the president of another insurance company, a man who didn't much like us, got some of our staff members into a card game. He started joking about the Farm Bureau's being a cooperative, trying to get an argument out of them simply as a way of having some fun. The teasing evidently didn't go down well with Gene Hensel, who finally said, "Hell, I don't believe in all that stuff they're talking about. I just work for them." The odd part of this was that the insurance company president bridled at this remark and afterward reported it to Bill Safford, who had been superintendent of insurance for Ohio. "Bill, you'd better tell Murray about this man," the president said. "While I don't care much for what he's doing, I think Mr. Lincoln's an honorable man and I wouldn't want a member of my staff to say what was said this evening."

Hensel may have picked up his attitudes toward cooperatives from his uncle, Henry Ballard. It seems a harsh thing to say about a man now dead, but I don't believe Henry Ballard ever understood or believed in the cooperative concept. I know that Henry did his best to keep me away from insurance examiners and commissioners for fear that if I should start to explain the concept of the cooperative I might do the insurance company irreparable damage. Where he got this notion, I don't know. I suppose he distrusted cooperatives himself and felt that no reasonable case could be made out for them. Well, he was wrong and we proved it later on in 1948. But that is something else.

I finally went to Lee Taylor, my assistant, and said, "There's something going on around here that you haven't told me about, and you're my assistant and I'm assuming that you're loyal to me. If there's something you haven't told me, I think you ought to tell it to me now." Lee got white as a sheet and said that he thought he ought to resign. At that point there was no doubt in my mind that something was definitely wrong.

Accusations then arose against me for being autocratic and arbitrary. My arbitrariness was particularly cited in the hiring of Herbert Evans, now president of our subsidiary, Peoples Broadcasting, and Harry Culbreth, now vice president in charge of our Human Relations office, both of whom were out-of-state men experienced in consumer cooperatives. The accusations were made by a board committee appointed to review my powers. The committee maintained that I had consulted with no one before hiring Evans and Culbreth. I said that I had. They came back at once with the question: "Who?"

I replied that it was up to the board members I had consulted to speak up. Ed Stough, then and now one of our board members,

157

finally said, "Yes, I discussed it with Murray, and also with Perry Green." Max Scarff, who was chairman of the committee and still a member of our board, said, "Well, what are we having this meeting for?" The charges were dropped then and there.

There is nothing pleasant in the recollection of matters like this. There are other details of that fight that ought to be recorded but these are not things I particularly want to remember. They caused me a good deal of pain and anguish, particularly since one of the men who sought to have me fired was a close personal friend of mine. I treated him as I would have treated a son—if I had had one. Betrayal is an ugly word and one I don't like to use. If you are going to do something worthwhile in the world you're going to have to trust a lot of people, and trusting people means liking a lot of them. Sooner or later liking turns into affection. If you trust a lot of people, one or two of them are going to betray that trust. That's inevitable and something you should simply take for granted. But when the laws of chance put that betrayal in that small group of people for whom you also have affection, it hurts and it's not easily forgotten.

The tragic things that happen to a man in life are always unexpected. They seize him when he is most vulnerable. I know of no man who was ever ready for tragedy. My daughter, Betty, died at the age of fourteen, struck down by a heart attack. I was not prepared for it. It stunned me. I cannot, to this day, find words to discuss that tragedy. Betty's life was full and happy— and brief. I did not enjoy much of it with her because during those years in which she was growing up I was busy with a thousand matters, all of which seemed terribly important. Not all of them were. I sometimes wonder whether any of them were, compared to some days with my daughter that I might have had. A man does with his life what he can, lives it for some purpose a little higher than mere selfishness, moves the earth a little closer to kindliness, to civilization, to the appreciation of each man's dignity. If anything I've done in my life has made the life of any man, woman, or child a little sunnier, a little more hopeful, then

I can count that a happy hour spent with my daughter, for I like to think that other men used their lives to make her life happier or brighter or more worth living—and used their lives without knowing her and without loving her. There are men who think this way and they form a golden chain from the birth of the race. I would like to place my life as a small link in that chain and I say that in the full knowledge that I may not, at the end, be considered worthy.

11

SEVERAL TIMES I've had occasion to mention Perry Green, and there'll be more references to him later. Perry meant a great deal to me as I was struggling along. I'd like to pause now to tell you about him.

Perry was born in a northeastern Ohio farm home but, unlike myself, he was not inclined to accept his destiny as a farmer without question. He was a schoolboy during the early days of the big farm movements, when the Grange, the Farmers Alliance, and the Populists were so active. Those were fairly exciting times in Ohio, when the farmer's cries of protest were almost matched by his hopes for reform, and Perry spent a lot of his youth bicycling from one political rally to another. I gather, though, that the main effect of listening to all those silver-tongued orators was to convince him that a farmer's fortunes were pretty uncertain. Anyway, by 1896, when William Jennings Bryan was defeated for president and the whole agrarian movement collapsed, he'd seen and heard enough to decide that the less he had to do with farming the better.

So he went to Hiram College, and from there to Cleveland to go to work in a wholesale hardware business. He got married. He began to look and act and talk like a businessman. But six years later he quit business—temporarily, he thought, and only to help out his ailing father-in-law on a dairy farm south of Hiram village.

What happened was that Perry did so well at dairy farming he never did get back into business. By 1911 he'd become a charter member of the Portage County Improvement Association, the forerunner of the Portage County Farm Bureau. He was interested in seeing that the individual farmer had a voice that could be heard against the organized voices of labor, business, and finance, and this led him to support the organization of the Ohio Farm Bureau Federation in 1918. When, in 1920, farm prices had fallen and costs had risen, the farmers chose Perry Green to represent them in the Ohio legislature. Perry didn't campaign. He didn't have to. The men who believed in him campaigned for him. They elected him. Not once but five times.

In the legislature, Perry became chairman of the Finance and Agriculture Committee and exerted a good deal of influence on farm policies and programs. He initiated legislation for a system of secondary roads and for the purchase of demonstration forests. He co-sponsored the Green-Farnsworth bill to provide a legal structure for farm cooperatives; today virtually every farm co-op in the state uses this structure.

I don't recall the first time we met. Perry became treasurer of the Ohio Farm Bureau Federation in 1927. In 1933 he became president and stayed president for the next fifteen years.

In the early days I had the feeling that Perry wasn't very friendly. He seemed reserved and cold. He was a successful dairyman and had a background of being a successful legislator and was highly regarded by one and all, but I didn't understand him. One of the people we hired to help out with organizational work was Perry's herdsman, a young, able, and progressive farmer named Fred Schoenberger. Once I recall asking Schoenberger, "What the Sam Hill is wrong with Perry Green?" I remember asking the question out of irritation over the way in which Perry had reacted to some matter in which I thought he should have taken a more forward-looking position.

Fred Schoenberger said, "Well, he's a great guy, but he needs a good bump."

161

It was five years before I appreciated the astuteness of that remark.

In 1929 people who understood the relationships of farm prices to consumer purchasing power began to see the handwriting on the wall. Quietly they began to sell out their farm holdings. But Perry did not and by 1931 he was financially ruined. The wonderful dairy herds of which he was so proud were gone. And in Christmas week of 1932, when he was on an auto trip with Norman Shaw, an editor of one of the Ohio farm papers, he was involved in a tragic accident that claimed Shaw's life. Perry landed in a hospital with a brain concussion.

Perry told me later that while he was in the hospital he started to think through his whole life, its purposes, its meaning, its direction. The double effect of the loss of his personal estate and his near brush with death changed his attitude toward many things. In Fred Schoenberger's words, Perry had received "the bump."

After that Perry and I became very close for many reasons. For one thing, he was one of the few people with whom I could sit down and talk future plans and do so with the satisfied feeling that here was a man who was able to keep up when he wasn't running ahead. I do not mean to say that we always agreed. We did, in fact, have a sort of running debate all the years he was president over what I was to do and not to do, and yet we always managed to argue it out and settle it between ourselves. I would have been fired many times if Perry had not acted as a sort of speed regulator on me. When I was going too fast for the board, Perry would take me aside and say, "Now you better slow down until the crowd catches up with you." It got to the point where board members would look to Perry to see whether they ought to sustain me or hold back. Perry and I had, finally, such an intimate relationship that I would go no further and no faster than we had previously agreed I should.

He had remarkably sensitive judgment of the quality of the men we both dealt with and to this day I am deeply aware of the loss that his death has brought both to me and to the insurance companies. One of his greatest interests lay in finance. He became one of the best-informed farmers in the country about the interplay of monetary forces. He drew up a plan of farm credit and central banking to help fight the depression. He went to Washington with the plan and although it wasn't put into effect, a good number of its provisions were embodied in the setup of the Farm Credit Administration. In Ohio, the plan took form in the establishment of the successful Farm Bureau Agricultural Credit Association. Perry could speak more knowingly on money than any person I ever knew. One of the stories he loved to tell on himself was that after a speech on money to an audience of farmers, one of them reported back to the Farm Bureau Federation office to say, "He knows what he's talking about, all right, but be danged if we do."

Perry's counsel was especially valuable as I sought to push our board into tackling new relationships, new enterprises. In an effort to broaden my own concept of consumer cooperation during the latter days of our REA adventure, I began to explore seriously the possibility of tying our interests to those of the urban workingman. This led me to find out more about the labor movement in America. To a lot of the Farm Bureau membership I guess it looked as if I were deserting, or at least moving into no man's land. Perry wasn't altogether sympathetic with what I was up to, but he was extremely helpful in pointing out pitfalls that I might otherwise have fallen into blindly, and he was particularly persuasive in defending my behavior before his fellow board members.

One day I asked John Carmody, the national REA administrator, if he would introduce me to some labor union leaders. Carmody asked me why I wanted to talk to them. "For one thing," I said, "the members of their unions eat what farmers produce. Since there are more of them than there are farmers I think they can swing more political weight than we can. I would like to know what they are up to and what they are thinking."

Carmody said he would do what he could and shortly thereafter it was arranged that I should meet John L. Lewis. Not only was I to meet him, but on three different evenings in the homes of three different men.

Lewis, from the first moment I met him, simply captivated me. He was one of the most delightful dinner companions I'd ever met—witty, amusing, astonishingly well read, with a great memory for the classics and the Bible. He was, in person, so totally different from all the caricatures and reports I had seen and read of him that I could hardly believe that this was the same man.

The second evening we began to discuss economics and I found that I disagreed with him. I wasn't able, however, to do much against his wonderfully flamboyant air of being so sure of everything he said.

By the third evening I became stubborn and began to dig in and talk back. We talked about cooperatives.

"Well, I believe in cooperatives, Mr. Lincoln," Lewis said. "I was born into a cooperative family in the coal-mining area of southern Illinois. My father was the head of a local cooperative. But they all failed."

"Yes," I said, "and I'll bet you don't know why they failed."

"Well, why did they?" he asked.

"Because," I said, "you used a cooperative to extend credit to your miners during the time you had a strike. You violated one of the cardinal principles of a cooperative, which is that it has to conduct its business on a cash basis. It wasn't the cooperative that failed. You just used up all the assets of the cooperative to support a strike, and a strike is a producer action."

"Well," he said thoughtfully, "I never understood that before."

We then went on to talk about the miners and their conditions.

"As far as I'm concerned," I told him, "I never want to dig coal. I wouldn't want a son of mine to dig coal. As far as I'm concerned you and your miners are entitled to every cent that you can economically justify. It's a hard, dirty, dangerous job. But what I don't understand is why you ask the owners of coal mines to do things that you won't do yourselves."

"What do you mean?" he asked in that deep, wonderfully rich voice of his.

"Why don't you get together enough money from your own miners to buy a coal mine and demonstrate to the industry that you can pay the wages you're asking for and still compete effectively?"

"Oh, no." He shook that leonine head of his. "We're not going to get caught there. We withhold our product from them until they are willing to pay the wages they should. Farmers do the same thing with what they produce. They withhold their produce from the market until they get the prices they think they're entitled to."

"That's the scarcity system and I don't agree with it," I said. "But we in the Farm Bureau did something better than that. When fertilizer was too high we didn't say that we wouldn't buy any fertilizer until the price came down. We put up our own money, organized a company, got our own orders, and we brought the price down. We did the same for feed and seed and insurance."

"Well, maybe you could do it, but we wouldn't."

"Why not?"

"Suppose we did as you said and operated our own mine and found that we couldn't earn the wages that we were asking. We'd never be able to ask for an increase then."

"Look, mister," I said, "if you're asking somebody else to do something that you don't dare take the responsibility of doing yourself with your own money and your own members, then look out. I'd say that someday you'll be caught napping."

Despite my disappointment in Lewis I didn't lose interest in meeting the leaders of labor. My own reputation in the business community of Ohio was none too savory. There was a time when I used to attend the Kiwanis luncheon every Wednesday. They used to make a great thing out of the attendance rules, which made it necessary that everyone show up, regardless of any other obligations he had. In those days I was terribly busy and as often as not skipped lunch. And if I had lunch, I rarely spent as much money on it as I did when I attended the Kiwanis meeting. Now Kiwanis is a fine service organization and I don't mean to run it down, but I had a reputation of being some sort of radical or Communist and no sooner did I sit down to lunch with the Kiwanis than I would get into an argument. I got sick of paying for a lunch I barely ever had the chance to eat and tired of getting nervous indigestion from forcing it down while I was at a boil, so I eventually gave it up. But I did want to get as close to the business community of Columbus as I could and so welcomed the chance to become a member of an advisory board of one of the principal banks. However, my reputation hadn't sweetened any during the years and there were still large groups within the business community who thought me a dangerous radical. My meetings with labor leaders did nothing to help that impression and one day a member of the bank's staff warned me that they were going to get me.

"Who's going to get me?" I asked.

"Our papers are going to start after you," he said soberly.

"Why?"

"The businessmen of this town are getting scared of you. They think you're going to take over all of High Street."

"Well," I said with a grin, "it'll take us at least another six months or so before we can do that. Are they really scared?"

"You're growing so fast," he explained, "that they just feel you're going to take over everything in downtown Columbus."

The story, as I later learned it, was that a group of men high in the business community met for a regular card-playing evening, partly as a social matter and partly to discuss problems that affected them and their businesses. One evening our name came up and a newspaper publisher said, "Our advertisers are kicking like hell about this guy Lincoln. I think we ought to go after him." The bankers present objected. "His companies are some of our biggest depositors. Why should we go after him?"

The discussion grew hotter and hotter. The grievances seemed to center about the fact that we had our fingers in too many pies and were doing things in an unorthodox fashion. I suppose the greatest crime of all was that we were successful. If we had been a small, struggling, unsuccessful group with wild, radical ideas no one would have paid us any mind. Heresy, by itself, is never taken seriously except by theoreticians. But heresy that looks as though it is going to be successful always worries people.

The banking member of that social-economic society finally put down his cards and said, "Lincoln's one man you're not going to lick with your radios and your newspapers. His business comes from other states and you can't put the pressure on him locally the way you can on other people. My advice is to make your peace with him one way or another."

They would not take that advice and so decided to go after me. My banking friend warned me and I deeply appreciated his action. It was interesting to me that again I was warned of a danger by someone who had no real reason to warn me. Sometimes it seems that the world has more than a few people in it who will warn a man if they see that someone is going to do him dirt. I have been fortunate in having had more than my fair share of friendly warnings.

Well, I had been warned but I didn't see what I could do to convince the businessmen that I was not a Communist—that I wanted to see capitalism spread so that everyone might enjoy the fruits of an enormous and productive economic machine. There didn't seem much I could do to slow down or halt the opposition when it came. For one thing, it was several years in developing, and for another it came from several different directions. It didn't really come out in the open until after World War II. It first expressed itself as a newspaper attack and, as I might have expected, it was pegged to my friendship with labor.

I was invited one evening by Walter and Victor Reuther to go up to Detroit and address a meeting of the United Automobile Workers. I knew the resistance of my board members to my meeting with labor leaders and I knew the bitterness of some of my staff members toward Democrats, and I had been fraternizing with both. I wanted to make it quite clear that I was going up to that UAW meeting on my own, so I traveled on a Sunday, paid every dime of my expenses, and still felt a little shaky when I appeared in Detroit.

Arguing the matter of my meeting with labor leaders, I once told someone, "I've got a brother who works for General Electric. I've got a sister who manages a little telephone exchange for the Bell system. I have another brother who runs the railway bridge across the Cape Cod Canal for the New York, New Haven and Hartford Railroad. Now am I going to cross these people off just because they don't farm? They're still my brothers and sister. In a larger sense all those people who work in factories and stores and in cities are fellow Americans. What are we supposed to do? Junk them because they don't happen to be farmers?" But the old, cautious, silly answer came back: "We don't want to have anything to do with labor."

Now that I had spoken before the UAW I invited Walter Reuther down to Columbus to speak at the 1946 meeting of the Cooperative League, of which I had become president in 1941. Walter couldn't come but he did send one of his assistants, Clayton Fountain, to read his address. Fountain was there when I made the opening speech. I was on edge that morning. I knew there were board members in the audience who resented our having a labor leader on the program. I knew there were some who sat just waiting for me to pull a boner. I have to admit that as I went to the podium I began to wonder if maybe I hadn't made a mistake. As convinced as I was that farm co-ops should make common cause with labor, maybe I was guilty of going too far too fast. I had a sudden impulse to throw my prepared speech away, mutter a few innocuous generalities, and sit down. But it was too late for that. Even though my eyes ran ahead and I saw the word "revolution" coming toward me, even though I said to myself, "Murray, you'd better not read that sentence," sheer momentum carried me on. I declared that "all about us is the pressing challenge of a world in revolution" as people demand an end to the inequalities and insecurities of the past. I said that sooner or later the American economy would be affected by this revolution. I challenged cooperatives to be "strong enough to offer the American people a practical alternative to either complete state control or an even more fearful form of European totalitarianism." And I commended American labor groups for showing increasing interest in sponsoring co-ops.

The repercussions from that speech astounded and dismayed me. That afternoon on the front page of the *Columbus Dispatch* there was a headline, CO-OPS SHAPE PLANS WITH CIO TO RUN INDUSTRY, AGRICULTURE. Over it was a picture of me with a caption that read, "Co-op Leader Hits Profit Motive," and some lines in boldface, the substance of which was that I was leading a movement "to meet the coming revolution and to achieve a non-profit system of enterprise in America."

The long, ominous-sounding story that followed apparently was what the National Tax Equality Association had been waiting for. During the next several months it reprinted hundreds of thousands of copies of that distorted newspaper account and circulated them throughout the United States. Organized about three years before, the National Tax Equality Association was the sworn enemy of all co-ops. Co-op competition had been getting pretty hot for hardware, feed, grain, petroleum and coal dealers, cotton ginners, livestock producers, and retail merchants —so they'd started the NTEA to fight the cooperatives. They figured that one point to attack was federal income taxes, because they thought cooperatives were getting away with something by not paying as much in income taxes as they were. (Co-ops may not pay as much in income taxes as profit corporations do, but the reason is that they refund most of their net earnings to their customers; a profit corporation could do the same thing, and if it did, it would pay no more income tax than a co-op does.) The NTEA went around saying, "Co-ops don't pay taxes," and using everything they could lay their hands on to attack them. The newspaper account of my speech was made right to their order.

What has always amused me about groups like the NTEA is that they invariably behave as though cooperatives and labor unions aren't composed of ordinary men and women, but of Martians or microbes or creeping vegetables. Look out, they yell, the cooperatives are coming! What are cooperatives? They are associations of men and women who want to solve their own problems and who invite others to join them in doing so. It's that simple. We have no political philosophy to expound. We believe in the democratic form of government a lot more than our enemies do.

As for that speech of mine, the feeling in the board of our own Farm Bureau was that I must have been out of my mind to have made it. The bad newspaper reaction reinforced the opinions of those who felt we should have nothing to do with labor. To those who resented me and wanted to get rid of me, the incident provided further ammunition. But I have never changed my belief that labor groups can themselves organize into cooperatives. Indeed, they have more and more expanded their area of concern beyond wages, hours, and other conditions of employment to matters affecting the welfare of the union member and his family, during working life and through retirement. Some unions, like the Amalgamated Clothing Workers, have gone into savings institutions, housing, and medical centers for the benefit of their members and their families. In other words, it has become possible for unions to act effectively as organized bodies of consumers rather than merely as bargaining agents. I believe that in this direction lies the greatest possibilities for improving the standard of living for working people.

I don't believe the solution lies in a four-day work week or even in guaranteed annual wages. I do not, in fact, believe in guarantees of any kind. This business of guaranteeing people that they will not have to think for themselves, not have to work for themselves, not have to provide for themselves leads us, sooner or later, into statism of one sort or another. Whenever people get into the habit of running to Big Daddy for protection or comfort or support, they are abdicating a bit of their manhood, a bit of their humanity. What is even more serious is that they are eroding the rocks on which our political form of government was built. I do not blame people for feeling that the world is too large, that their problems are too complex, that the decisions to be taken are too important for them to tackle these things alone. I am not asking any single one of them to do it—alone. Nor am I suggesting that they do it without proper leadership.

People who get to work on a problem that is too big for any one of them find out that it is not too big for all of them. They don't keep it confined to the people they know. That is the secret of an effective association. It must have an open door. It must never seek to be exclusive. No association or society is ever going to succeed that seeks to keep people out. The Communists have been shrewd enough to promise the world that they will hold the door open—the door to freedom, to abundance, to political prestige, to dignity, to peace. That is what makes them so attractive to the people who are left out. The value of the Communist promise to keep the door open is so great that we are always going to be beaten to the punch in our international relations until we begin to understand that we must offer the same open door. I was not aware of this until the spring of 1943 when I was appointed to the five-member United States delegation to the United Nations Conference on Food and Agriculture.

I don't know why I was appointed to that delegation and sent to that conference in Hot Springs, Virginia. I suppose at the time that someone said in Washington, "If it's going to be a conference on food and agriculture we ought to get one of those farm leaders to go down. Seems to me I've heard of one up in Ohio who sounds liberal—I understand he's a relative of Abraham Lincoln. Let's send him along." The trouble with the story is that I am not related to Abraham Lincoln at all. The only kinship I can claim to Honest Abe goes back a long time, to the Lincoln brothers who came from Lincolnshire. I am a descendant of one branch; Joseph C. Lincoln, the writer, was the descendant of another brother; Abraham Lincoln was the descendant of still another. I heard later that I had been put on the delegation because Mrs. Roosevelt had heard me deliver a speech in which I said the solution to the world's problems relied upon the distribution of plenty, rather than the creation of scarcity. But I don't even know that this version is true.

In any event, I had never been in international waters before and felt a bit out of my depth. I kept to myself, listened to all I could hear, and watched all I could watch without really doing anything. I didn't understand what was going on. I especially didn't understand why, if the world was on fire, the delegates from forty-four nations didn't get up early in the morning as farmers did, get to work, take a short lunch, go back to work, have supper, and go back to work after that. Most of them arose at nine or ten o'clock in the morning, had a large and leisurely breakfast, attended an hour or two of sessions, and then went to lunch. They might have a short afternoon session and then play golf. Well, I don't say I knew how to put the world right but I had the feeling that this wasn't the way it was going to be done.

One day a young woman came up to me and said, "Mr. Lincoln, aren't you ever coming to your office?"

"My gosh," I said, startled, "have I got an office?"

"Yes," she said. "I've been sitting up there for the last week wondering if you were ever going to come around." I suppose not to disappoint her, I went up to look, and sure enough, there it was. And a handsome office it was, too. But I still had nothing much to do.

We were encouraged to make the acquaintance of the little-nation delegates at the conference. Principally because I couldn't play golf, I made the acquaintance of all the fellows from the small nations who also couldn't play golf. One of them was the economics adviser to the Emperor of Ethiopia. His name was Lidj Ylma Deressa.

He was a little man—keen-minded, well versed in world politics and economics. He had been drafted into the Ethiopian army when Mussolini's Fascist armies invaded his country. When he was captured he asked to be assigned to a labor battalion because he knew such groups would be sent to Italy. He counted on their assigning him to some country place where he would be billeted with ordinary farmers. They did just as he expected and he listened to what the ordinary Italians had to say.

Lidj Ylma Deressa told me that Italy would collapse once the Allies invaded Europe and he told me that the Italians would destroy Mussolini themselves. He predicted the overturn of the Conservative Government in England. He said a Labor Government would take over. He said that while Churchill was a great wartime leader he would never do as a leader in peacetime and that the English would reject him when the war was over. But the most significant part of our conversation had to do with communism. As we sat under a Virginia oak tree in May, 1943, the world had a curious look. The Japanese were in the Philippines; they had executed Jimmy Doolittle's Tokyo raiders; John L. Lewis was pursuing the old practice of trying to get what wages he could for the miners, war or no war; we were having rationing at home; the Japanese invasion of North America was just being broken off up at Attu. Things certainly didn't look bright, although the Russians were the heroes of that month and of that year. They had just broken the German assault on Stalingrad. I had not, up until that moment, given much thought to Communists or communism. But what my Ethiopian friend said next startled me.

"Mr. Lincoln, in the end I am very sure that the majority of the world is going to be Communist. Now I am not sure exactly what form it's going to take. It may not be the Russian brand, but it is going to be Communist." He went on to say that there was going to be a revolution all over the world. Little people, such as his own countrymen, were not content with their lot any more. While he was loyal to the Emperor and on his staff, he felt that there were going to be great uprisings and changes in many institutions, political, economic, and social—perhaps even religious. "The reason the world is going to be Communist is that you people in the free democracies won't work as hard to change things. You are pleased with them as they are—whereas the Communists exist solely to change things. These people in undeveloped countries are going to be looking for a change. It takes sophisticated political judgment and a high rate of literacy for people to run a democracy. These people do not have such sophistication or such a literacy rate, but they want a change. They want to better themselves. You people who have democracies are content. You are not ready to fight to spread the benefits of the democratic state."

I gave this talk a great deal of thought. The man's points, I realized, were too true. We do not have a missionary zeal. We aren't doing half enough to spread the gospel of democracy. The fact of the matter is that we have a society that pleases us and we're very reluctant to open the door to let others share in that idea. What is worse, we don't want to change the world. People continue to starve, people continue to be illiterate, people continue under tyranny, under primitive health conditions. What happens to them does not disturb us. I don't mean to say that Americans are callous or indifferent to the condition of suffering people. I know of no more generous national group when the drama of human suffering and privation is brought home to us. But it is not generosity that the world needs. I think it is fairly well conceded by this time that we cannot buy our friends and that those we have bought have been for sale to the next higher bidder who bought them not with cash but with a promissory note.

The problem of the world is not political, despite all the juggling we have been doing opposite the Russians. The problem is one of nations that have and nations that have not. In a time when we are talking of exploring the solar system, the problem is that there are people on earth who are starving. The problem of the world is still scarcity and that is hard for Americans to understand and to credit. Americans have so much of things that sometimes they become sickened with surfeit, whereas the bulk of the world literally has not enough to eat. India is experimenting with sterilization to hold down her population. Not because there is not enough room on the subcontinent of India, but because there's not enough food to feed the excess population. There are always people talking about overpopulation, but when you speak of number of people to the square mile there is no more densely populated country than Holland, and no one discusses the overpopulation of Holland because Holland has abundant food. The moment enough food is at hand all the talk of overpopulation fades away. You cannot really have political democracy unless it is undergirded with economic democracy. I believe it was a Frenchman who once bitterly observed that the law in its grand impartial way declared that both the rich and the poor had the right to sleep under the bridges of Paris on rainy evenings. Such "equality of justice" and such "freedom of opportunity" aren't worth much. I am afraid that it is that kind of freedom of opportunity we have been trying to give away to the underprivileged nations. We should not be surprised that they have not snatched it up. The day we can go into the world and say to the hungry and dispossessed, "Here, here is a way you can feed yourself and your family, clothe yourself, and earn your own way and govern yourself," we'll find a long list of takers because that is something the world wants.

12

If THERE WAS one thing my membership on the U.S. delegation to the United Nations Conference on Food and Agriculture did it was to stir my imagination toward ways of solving the world's food crisis. Much of the talk around the tables in Hot Springs had to do with ways of eliminating or ameliorating the age-old scourges of mankind—hunger, disease, poverty, ignorance, and war. My own interest lay in eliminating hunger.

The late novelist and experimental farmer, Louis Bromfield, was a friend of the Farm Bureau and whenever he found himself in Columbus he would have lunch with Perry Green and me. During one of our luncheons I told him what my feelings were about the world and its seeming inability to feed all its people decently. We agreed that history proved that in new countries everyone had to stay on the land if anyone was to eat, and ways of enabling one man to grow more food than he and his family could use had to be devised before any sort of civilizing process could begin. In the early days of our own nation more than 85 percent of our population lived on farms, devoting themselves to agriculture, while only some 15 percent lived in cities and towns, devoting themselves to manufacture or retail trade. Even with 85 percent of the population devoting its time to growing food there wasn't enough food because tools, methods, and techniques were fairly primitive. The standard of living wasn't very high. But as tools and techniques and methods improved, fewer and fewer people stayed on the farms to raise the necessary food. A greater percentage of people were able to go into the cities and the towns to manufacture more nonfarm products, to enter into the sciences and the arts and business.

Experts now tell us that mechanization of agriculture in the United States may eventually bring our farm population down to merely 9 percent of the total population, and that this 9 percent will not only produce enough food for itself and the other 91 percent, but will produce a surplus. The surplus has, until now, proved to be an embarrassment rather than a blessing.

Louis Bromfield and I agreed that the first thing to do, one way or another, was to mechanize agriculture throughout the world. Our theory was that no nation is ever going to progress toward democracy and the sophisticated arts of self-government if the bulk of its population is struggling to raise enough food to stay alive. The fact of the matter is that great civilizations need at their base a vast amount of labor to free the bulk of the citizens from the grueling task of feeding themselves. The famous city-states of ancient Greece were able to develop so highly because they depended upon a huge supply of slave labor. Examine any great civilization of the past, and no matter how noble its philosophers, or how just its lawgivers or brilliant its artists, you will see beneath the philosophy and the art and the laws a wretched mass of human beings condemned to eternal servitude on the soil, in the mines, in the pits, in the quarries. Modern industrial nations no longer condemn human beings to such servitude. They have developed mechanical slaves with the strength of thousands of men. The miracle of the Industrial Revolution is not that the average workingman can have a house in the suburbs, with leisure in which to learn how to hurl a ball down a polished wooden runway to knock over wooden pins. The miracle is that machines have freed us from the greatest tyrant of all, the invisible demon that makes us hunt for food.

It was during this discussion of the importance of mechanizing agriculture that Louis Bromfield invited Perry and me, together with our wives, out to his world-famous Malabar Farm. Louis had been doing some sort of public relations work for the Ford Motor Company and during that time he had met Harry Ferguson, the inventor of the Ford-Ferguson tractor. "I'm having Mr. and Mrs. Ferguson and their daughter out to my house for the New Year's weekend," Louis told me. "I'd like you to talk to him. I think he's got something to do with just what we've been talking about."

The Fergusons turned out to be a hearty, redheaded Irish family. Ferguson himself was a genius. I don't think the world yet appreciates the enormous contribution the Ferguson tractor has made to peace and plenty and the advancement of civilization.

Harry Ferguson was the son of well-to-do Irish gentry. When he was a young man out of college, about 1906, he made up his mind that he was going to make some contribution to society. He sat down to figure out what it was he could do that would make the greatest impact for good upon the world. He thought of water, of medicine, of power, and a number of related things. Finally he decided upon food. He felt that the world would never develop into the sort of place we all wanted it to become unless everyone was properly fed. Because he had studied engineering, he began to search out a way in which he could best apply his special knowledge to the problem of hunger. After some study, it seemed clear to him that the basic trouble was that the motive power by which food was produced over most of the world was animal—horses or oxen, the most expensive and least efficient power available. What was needed, he believed, was some sort of adaptation of the internal-combustion engine to give the farmer the kind of cheap, reliable motive power that would produce surpluses.

It was the steel plow that enabled us to break up the prairies and it was the steel plow that enabled one farmer to raise enough food to support more than his family and himself. It was the steel plow that helped bring abundance to our nation, an abundance that enabled us to let people live in cities, to enlarge the scope of American society. The sod of our prairies was so tough that the wooden plows, which are still being used in many parts of the world, would never have worked.

We had been using cast iron in the manufacture of most of our farm implements, because it was cheap and also because it was the material that weighed the most. We were depending upon the weight of the implement to do the tillage. Steel had been developed, and other high-tensile, high-strength metals, but none of these were being used in farm equipment because they lacked the necessary weight.

Manufacturers in the United States were aware of the problem and were working on tractors. The principle on which they worked was the same principle governing the use of implements pulled by horses. We simply unhooked the horses, placed the tractor, with four wheels, where the horses had been and hooked whatever implement we wanted to use—say a plow—to the tractor's drawbar and depended on the weight of the cast iron to press the plow into the ground. It should have worked the way horses pulling a plow worked, but it didn't. When, for instance, a tractor-powered plow struck an obstacle—a root or a rock—the tractor was likely to tip backward and either throw the operator free or fall on him and crush him. General Motors had spent a great deal of money on the old Samson tractor and finally given up because it could find no way of developing a tractor that could be relied on not to kill its operator. Henry Ford had also worked on a tractor but he, too, was about to give it up.

Harry Ferguson had three brilliant ideas. The first was that the tractor had to be small. He felt that you would never eliminate the last horse and the last ox until you had a motor-driven machine small enough to plow the wife's kitchen garden. The mother who had charge of feeding the family would never let her farming husband give up the last old horse until she was sure she was going to get her kitchen garden plowed, because it was from this garden that she got the food to can for the winter and to feed the family.

The second idea Ferguson had was to eliminate the need for

179

using heavy cast iron in the pulling instrument. To do that, he designed a hydraulic system that would control the working depth of the tillage tool. What was more, with such a system the implement could be raised. That meant the tractor with the implement on it could be backed up, a feature that only a farmer who used it could appreciate. Once the hydraulic system controlled the depth of the tilling implement into the ground, the farmer could use all the lighter, high-tensile, high-strength metals that the metals industry had developed.

The third brilliant idea Ferguson had was that the way to avoid the tipping of tractors upward involved the manner in which the implement was fixed to the tractor. Heretofore the implement had been fixed to the tractor below the lowest draft point of the rear wheels. When the implement caught, the power of the tractor, still in the rear wheels, began to roll the front of the tractor up as the rear wheels turned. Then the tractor fell over backward. Ferguson had the implement attached in two places, at the lower part of the body and higher up so that the point of draft was not at the rear wheels but somewhere farther forward near the front wheels. As the plow caught and the motor pulled, the motive power of the rear wheels was not used to tip up the tractor, but to press the wheels more firmly into the ground. The hydraulic system could be used to lift the tillage implement out of the ground, and thus the machine, with implement, could be backed out and the obstacle by-passed.

Those great developments were neither understood nor appreciated by those persons Ferguson approached in Europe. He finally gave up in disgust over his failure to raise money, and came to the United States in 1938 to see Henry Ford. According to the story he told me that evening at Malabar, he had barely started to describe what he had in mind when Henry Ford asked him, "What do you want?"

Mr. Ferguson said, "I want enough time to explain my system."

"Yes," Henry Ford said. "What do you want?"

Ferguson's Irish temper began to flare. "Well, I just want fifteen minutes of your time to explain what I've got here."

Ford said, "I see it. You've got it. We missed it. So did General Motors. What do you want?"

"I want some money and I want a factory," Ferguson said.

Ford extended his hand, and on the basis of that handshake, without a written contract, the Ford-Ferguson tractor was born.

At Bromfield's farm Ferguson showed us a model of his tractor. Perry Green and I got excited as we saw how it worked. We'd never heard of this before. Where have we been? we asked ourselves. Then and there I made up my mind to see if we couldn't get together in the Farm Bureau to buy the Ford-Ferguson tractor. After all, it was something the farmer was going to buy sooner or later. He might as well own the company and the patents.

In 1945 we got six models of the tractors for the members of the Farm Bureau's board to see if they were everything Ferguson claimed they were. They were. But let me take the story in sequence.

Earlier in 1945 I took my second trip to Europe, this time as a delegate to the International Cooperative Alliance. It was a momentous trip in many ways for me but I want to touch only on the Ford-Ferguson tractor aspect of it right now. I went to see Mr. Ferguson in London and reminded him that we had met at Malabar Farm in 1944. He didn't remember the occasion but Mrs. Ferguson did.

"What do you want, Mr. Lincoln?" Ferguson asked.

"I want to buy your company."

Ferguson nodded. "That's interesting. What are you going to do with it?"

"Save the world," I said, without smiling.

"How are you going to do that?"

"By using your machine to get everyone in the world fed." I then went on to discuss my own feelings on the mechanization of

181

agriculture and the importance of food to the establishment of political as well as economic democracy. I told him of what I felt about the cooperative way of life. Mrs. Ferguson interrupted to say that Harry had to take his daily walk. So Ferguson and I walked around Hyde Park, not quite oblivious of the wartime destruction of London, but still absorbed in our conversation. Ferguson was a good listener. "Well, mister, if you can get it done," he said when I finished, "I think you're really on to something. But I'm not too sure you can." He looked at me with those Irish blue eyes and said, "You know, it's going to take a lot of money to buy this company."

"Yes," I said, "I know. But don't tell me how much."

"Why?"

"Well, if you told me how much it was going to cost I'd get so scared I'd go home and forget it." He laughed at that. "But if it's right," I went on, "it doesn't make any difference how much money it's going to take to get it done. We'll get it somehow, just as you've managed to get what you needed—somehow."

At this point I have to take a couple of hitches in my story. Ferguson referred me to his representatives in America. I was in consultation with them off and on for the better part of a year, and a lot of interesting things came out in those conferences. I am not free to report them, however, because one of the principals—despite the fact that everything he did for us reflected to his credit—has asked that I not mention his name in this book. Suffice it to say that Mr. Ferguson was right: It would have taken a *lot* of money to buy his company—better than twenty-five million dollars—and although I tried valiantly to swing it and, with the help of Henry Knight, came close to doing it, everything fell through at the end when Henry Ford died and the younger Fords terminated his gentlemen's agreement with Ferguson and began to manufacture a tractor of their own.

It was an extremely profitable experience for me, just the same. It was the first time I'd come so close to seeing how a big American corporation works, and it taught me and the Farm Bureau two important lessons. The first of these had to do with executive salaries, the second with the hiring of management consultants.

The matter of salaries came into focus when we were considering how much we'd have to pay the management of the Ferguson Company if we bought it. One executive told me he was getting approximately $225,000 a year, plus a bonus.

"Well," I remember saying, "I'm getting slightly less. I'm getting seventeen thousand, five hundred a year."

He looked at me with some shock. "Is that all? What makes you do it?"

"I don't know," I said. "I've never earned this much before. Mrs. Lincoln and I have always kept our needs down to a minimum and I'm having more fun than you've ever had."

"Well, I won't work for fun," he said. "It was all right for you to start in at the wages that you did, but you'll never be able to run the kind of large-scale institution you're talking about at the kind of wages you're paying."

After that I went to the board and asked them to set up a committee on compensation. Ed Stough, one of our board members, growled at me, "What do you want—a raise?"

"Maybe," I said. "But I want you to face up to this thing. If we're going to go into big business we're going to have to compensate our executives in the same way big business does."

John Hodson, another board member, said, with an air of self-satisfaction, "We're never going to pay salaries like that."

I turned to John and asked, "Didn't I see you coming into our garage this morning with a new Packard?"

"Yeh," he said, "but that's my business."

"I'm not denying that. Didn't you buy a new Packard?"

"Yep."

I smiled. "We've been hearing so much about the downtrodden farmer lately, I didn't think any of us could afford a new Packard. But some of us can, and that proves that some of us are doing pretty well. But I'm not going to discuss that. What I want to ask you is this: Did you inquire what salary the president of the

Packard Motor Company got before you bought that car?"

"Hell, no," he said. "Why should I?"

"Well, don't you think your share of his salary was in the price of that car? And that you paid it without question?"

"I guess so."

"Now some of you have bought Ford-Ferguson tractors. Have you any idea what proportion of the cost of that tractor is in executive salaries? It's in there and you know it. And you knew it when you bought it and you didn't kick about it. And if we buy the Ferguson Company we'll have to have those same executives on *our* payroll, no matter what we pay them, because no one is going to run that thing as well for us as they can."

It was pretty naïve of me, I suppose, but I was no less surprised to learn that companies like Ford, large and successful though they were, needed professional guidance. At that time, I was told they had more than twenty management consultants and it was suggested that maybe Farm Bureau could use one too. I figured we'd give it a try, so we went ahead and hired the management consulting firm of Rogers, Slade and Hill. So far as I know, we were one of the first cooperatives to bring in that kind of consultant. Since one of the first problems we had to solve was the one of executive compensation, the firm went to work to determine what executives of related businesses were getting. The report showed that my salary should have been quite a bit over a hundred thousand dollars. Our board blinked a bit and Ed Stough said cautiously, "Well, we'll take it in two jumps." But I had now established the fact with the board that if they wanted first-class executive talent they had to be prepared to pay for it.

Next I went to see Henry Knight about raising enough money to buy the Ford-Ferguson tractor.

"Well, Murray," he said, "I think I can get together the money to buy it, but how are you going to pay me back?"

"Henry Ford has sold three hundred thousand tractors," I said. "Multiply that by a hundred dollars. What does it come to?"

"My God," he said, "that's thirty million dollars!"

184

"Right. Don't you think we could sell at least half the farmers that already have a tractor a hundred-dollar share of stock in the Ferguson Tractor Company, the way it's going?"

"I guess you could."

"And if I can get just half—about fifteen million," I said confidently, "we can borrow the rest." Actually, I wasn't sure we could borrow anything like that sum.

Henry Knight and I went to New York and he started to call on his friends. In one evening's time—and I would not have believed this if I had not heard it with my own ears—he collected pledges for thirty-three million dollars. I don't think many of the men who pledged money understood fully what he was talking about, but every one of them had been helped so much by Henry in his trucking business or horse business that he had faith in Henry's judgment and integrity.

But it was to no avail. By the time I reported to the Ferguson management that I was ready to put up the money, the Ford Motor Company had withdrawn its production facilities and made plans to put out a tractor of its own design. And that was that.

In an odd way, though, the whole experience boosted my stock with the Farm Bureau board. What was more, it enlarged their vision and their sense of the size of things we were capable of tackling.

We have continued our growth since then and have taken on larger and larger propositions and made them grow. Our failure to get Ford-Ferguson as a subsidiary prepared us for similar opportunities in the future. We had, in the past, missed opportunities because of timidity, suspicion, lack of confidence. And when we missed those opportunities I had not hesitated to remind the board and the staff of our failures when later opportunities arose. I knew that one day I would go before the board with some proposition, hear them balk, and then say, "Remember Ford-Ferguson, and how we kicked over paying the salaries we should have paid. When opportunity knocks at the door, you ought to open the door, look it full in the face, and just snatch it inside if it looks right to you."

The odd truth about us was that we had grown up into a very big business, yet we still ran ourselves as though we were a small, struggling farm group. We were not aware of our own size and not yet ready to use that size and power to do all that we could to help other people to help themselves. Our size was no secret to outsiders, who sometimes made assumptions about us, based on our size, that were rather shocking.

All insurance companies, as you know, are carefully regulated and examined by the insurance departments of the various states in which they do business. Cooperative insurance companies are no exceptions to this rule. From the moment we started business in 1926, we were under the vigilant scrutiny of the commissioners of insurance of every state in which we were soliciting business. I had had little contact with the examiners from the various insurance departments because Henry Ballard, our general counsel, had a fear of the misleading impressions I might inadvertently give the insurance examiners. But one day in the late thirties, when we were getting big, a pair of examiners finally asked to see me. They were shown into my office.

"What can I do for you gentlemen?" I asked.

"Mr. Lincoln, we've examined your books and everything is perfectly in order. But we would like to ask you one question."

"Sure. Go ahead."

"How do you get paid?"

"By check," I said.

"Oh, we understand that. We can see your salary listed on the books. But how do you really get your money out of this company?"

"By check!" I insisted.

"Are you a lawyer," the other examiner asked, "or an accountant or something else, so that you get supplementary fees?"

"No," I said.

They looked at one another. "Do you mean to tell us that all you draw from this company is what we see in the statements as your salary?"

"That's all I get. I'd like to get more, but you go to the board and see if you can get me any more."

The men shook their heads. "We examine a lot of companies and we know what their presidents get. Your company is bigger than a lot of them and we just can't believe that your listed salary is all you're getting out of this company."

I felt like laughing. "Gentlemen," I said, "I can show you every deposit slip and every check I've ever written since I put a hundred and twenty-five dollars in the Amherst National Bank after I made it carting stone at fifty cents a ton back in Raynham, Massachusetts. I'll bring down my expense accounts, my income tax returns, my canceled checks, and anything else you want to see."

The examiners looked at one another again. "You mean that's really all you get?"

"That's all."

I doubt if they ever believed me. Unfortunately, low salaries have been typical of the cooperative movement, whose traditions of poverty and of pinching and scraping have clung to it like moss on a stone that hasn't been moved in centuries. Today, with its name changed to Nationwide, and after enormous growth, our organization is ready to take on larger and larger ventures, but until recently the traditions held us back. I have kept chipping away at those restrictive and narrow traditions for years because I believe they give people in cooperatives an inferiority complex that hampers the whole movement.

When we moved into the building that Nationwide currently occupies on North High Street in Columbus, I felt that we ought to dress up the executive offices so that they might reflect the success we were enjoying. I knew that if I brought the matter up directly with the board they might kick about the expense and fume about "frills and trimmings." Instead, we had a board committee appointed to look into the decoration of modern office buildings throughout the United States. It came back with recommendations that went much further than I had ever dreamed they might. Once our building was redesigned and redecorated the board was as pleased and proud as Punch. The members took positive pride in showing relatives and friends and business associates the handsome early American decor of our executive offices, the modern efficiency of the building. We eventually bought private planes for our company, partly because they provided us with safe, rapid, private transportation and partly because I felt that we ought to have the "frills and trimmings" of a modern, successful big business. They have paid off for us—not merely in convincing people outside our organization that we are successful, but also in placing our own board and staff in the psychological frame of mind which makes for self-confidence, for aggressiveness, for the willingness to tackle larger projects without cringing.

The cooperative movement has somehow gained a reputation among many people for being left of center in political outlook and for being primarily intended for poor people. At least that's what Ernest Dichter and his Motivational Research Institute discovered when they ran an analysis on what the public thought of when they heard the word *cooperative*.

We are not leftist in political outlook. As I've said many times, the majority of our Nationwide board members are bedrock Republican farmers. I sometimes wish they were less conservative than they are. Cooperatives do not seek to change the form of political government under which we live, since they themselves depend upon a democratic society for their own existence. Our form of cooperatives do not exist under communism or fascism. Authoritarian societies insist upon control of their economic machinery and do not allow people to set up associations to handle their own economic affairs. Genuine cooperatives are possible only in a democratic society. They constitute a form of economic democracy which supports political democracy. Just as that Frenchman didn't want to live in a country where a man was free to sleep under a bridge in the rain, I do not want to live in a country where men, women, and children are "free" to starve. Such freedom makes a mockery of the word.

I presume that the public feeling that cooperatives are for the poor derived from the impression that people had of some of the early European cooperatives. It was to dispel this misconception that we at Nationwide and in our subsidiaries have taken on all the trappings and trimmings of the successful, old-line profit-motivated corporations. Outward appearances count to Americans. The package is something that convinces. I do not know why this is so. I do not know why Americans seem so willing to be fooled. Perhaps it is because we are an overly imaginative people.

Americans are too lazy to look into the good qualities of products that don't advertise themselves as being "the best." The clearest example I have ever seen of this was the problem we once had in marketing apples. A boom crop gave us more apples than we could sell in the normal market, so we talked the chain stores into selling apples by the bushel rather than by the pound. Bushels of apples were filled just as they came off the tree, large and small ones mixed as they came to hand. But the chain stores could not sell them until someone started rearranging the apples—placing the largest and most attractive ones on top and placing the smaller ones below. Now, even though people knew that the bushels had been "faced," they began to buy bushels of apples. They bought more than we had ever sold before. They bought out the crop. They were fooling themselves. They knew they were fooling themselves. They wanted to fool themselves. Why, I cannot say. I learned long ago not to argue with human frailties, but to accept them for what they are and work around them as best I can.

It is a human frailty to judge an organization by its outward appearance. We acknowledged that and we have composed ourselves outwardly to resemble the capitalistic companies of our own size. But we are different from them. They are dedicated to the proposition that so long as two dollars grow from one dollar they are doing all that they should. We are interested in enabling people to control their own destinies, and if two dollars grow where one did, that's a bonus, not an end in itself.

When you meet us at Nationwide, see our offices, visit our subsidiaries, you are going to see things that make us seem indistinguishable from any American insurance company. We use the same accounting systems, the same techniques, the same managerial procedures, the same personnel methods, the same business methods as any successful, well-managed American corporation. But we are different. And—I believe sincerely—better. How do we get that difference across to people who don't know us? By using the same public-relations techniques that Big Business uses. We project our difference through our policyholder advisory councils, through our attitudes, through our outlooks, through our investments, through our motives. I hope this book will also make the difference clear. We believe the difference is so vitally important that it may affect the survival of the world and the people living in it.

Our country began a revolution in 1776. It was not merely a revolt against the authority of a German king of England, but a revolt against the concept that people could not "do" for themselves as well as others could "do" for them. We stepped out of the frame of European and world history to create our own frame of reference. We began to do for ourselves and we have done well. Over the years we in the United States have given up a good deal of control, first to the large corporations and then to our Government. But by and large, we still do for ourselves, and this revolutionary concept is so important that it could be an explosive force in the world. It has no such force in the world only because we have stopped regarding it as revolutionary.

The profit motive did not build this country into its greatness, because the profit motive is present in every country in the world. In fact, there are philosophers of the profit motive who will tell you that the acquisitive instinct is present even in the lower orders of animals and insects. They tell you this to prove how "natural"

190

the acquisitive instinct is. If they can prove it is natural, or that it is a gift from heaven, any legislation that interferes with it is hampering one of the natural laws or something heavenly. People who uphold such legislation, it stands to this kind of reasoning, are godless. And since Communists are godless, opponents of "natural" laws are Communists. But surely no one need be a Communist to express the fear that a society which allows everyone free rein on the acquisitive instinct is going to be in chaos before long.

The free-enterprising individualists of an earlier day have disappeared from the American scene because society has come to an agreement that the acquisitive instinct can get out of hand and must be governed. I suppose I will be shocking a good many American businessmen when I assert that the Government of the United States has done more to preserve capitalism than they have. And when I say Government I include the twenty-year administration of the New Deal Presidents, Franklin D. Roosevelt and Harry S. Truman.

I do not say that the profit motive is unimportant, but let no one believe that this country came to greatness because of the profit motive. And let no one convince himself that we in the United States are going to inspire the world with the will to resist statism and communism by telling them that we have the secret of making two dollars grow where one grew before. This is the only story the old-line capitalists can carry to the world. If it fails to stir human hearts I am not surprised. If that's all America has to offer the world, she deserves to lose the cold war. I thank God she has more to offer. I know that America can offer the world this revolutionary and explosive concept: We know how to control our own destinies, political, social, and economic. We will help you to do the same. We ask nothing in return for this, because we believe that once you can control your destiny as we control ours, you will want to preserve your way of life as much as we want to preserve ours.

Part Four

CHAPTER

13

TRAVEL IS BROADENING. Like most old sayings, this has some truth in it. Travel broadens the man who is ready for it. It does nothing for the man who is not ready. By that I mean that people who travel outside their own country with preconceived notions and locked minds aren't apt to see anything but the reflection of their own prejudices. I know that when I first traveled to Europe in 1923 I wasn't ready to be broadened. Across the Atlantic I saw only what I was looking for—proof that Americans were better than anyone else and that we had little to learn from Europe or Europeans. I was twenty-two years older in the summer of 1945 when I made my second trip to Europe, and in the years between I had learned a good deal about myself and the world in which I live. But I had even more to learn. I am learning today. I hope I can continue learning as long as I live.

In 1945, soon after V-J Day, I was sent with Howard Cowden, president and general manager of the Consumers Cooperative Association of Kansas City, to represent the Cooperative League of the U.S.A. at a planning meeting of the International Cooperative Alliance in London. It was the first such meeting since the beginning of World War II. I was to meet Harry Culbreth, one of our staff members, in Europe. He was to follow me by boat. Cowden was already in Europe. For some reason I no longer remember, I decided to fly.

I was staying at the Hotel Roosevelt in New York and my flight was scheduled to leave at seven o'clock in the morning. At three in the morning I got up, dressed, and started for the terminal—I had been requested to check in at three forty-five. I'll never forget that lonely walk I took from the Hotel Roosevelt to the airlines terminal on Forty-second Street. If ever a man wanted to back out of a thing, I wanted to back out of that flight. But there had been so much publicity about my appointment and my leaving, I didn't dare go home and face people to tell them I had been afraid of flying the dark Atlantic in something half bird and half fish called a clipper plane.

In September of 1945 there were still priorities on air travel and at the terminal I had to announce my reason for flying. A young man who overheard me introduced himself. "I'm Charles Van Bergen, an oilman, and I'd like to talk to you. I understand there's an oilman named Cowden whom you're going to meet in Europe. Can we sit together?"

Well, I was grateful for the company, because I certainly dreaded what was ahead of me. When we got settled in the clipper it started to roar up and down the Hudson. I presume they did that to check the engines but I used to tell people they did it to give the fainthearted a chance to jump off. I was about ready to dive out and start paddling for the New York shore when the ship was up and off.

Van Bergen proved to be a most interesting young man. His father was one of the operating heads of Sir Henry Deterding's oil empire. He had been born in the Dutch East Indies and as a youngster had been sent around the world by his father, entertained by oil people wherever he landed. His life had been spent in the oil business and he currently worked for a firm which blended oils to specification for other companies. His firm had handled about three-quarters of all the oil that American companies had furnished to the Allies during the war. He knew a great deal about the business and the people who were in it and he was interested in knowing what the cooperatives were doing about oil. I filled him in, of course.

Hours later, after it had grown dark, Van Bergen excused himself to go to bed. I was hoping that he or someone else would stay up all night with me. Somehow I was filled with a mortal fear of getting into that berth. It seemed better to plunge into the Atlantic while sitting up—that's all I can say. The purser finally came around and asked, "What's the matter with you?"

"Nothing," I replied in as brave a voice as I could manage.

"Now, come on, what's the matter with you?"

"I'm not going to take my clothes off," I said.

"Look, Buddy," he said, "if we go down it won't make any difference whether you've got your clothes on or off. So, just undress and get into your berth and get some sleep."

The next thing I knew the purser was pulling at my blanket: "We're about ready to come into Shannon."

The first few nights Van Bergen and I were in London we walked the streets and saw for ourselves what the blitz had done to this great capital. I had seen pictures and I had heard descriptions, but the actual evidence, even though a good deal of cleaning up had been done by then, shocked me profoundly. Here a church had stood, here a shop, here a row of homes, and now they were gone from the face of the earth with the people who had been in them. I shuddered as I looked about me. The adults we saw on the streets looked peaked and exhausted. The kids, on the other hand, looked healthy enough. Much of the orange juice and extra rations had gone to them, I learned. Thinking back, I feel that many children probably received better care during the war than they ever had during peacetime. With all that death pouring out of the skies and all the uncertainties of wartime life I think people began to cherish their children more. After all, they represented their continuation, their future. Van Bergen and I spoke to a great many Londoners and what we heard over and over again was the harrowing fear people had had that when they left for work in the morning they might never again see their children, their families, their homes.

I had been, until Pearl Harbor, an isolationist. Our sentiment in the Midwest was to stay out of the European war. Like many of my friends, I felt that all wars had been fought for commercial reasons and over commercial advantages. War was a business, I kept assuring myself, and it couldn't flourish if it didn't provide profit for someone or for some group. I still believe there is too much profit to be made out of human calamities. A. J. Brosseau once told me during the depths of the depression, "There are people who can make money even now. Because they have money, they can pick up properties and investments at bargain rates. The poor man considers a depression the end of the world. The rich man merely considers it an interlude during which he gets everything at sale prices." Because I believed there was money to be made during a war, I believed that wars were carried on for the profits to be made in them. Perhaps that was true, once. I no longer believe it to be wholly true.

Profits are made during wartime, but these profits are only incidental to the war itself. If some people are enriched by war it is because there is no situation, after all, that won't yield a sharp-witted or unscrupulous free-enterpriser an opportunity for earning more than he should. I suppose when the archangel Gabriel blows his trumpet for Judgment Day, there'll be someone making money out of the lining up of sinners. Perhaps he'll be peddling influence with the shaky ones, or selling cards of admittance to the judgment procedures, or issuing stocks in the Kingdom of Heaven, or selling plots in the Fields of Heavenly Rest—but he'll be there: I am more certain of his presence than I am of Gabriel's. But if profits are going to be made out of future wars, they are going to be illusory profits and even the most hardened of speculators is bound to see that. When I saw the destruction of London, understood the misery of the people, heard the stories of their sacrifice, I said to myself, "There just can't be another war. I don't think the human race can go through it."

One of the great debates then going on back home was whether or not we ought to help the Allies to re-establish themselves. Of course a great many liberals thought there was no question about that. They were convinced that the war should have demonstrated that the economic welfare of the United States depended on the economic welfare of the world. We in the Midwest weren't ready to concede that. We felt that we had expended so much of our worldly goods and so many of our young people's lives that we had given enough to the world. We felt that now it was time our allies fended for themselves. I believe I subscribed to that theory. I realize now that it was wrong. It was an extension of the spirit of isolationism, and if the events of the past thirty-odd years have proved anything, they have proved that we're not alone in the world.

When Harry Culbreth joined me in London we got a room in the Park Lane Hotel and it was one of the few warm rooms in London, thanks to the steam pipe that ran right up through it. One day Harry announced, "Let's go see the members of the British Cabinet."

"Why would the British Cabinet want to see two foot-loose Americans?" I asked.

"They probably don't," he said with a cheerful drawl, "but I want to see them."

I had a cold and was feeling a bit shaky and thought the idea not worth much, but since I didn't want to miss anything, I went along.

When Sir Stafford Cripps learned we wanted to see him he granted us an interview that was to last ten or fifteen minutes. Almost at once we began arguing the question of United States economic aid for the Allies. Sir Stafford became so aroused that we were with him for two hours. The substance of the argument he presented so impressed me that I brought it home and pre-

197

sented it to our discussion groups for their consideration. In effect, what he said was:

"We realize that the argument as to whether you should help us or not is a proper one for debate. But you ought to help us more in your own interest than in our own."

"What do you mean by that?" I asked.

"Well, you have, as a result of the impetus of war, built up an enormous output of agricultural and industrial products. You produce more than you can use yourselves. You now have three alternatives. You can cut back your production drastically, which would throw countless numbers of your people out of work at precisely the moment when you will be getting millions of returned soldiers dumped onto your labor market. That would throw you into an economic tail spin that would set off the whole world. You can't be allowed to do that, for your own sakes as much as for the rest of the world's. Secondly, you can keep on your present rate of production and dump your surplus into the ocean. I don't think your own consciences will allow you to do that. Thirdly, you can maintain your present rate of production and give your surplus to us or any of your other allies. Giving that surplus to your allies will keep your own economy going at the same time it helps us start up and back. For you, helping us is really a matter of self-interest."

The argument Cripps made was powerful because it plainly and sensibly stated the complex interrelation that the economies of the world have with our own. Certainly it impressed our discussion groups after I returned home. After considering it and the arguments to the contrary, they found themselves in agreement with Cripps.

After leaving Sir Stafford's office, Culbreth and I visited Lord Beaverbrook, the Conservative leader, after which we spent several hours with Harold Laski. It turned out to be one of the memorable days of my life and I was grateful that I hadn't let a little cold and a sense of crankiness keep me from meeting and speaking to such men. I suppose Harry Culbreth was kidding about meeting the British Cabinet, but we wound up seeing almost everybody but the Prime Minister, and we met him a short time later at a reception.

Van Bergen, who had been generally kind and helpful, kept in touch with me during my stay in London. One day he came to me and said, "If you're really interested in developing a world oil cooperative, I'd like to help you."

"How would you go about it?" I asked.

"I've got a friend down in Portugal I'd like you to meet. His name is Calouste Gulbenkian."

"Never heard of him," I commented. I don't know what kept Charley Van Bergen from breaking out laughing at that point. I presume politeness, although I hope it was friendship. In either case his restraint showed he had a gentleman's patience and a good deal of tact.

"He's the most important man in the oil business today," he said, "and I'd like you to go down to see him with me." He went on to explain that Gulbenkian, the fabulous "Mr. Five Percent," had secured most of the oil concessions around the world and had sold them out to major oil interests for flat fees (and fabulous fees they were, too) plus five percent of the gross product. He sounded important enough but I was in a hurry to return home. The Ford-Ferguson tractor matter was then occupying most of my working thought. I told Van Bergen that I was sorry but I couldn't arrange to take a side trip to Portugal to meet some old Armenian.

After I returned to the States I went to see Charles Van Bergen's boss and satisfied myself that Gulbenkian was all Van Bergen said he was and something more. I heard again about Gulbenkian when Van Bergen came home. He told me that the man had taken his pay in crude oil. The companies to which he'd turned over the concessions would let him build up his stocks of crude; then, when he had no more tanks in which to hold his oil, they would go to him and squeeze down his price and take it away from him at bargain prices. The old man was sitting there in Portugal, building up a head of steam, furious with the companies for the way in which they were dealing with him. He also had some personal problems; his son had gone off and married a Parisian dancer and that had annoyed him so that he was sore as a boil.

One day Van Bergen came excitedly into my office. "Gulbenkian will sell to you, Murray! He's ready to sell."

"How much would it cost?"

"I think he'll sell you his five percent for ninety million."

I shook my head. The sum was so large I was sure there would be no use putting it up to the board. Charley Van Bergen insisted that I try. The result was not encouraging. I spoke to Howard Cowden and some of the people in the oil cooperatives. They said the same things: "It's too big for us to swing. There's no point in even considering it."

John Carson, the director of the Washington office of the Cooperative League, urged me to see Watson Snyder in the Justice Department and tell him about it. I took his suggestion.

Snyder got terribly excited. "Good land, that would be the most fabulous thing in the world if you could get it done. Can you?"

I told him I was highly dubious. He urged me to do whatever I could. He felt that it might change the course of world history if the cooperatives could ever get their hands on a portion of the world's oil supply—and I agreed with him. Some years earlier, when we had started out in the oil business, Snyder had suggested we go into Iran and develop a cooperative refinery. When I had asked him how much it would cost, he had given me the figure of twenty-five million dollars.

"Mr. Snyder," I had said unhappily, "have you any idea of the sort of language I'd have to use to get twenty-six Ohio farmers to put their names on that amount of paper to go into a business they know nothing about, in a country they don't know exists? I hardly know where Iran is myself."

"Perhaps so," Snyder had said, "but you can change the course of history if you'll do it."

I had reported to our board and been surprised and pleased to learn that they were ready and willing to consider it—even to the tune of appropriating five thousand dollars to investigate the matter. I had then talked with Howard Cowden, with the Grange League Federation, and with some of the other cooperatives, but the answers I got from them were that this was all so much poppycock, that we needed no such cooperative refinery in Iran, that we weren't big enough, and so on and so on. The voices of despair, timidity, and disbelief. I can't say that we were ready at that time to do what Mr. Snyder had suggested, but I do not doubt that he was right when he said we could have changed the course of history.

I think the establishment of cooperative refineries in the Middle East is still necessary. I think if the people of the Middle East are ever really to govern themselves, they will have to develop their own resources. The monies which are currently pouring into the pockets and treasuries of sheiks and chiefs and a handful of others ought to be going to the great mass of people. We need their oil and want it. We and Europe are ready customers for that oil but our needs do not entitle us to continue the sort of exploitation we and the English have been practicing in the Middle East. Because the English have needed the oil of the Middle East, the worst features of Arab feudalism have been maintained and supported by English governments from the days of the Industrial Revolution. Billions of gallons of oil have been pumped out of the Middle East and fortunes have been made, but the standard of living for the average Arab is little better today than it was centuries ago.

I had the same feeling of despair about the possibility of buying Gulbenkian's 5 percent as I had had about the Iranian oil refinery.

I had made up my mind, though, that our board members

ought to go to Europe to see for themselves the work of the cooperatives, to meet some of the people I had met, and to get a firsthand view of the war damage in England. So in 1946, when the International Cooperative Alliance held its first post-war congress, seven directors went with me: Everett Rittenour, chairman of our fire insurance company; Ed Stough, chairman of the cooperative association; Roland Benjamin, chairman of the life company; George Dunlap, chairman of our auto insurance company; Perry Green, president of the Farm Bureau Federation; James West, then president of our new subsidiary, Peoples Broadcasting Corporation; and Mrs. Harold Robison, whom we always naturally thought of as "our lady representative."

At the end of our trip Charley Van Bergen approached me again. I told him it was no use. "All right," he said sadly. Then he added, "I'm going home with you on the ship. Now, when the proper time comes, I'm going to get you in a card game and I'm going to introduce you as my assistant. Don't say anything—just listen. I want you to know just how big a thing Gulbenkian has been offering you."

One night, then, I slipped away from my own crowd and went down with Van Bergen to a stateroom. There I listened to the conversation of officers and high-ranking representatives of a number of the prominent American oil companies. The substance of it was that they had been negotiating with Gulbenkian to buy out his 5 percent interest. I quickly gathered that the ninety million had been a fire-sale price. The companies these men represented, as a matter of fact, wound up paying Gulbenkian an annual royalty of eighteen million dollars for quite a few years.

We missed out on that opportunity. It was a great one, not merely because of the money involved but because it would have plunged us into international oil cooperatives on a scale that would have made our influence felt. I believe that if oil cooperatives had been established in the Middle East a number of years ago, that area would not now be drifting helplessly into the sphere of Russian influence. If oil cooperatives had demonstrated to the people there that they could control their own destiny, they would not have turned to a nationalist like Nasser. If we could have demonstrated to them that we wanted them to control their own economic affairs, what democratic elements there were in those countries would have taken heart and pushed for political democracy. If we had been generous in the matter of allowing those people to control their own destinies, we would not have had the silly spectacle of the Suez crisis, or the political maneuverings of the Bagdad Pact. We would not have found ourselves foolishly condemning England and France and Israel in the United Nations for behavior no worse than behavior we ourselves have demonstrated in the past toward other nations. I know that our condemnation of these allies of ours was intended to show the world how morally righteous we are. But the fact of the matter is that moral righteousness ill becomes us. I think it's important for us to remember that the first armed clash between Japan and the United States came not on December 7, 1941, but almost four years earlier, on December 12, 1937, when Japanese aircraft attacked a United States Navy gunboat, the *Panay,* in the Yangtze River. It was dramatic news, but the explanation for the presence of the *Panay* in the Yangtze was not given such wide publicity. The *Panay,* there to protect United States interests generally, was at the time of the incident guarding a Standard Oil tanker.

14

I CAME BACK from London in 1945 humbled, depressed by the devastation I'd seen, and aware of the immense rehabilitation job that lay ahead. I was immediately interested, therefore, to learn that the Cooperative League was already taking the initiative in the formation of a new cooperative which would make it easier for Americans to help the less fortunate overseas.

I am, of course, referring to CARE, an organization that has since become so important and famous for what it does that practically nobody knows what it is—a cooperative.

There were a lot of people in on the beginning of CARE, as there must be with any cooperative. I suppose credit for the idea rightly belongs to Arthur Ringland, then of the President's War Relief Control Board. Ringland had served with Herbert Hoover after World War I in a similar venture (but not one that was in any sense cooperatively directed), in five years overseeing the distribution of eighteen million dollars' worth of relief packages. When the atomic bomb brought a quick, and somewhat unexpected, end to World War II, the United States Government was left with immense stockpiles of army ten-in-one rations. Aware of these stockpiles, Mr. Ringland was inspired to set up an organization to purchase the surplus packages, each of which contained the equivalent of thirty good meals, and ship them to the hungry of Europe. He tossed the idea to Dr. Lincoln Clark, cooperative specialist for the United Nations Relief and Rehabilitation Administration. Through John Carson of the Cooperative

League's Washington office, Clark got in touch with Wallace Campbell, secretary of the League's international committee in New York.

Campbell's committee had been raising a Freedom Fund to help co-ops and cooperators in Europe. Clark wanted to know if the League would use part of these funds to start the food-package cooperative under League auspices. Campbell said no. If the idea was important for co-op members, he said, it was important for everybody. He told Clark that if he would agree to establishing a cooperative that would be owned by a representative cross section of national organizations—but operating on the same principles as any local co-op—the League would go along. Clark liked that idea even better than his original one, and the CARE structure was born.

But it wasn't easy.

Campbell took the proposal before the cooperative committee of the American Council of Voluntary Organizations for Foreign Service, the clearinghouse for United States relief agencies operating overseas. The committee liked the idea. Memoranda were prepared, hundreds of letters written. Meetings were called and adjourned. Nothing really happened. Late in the fall Campbell was called back from a series of talks in Minnesota to chair a "final" meeting at which everybody expected to see another good idea get buried.

Instead, Eastburn Thompson of the American Friends Service Committee challenged Campbell to take three weeks off from his job to put the organization together. George Miles of the Catholic War Relief Services (National Catholic Welfare Conference) volunteered to join them. Charlotte Owen, American Council executive director, put her office and staff at their disposal. For three weeks the "three musketeers" pounded the pavements of New York, meeting with executives of religious and relief agencies, labor organizations, and civic groups.

They laid the challenge before each group. Name a top-flight director to the new co-op board. Put up enough money to make it big from the start. The need is great, the time is now. In three weeks they enlisted twenty-two organizations as charter members of the new co-op and raised three-quarters of a million dollars for starting capital. All of a sudden they seemed to have everything but a name. What to call it?

Lincoln Clark paced the floor of his University Park home in Maryland while his wife ironed his shirts. Linc was at the end of his rope. Nobody could come up with a satisfactory name. His wife asked him what he needed. A name that meant something in itself, he said—one that would have some meaning when reduced to its initials. An acrostic.

What had to go in it?

Well, first and most important, the organization was a *co-operative*. Who was it for? Well, it was for *Americans* to use in sending relief packages abroad. "There are two of your words," Linc's wife said. Where do the food packages go? To *Europe*. So far the initials read CAE. Packages? That would be CAEP or CAPE. Not yet. Mrs. Clark's next question: How do you send the packages? "We have a system of remittances," Linc said. "We'll have stockpiles in warehouses overseas. People will buy remittances—cards—that the co-op office will send by airmail overseas and—" *"Remittances,"* she said. "Why not put remittances *before* Europe and then the initials will spell CARE?"

Linc didn't report whether he kissed her or not but he should have.

The first CARE board was composed of people experienced in welfare and relief administration, but except for myself and three bankers, none of them had had any experience in running a business. On that board were representatives of Catholics, Jews, and a number of Protestant denominations, including Quakers, Mennonites, Brethren, Christian Scientists, and Seventh Day Adventists; the AFL and its bitter rival at the time, the CIO; the Cooperative League of the U.S.A.; national relief bodies for aid to France, Norway, Czechoslovakia, Yugoslavia, Lithuania; the

Tolstoy Foundation, and several others. Wally Campbell, Linc Clark, and I figured that CARE was going to be an immense organization; it had to be immense if it was going to do the job. We felt it needed an executive head who knew something about the business of logistics and supply. Even before we held our first meeting we had our sights on Donald Nelson, head of the War Production Board under Roosevelt and a former vice president for Sears Roebuck.

The CARE board held its organization meeting in New York on November 28, 1945. The charter and bylaws were approved and Donald Nelson was named general manager (the boys in Washington had earlier persuaded him to accept it), and nothing remained but the election of a president. General William N. Haskell, then director of the Save the Children Federation, and I were nominated. We went through three dead heats. A tie each time. I voted for him and I'm sure he voted for me. On the final vote I was elected.

Next morning we settled down to work. Donald Nelson hired Linc Clark as CARE's first employee. Wally Campbell was drafted to find office space. Negotiations were pushed in Washington to secure seven and a half million ten-in-one ration packages.

Trouble began immediately. Certain authorities in Washington apparently had little or no faith in the ability of a voluntary organization to do a major relief job overseas. Turn seven and a half million packages of government food over to a nonprofit cooperative? Horrors! Donald Nelson persuaded, cajoled, threatened—to no avail. Blocked at every turn, he threatened to resign from CARE if the government agencies wouldn't clear the food. Nobody budged. Nelson resigned and went home to California.

General Haskell, who had administered a relief program after World War I, was drafted, in spite of his age, to take over. He promptly resumed negotiations in Washington. Next, former Governor Herbert Lehman, then director general of UNRRA and an ardent supporter of CARE from the beginning, came to New York to meet with us, and through him we arranged for a million ration packages. At last it looked as if we were in business.

Linc Clark headed a crew to negotiate contracts with European governments for the entry of CARE packages. The contracts were drawn up by Alex Hawes, our general counsel, who proved himself especially gifted at providing the kind of legal backstopping which, in the long run, made CARE's operations amazingly free of government red tape. On his recommendation, we insisted on duty-free entry; these were relief packages, we emphasized, not to be sold. We required adequate police protection to assure safe delivery. We insisted that there be *no* penalty to the receiving family in the way of reduced ration coupons. These were our conditions, and they were standard for each country. The negotiations were slow. No government was eager to negotiate with a new, untried, cooperative organization. What, after all, was CARE?

That question haunted us, so much so that at one point our deputy director recommended we change the name. It would never catch on. Messenger boys wandered all over 50 Broad Street, in New York, looking for CARE. CARE of what?

We didn't give up the name, but we did compromise. We agreed that our cable address would be PARCELUS. Parcel U.S. Much simpler and more meaningful than CARE. So it was. And, if you will look at a CARE letterhead, so it is today.

The early months of the CARE story were a series of frustrations. During the first nine months we "lost" $600,000 of our $750,000 capital. Things looked so dark that the board could easily have thrown in the sponge with ample justification. But by September, 1946, we began to turn the corner. We were able to bring down the cost to CARE of the ten-in-one ration packages so that we could supply them to our contributors for ten dollars delivered, instead of fifteen. The first large quantity of signed receipts came back from families in Europe who had received the packages and our American contributors now knew for sure that their money was being well spent.

About that time, too, Paul French, a Quaker newspaperman with great promotional ideas, stepped into the job of executive director. He succeeded General Haskell, who now became honorary president. Thanks to Paul's drive and publicity methods, CARE and its person-to-person relief program quickly attained international recognition. CARE delivered twenty-five million dollars' worth of foodstuffs overseas in 1947. A year later the total increased to nearly thirty million dollars. Hundreds of thousands of letters poured across the Atlantic thanking American families for their contributions and these in turn inspired further contributions. Our parcels became so well known in Europe that all food packages tended to be credited to CARE. CARE became a new word in each of the languages of Europe.

But success brought our greatest headaches and heartaches as well. Perhaps it is unfair to report the inside story of a public institution like CARE, but unless the story is told, people are likely to take its success for granted. Conflicts, both of issues and personalities, are inevitable in any organization, I suppose. Somehow, though, they always seem especially painful in an organization that is idealistically motivated and democratically controlled. As a distinctly human organization, CARE has had its share of human differences.

One of our early crises arose when the public began spontaneously to send in undesignated contributions. You might expect that everyone would welcome such contributions, since they made it possible for CARE to help the neediest families in each country in the names of those Americans who had no friends or relatives abroad. Unfortunately, most board members thought otherwise. By a vote of eleven to ten, they decided to return these contributions with a letter saying that CARE was not able to administer general relief. The policy was a mistaken one. It sprang from the fear that contributions to CARE would be siphoned from other relief agencies. The facts hardly warranted this assumption, but the fear was there. The fact was that CARE stimulated giving for overseas relief among people who had never contributed to any overseas aid program before.

After an emotion-packed series of board meetings, the board reversed itself, again by a narrow margin. In protest some members resigned.

And that's the way it was at each point in our expansion. When the CARE staff decided we should send blankets as well as food, important board members rebelled. When the CARE staff arranged to ship coal packages in the face of a critical coal shortage in the low countries, ditto. A plan to send shoes was killed entirely.

Our most dramatic crisis was precipitated by a recommendation that CARE send technical books to Europe, something many board members considered the grossest example yet of CARE's departure from what, to them, was its original purpose. If it hadn't been for a tragedy, chances are the board might never have approved the program. Arthur Gamble, CARE's chief of mission to Poland, became seriously ill. The mission cabled for penicillin, then in short supply in Europe. The drug was delivered, but there were no doctors at hand who had had any experience with it and no books available that could tell them how to use it. Through lack of technical information, Gamble died.

As I've indicated, these expansion moves brought about gradual changes in CARE's board membership. The American Jewish Distribution Committee withdrew even before the board faced its first major issue. The National Catholic Welfare Conference (War Relief Services) and Church World Service resigned after they lost a fight to fire the executive director. When CARE decided to supplement its relief activities with a self-help program, the American Friends Service Committee pulled out. The Christian Scientists quietly withdrew when we added medical equipment for European hospitals.

In time all these were replaced by new organizations. United HIAS (Hebrew Immigrant Aid Society) and the National Council of Negro Women were brought in. The Lions and Eagles, each of which had launched important CARE programs as group contributors, became active members of the board. Two of the great farm groups, the National Grange and the National Farmers Union, joined us and were soon followed by the Credit Union National Association. The result of this last addition was that the nonprofit economic organizations, including the AFL-CIO and the Cooperative League, began to assume a more influential role in CARE policy.

Oversimplification is always dangerous, but in general what happened was that the organizations which were conducting their own overseas relief programs looked on CARE as a potential rival; when they could not control it, they withdrew. The large membership organizations that did not have their own relief programs looked on CARE as a strong right arm to carry forward the programs which they were not prepared to carry out on their own.

Measured by its successes, the CARE story is well known. We withdrew from most of Western Europe as soon as those countries attained a strong enough economic position to take care of their own people. CARE programs then got under way in Japan and Korea, the Philippine Islands, and sections of Southeast Asia.

Since the United States had no plan for the disposal of its huge surplus of agricultural commodities, CARE asked for the right to add some of those foodstuffs to its warehouses for distribution. After all, as taxpayers, we had already paid for this surplus. What better use could be made of it? The Agriculture Department agreed, and that's how we came to launch huge programs in Yugoslavia, Greece, and Southern Italy. Our program of school lunches in Egypt became the largest overseas voluntary foreign aid program ever undertaken in a single country.

For two successive Christmases CARE obtained huge quantities of agricultural surplus and made them up into Christmas packages. We charged the contributor one dollar for each package delivered overseas. The idea was important and dramatic, easily understood and easily supported, but how much so we didn't immediately appreciate. One Monday morning just before the first Christmas, the mailbags brought us $180,000 in contributions, most of it in one-dollar bills. The entire staff had to stop everything else to check and count the money.

After ten years of such successes, CARE faced another crisis. We had followed the human pattern of trying to meet every need as we saw it. Needs, of course, were great, and we found ourselves operating relief missions in sixty countries around the world. They were staffed by some of the most competent young men and women you could find anywhere. They were not only distributors of food and self-help materials, they were effective unofficial ambassadors for the people of the United States. By 1955, however, the extensive CARE program was beyond the public support. We were spending nearly a million dollars a year more than we were taking in. Obviously something had to give.

Paul French had declared repeatedly that rather than ever cut back, we should wind CARE up "in a blaze of glory." He preferred this to cutting back countries, cutting back services, tightening our belts, firing staff, and making the budget meet our income. Reluctantly, in July, 1955, we accepted Paul's resignation. To replace him we reached into the ranks and named Richard Reuter, who for some time had been the deputy director. Dick Reuter proved to be the kind of an executive we needed—a team-play man who commanded the full support of his staff. Economies were instituted. CARE cut back its services to 20 countries. The budget was balanced without any slowdown in the flow of relief goods.

Under Reuter, CARE has seen the contributions to its self-help program jump from 8 percent in 1955 to more than 30 percent of its total donated funds in 1959. With these funds we have shipped iron lungs to the Philippines, Japan, and Korea, and to dozens of hospitals in other parts of the world. Midwife kits by the hundreds went to India, Pakistan, and Ceylon. Grange women raised funds for fruit jars to be shipped to farm wives in Greece to help preserve crops that otherwise would have rotted. The World Veterans Federation launched a special program of wheel chairs, Braille watches, Braille writers, and other aids for the blind. The National Education Association raised about a hundred thousand dollars for suiting materials for teachers in Korea. Each teacher was given enough cloth for two suits of clothes; a tailor could keep one suit as his pay for making the other for a teacher. Four-H Clubs raised funds to help buy plows and handtools for farm use in Greece, India, Italy, Haiti, Korea, and Pakistan. Perhaps these aren't the most dramatic things in the self-help story but they figure in my mind as the most significant.

Reuter also saw to it that CARE began to make more effective use of surplus foodstuffs. Public Law 480, adopted by the Congress in 1954, provided a great new flow of agricultural surpluses. The United States Congress was persuaded that it was cheaper to repay voluntary agencies like CARE for the ocean freight in shipping surplus wheat, milk, cheese, corn, and other products than it was to pay storage for a year for those same commodities. As a result, the new CARE program today comprises a cooperative effort of the Federal Government, which supplies the agricultural surplus and the ocean freight; the recipient country, which pays the internal costs; and CARE, which pays the assembling, packaging, and supervisory costs.

The Latin American countries have long been the stepchildren of the United States. We fail to realize that in some of Latin America poverty is more severe than it is in India and Pakistan, or other spots long looked on as the neediest in the world. CARE now has self-help and relief programs under way in eight countries in the American Hemisphere. We are providing the material for Mexican villagers to drill their own wells. In cooperation with the United Nations Housing Center for Central America we are distributing a block-making machine, with which a couple of men, using native earth and a binder, can make building blocks. CARE provides the machines; the people provide their own labor and materials. Hundreds, probably thousands, of homes and community centers have been built with this machine, which seems to me to be a particularly apt symbol of CARE's new self-help direction.

By 1957, I thought it was time some of the younger men began to share more responsibility, so I decided to step down from the presidency. I then became chairman of the board and was succeeded as president by Harold Miner, who, like me, had been with CARE from the beginning. For the past ten years he'd served as our treasurer. Harold is a representative on the board from the Congregational Christian Service Committee and is a vice president of the Manufacturers Trust Company. His prime responsibility is with that beautiful new glass bank on 43rd Street and Fifth Avenue in New York City. From time to time he and I have had a lot of fun sparring with each other about the role of the banker in the American economy. I'm sure it came as a surprise to him when, after my resignation from the presidency, I invited the board to meet in Columbus and arranged to bring them here in our company planes. Although I'd assured him that we were no longer just operating a series of farm supply depots at country crossroads, he wasn't prepared for our $6-million headquarters building, nor for the impact we were making on the community. At lunch that day he took a look around our board dining room and said, laughing, "Murray, I believe you farmers could swap everything, including cooks, with Manufacturers Trust, and come out even."

Harold Miner has been one of the towers of strength throughout both the troubled and triumphant days of CARE. Fortunately, on balance, the days have been more triumphant than troubled. During CARE's short fourteen years of service it has put $325 million worth of goods where they were most needed overseas. In the fiscal year of 1959 alone its relief volume totaled $40 million.

It has always been a source of pride to me that CARE has managed to buy, package, transport, and distribute goods and other essential products overseas at a cost which no private company could match. We know this to be true because we have periodically submitted our operations to the inspection of private companies with the thought that we might be able to get someone else to do the job. None of these has ever indicated they could do the job as efficiently and cheaply as we could ourselves. CARE had, and has, a staff of devoted, idealistic, and dedicated people working for it that I have never seen matched anywhere. The idea of relieving suffering and hunger among the nations of the world has attracted men and women of a very high caliber, who have been content to work for very moderate wages, both in this country and on the mission staffs overseas. None of us on the board has ever received a penny in wages or expenses. CARE has also been fortunate in having a distinguished group of business executives to serve on its national advisory committee. It has received invaluable support and assistance from the Advertising Council and from dozens of associations and from millions of Americans.

I am often asked why CARE is a cooperative. Many people see the cooperative principles in action in modified forms in so many organizations that the unique nature of CARE is not clearly perceived. CARE is a cooperative because it is a democratic non-profit economic organization. Each member organization has one vote and only one vote in the determination of policy. The savings made in the operation of a cooperative are distributed to its members in proportion to their patronage. In this case, however, the consumer-members, the national organizations that own CARE, do not wish to receive the funds themselves but wish to have any savings made used in the contribution of additional relief or self-help supplies in the countries to which the original contributions were made.

Perhaps it is important to say what CARE is not. It is not a government organization. No government funds are ever contributed directly to CARE although CARE is reimbursed for ocean freight and for certain services it performs. These payments merely cut the cost of operation. The financing of CARE

215

in its basic program is, has been, and always will be nongovernmental in character. To illustrate: When CARE began handling government agricultural surpluses, an attempt was made to put the CARE employees through the security and loyalty clearance procedures used for government personnel overseas. We refused to comply because we felt that submitting the staff to security clearances would change the nongovernmental character of the CARE operation. Fortunately our point of view was sustained. Both the United States Government and CARE would have suffered otherwise, for one of the great values of CARE is that it has always been a nongovernmental instrument. The ambassador to Greece once remarked at a farewell party for the CARE mission chief in that country, "I am the ambassador of the United States Government. The CARE chief is the ambassador of the American people."

I am always surprised and impressed, during my visits to CARE missions abroad and my talks with foreign government officials, to find that our cooperative association has attained such tremendous status. The cooperative character of CARE will always be with us. When we changed CARE's name as it withdrew from most of Europe, we dropped the word *Europe* and substituted *Everywhere.* When we changed CARE's name again to drop the word *Remittance,* we substituted *Relief.* But we've never changed the word *Cooperative* or the word *American.* We never will. And we can thank millions of Americans for the fact that all over the world, among people who have no idea what the letters themselves stand for, CARE means care.

15

O NE OF THE most momentous decisions our Farm Bureau board faced after the war had to do with the separation of the Ohio Farm Bureau Federation from the insurance companies in 1948.

We started in 1926, you will recall, with a capitalization of ten thousand dollars, just to secure for farmers a more equitable rate for auto insurance. We grew, at first, because our volunteer sales force picked us fine risks among their farmer-neighbors. We were able to cut rates way down, so far down that insurance agents for other companies began to yell with pain in states where we were doing business.

It wasn't long before Farm Bureaus in other states were inviting us in to insure their members. Connecticut is a good example. When we went into business in Connecticut we had the sponsorship of the Connecticut Farm Bureau. Now Connecticut is a powerful insurance state in the sense that some of the great insurance companies of our country have their home offices located there. They are powerful politically as well as economically, and I doubt whether any new company could have made any headway in Connecticut had it not had the arrangement we had with the Connecticut Farm Bureau. The Bureau had a membership of ten thousand, including the state's most outstanding and successful farmers. We paid the Connecticut Bureau a sponsorship fee. Now sponsorship fees were something new in the insurance field. Not new if you thought of them as advertising costs, but new in the sense that they were not paid to magazines or newspapers or radio stations or television stations but to farm organizations. We felt that we'd get more policyholders if we appealed, at first, to groups of people who were, like ourselves, farmers and members of a farm bureau, or city consumers and members of a cooperative.

Well, the technique worked—and for very obvious reasons. If some insurance organization was soliciting your business and you knew nothing about it, you might ask a neighbor and if he, an influential and successful farmer, said to you, "Well, yes, they're all right. We have an agreement with them to sponsor them and we've looked into their insurance and their organization and we think they're good people to do business with," there's no question but that you would be favorably impressed.

That's exactly the way it did happen in Connecticut—and in Pennsylvania, Delaware, Maryland, New York, New Jersey, North Carolina, Rhode Island, Vermont, and Washington, D.C., in each of which either a state farm bureau or a state federation of cooperatives became our sponsor. Our insurance just kept right on growing like a vine, and one of the reasons was that local organizations of good reputation and importance were sponsoring us.

I had learned long before that when you become successful in a new venture in a new way, sooner or later you step on someone's toes. By 1948, in our insurance business, we had stepped on a lot of toes. I had the feeling that somewhere, someone would presently say "ouch" and try to find some way of stopping us.

It's interesting to note here that we once employed a bright young man named Frank Lang. Frank was graduated from college when he was eighteen—something of a child prodigy. He was working for us in our actuarial department and came to my attention when he won some national contest with a paper he'd written on insurance.

Shortly before he left our employ to become an insurance consultant he warned me that one day other insurance companies would try to stop our growth in one way or another, and he said,

"Mr. Lincoln, watch out for your next insurance examination."

Now, all insurance companies are rigidly supervised by the insurance departments of the states in which they do business. Mutual or cooperative insurance companies are no exceptions to this general supervision. Ordinarily, every three years each company has a convention examination, which is conducted by examiners designated by several of the insurance departments of states where the company is licensed. If an examination is not completed in one year, it continues on into the next year. In the late 1930s I had met the insurance examiners for the first time. That, as you probably recall, was when they questioned me as to the source of my income.

Dean Kerr, who was formerly with the Ohio Insurance Department and is now Nationwide's government relations director, tells a story that reveals the attitude some members of the Ohio Insurance Department had toward the Farm Bureau during the 1940s. Dean says he was riding with one of his fellow examiners one day when they came in sight of a Farm Bureau Insurance Company sign on the road. Dean's companion saluted it with a Bronx cheer. "Why did you do that?" Dean asked. "Well, those guys are just no good," the examiner said. He went on to say that no one in the department liked them.

In 1942 our regular insurance examination was begun. It was recessed in 1943 or 1944 and resumed again in 1946 or 1947. I had paid no attention to it except to notice that it had been going on for some time. Our three companies—auto, fire, and life—were going great guns. Each was increasing its business from 15 to 25 percent a year. It was a long time since our treasurer had come in, slammed down his books, and said happily, "Well, we're a million-dollar institution." The other organizations within the Farm Bureau family were doing well too. The cooperatives were doing about fifty or more million dollars' worth of business. Membership in the Farm Bureau Federation was continuing to grow (fifty-five thousand farm families in 1947 and sixty thousand in 1948). It was also becoming a stronger and stronger influence in Ohio affairs, largely because of the fifteen hundred grass-roots advisory councils we had going throughout the state. Most of the directors of the Federation were also directors of the insurance companies. That had been our custom from the beginning and it had worked very well. What's more, on our insurance boards were men who also served as directors of the sponsoring organizations in other states.

I was on vacation in Maine when I got a phone call from Ed Keltner, our controller. The examiners had concluded their examination and had made some recommendations which threatened to raise all kinds of havoc. Keltner wanted me to come right back.

When I returned to Columbus I discovered that the examiners had two objections. The first objection lay in the sponsorship fee arrangements. There was no clear schedule, they said, for determining just how the fees were arrived at. On the one hand, the boards of directors of the Farm Bureau insurance companies offered sponsorship fees to various organizations. On the other hand, the same men rushed around to the other side of the table, where they became directors of the boards of the sponsoring organizations, and said, "Okay, we accept those fees." The examiners said they felt people should not negotiate with themselves —that negotiators ought to be at arm's length with one another. Well, we asked, were the fees unfair? No, they weren't. Were we justified in spending the money? Yes, we were, they conceded. Was the money well spent? we asked. Yes, it appeared to be. Certainly the Farm Bureau insurance companies had prospered and grown and the examiners conceded that the sponsorship arrangement was largely responsible for our rapid growth. Well, what was wrong? Negotiators should negotiate at arm's length, they said mysteriously. What does that mean? Did they think we were robbing the insurance company to support the sponsoring organizations? No, they did not believe that. Did they have any evidence that anything like that had taken place? No, they hadn't. As far as they could see, the gentlemen of the boards of directors were all honorable, upright, and responsible. *Nevertheless,* they contended, the opportunity for misappropriation existed under the present setup.

Well, what were we supposed to do about the sponsorship fees? What was it they wanted? They wouldn't say. But one day, one of the examiners went out to lunch with one of our staff. And what the examiner told him, was this:

"Part of your trouble with this sponsorship fee is that you haven't anything in black and white to substantiate your payments."

"But we get services for our money."

"I know that."

"If we had paid it out in advertising you wouldn't kick about it."

"No," the examiner said, "we wouldn't. That's because we're used to insurance companies spending money on advertising."

"But our sponsorship arrangements are a lot more effective than ordinary advertising," our man protested.

The examiner agreed.

"Well, then, how are we going to justify these sponsors' fees to you people?"

The examiner smiled. "Buy a file. Buy a bunch of files."

"Then what?"

The examiner looked at our man. "Didn't you ever hear of an invoice?"

We bought files. We drew up new contracts that specified how much we were to pay a sponsor for each service. We had our sponsoring organizations bill us for each meeting held on behalf of Farm Bureau insurance, for each ad, for each mailing made to its membership. We accumulated a mountain of invoices. The examiners were happier. This was what they were used to. This was what they wanted.

The second problem, that of the interlocking directorates, wasn't so simply resolved. The examiners wanted the Ohio Farm Bureau and its insurance companies to separate physically. As

221

we saw it, that called for a great wrench. What if we refused to separate? The examiners hinted that since we had failed to substantiate the payments to the sponsors they might hold all the directors individually and collectively responsible for some five million dollars paid out. This was sheer bluff; I've learned since that they had no more chance of doing this and making it stick in a court action than they had of jumping over the moon. At the time, though, the prospect was frightening.

Even so, some of our board members were inclined to fight, so for advice I went to see Bill Safford, the man who, as Ohio Insurance Commissioner in 1926, had been responsible for our getting into the business in the first place. He intimated that it might be worth while to go to court, if we had to, to resist the examiners' decision.

Because our lawyer, Henry Ballard, was counseling us to compromise I went to see Joseph O'Meara, a keen lawyer who is now head of the Law School at the University of Notre Dame. Joe O'Meara said that if he were in my position he would fight the decision; he thought it might develop into a very important case at law.

I returned to Henry Ballard and suggested that Joe O'Meara discuss with our board his feelings pro and con. Henry said if we heard O'Meara he would resign. Well, I had so much else on my hands I didn't feel like provoking the fight any further, so we agreed to the separation of the Farm Bureau from its insurance companies.

I regret to this day that we did not fight. We'd done nothing wrong. Neither I nor any member of the board was benefiting from the interlocking directorates. The examiners, after they'd looked under every rug and in every bureau drawer, agreed that no one in the institution had made any personal profit out of the arrangement.

Personally, this separation meant that I had to resign either as secretary and general manager of the Farm Bureau or of its insurance companies. When I asked why I could not continue with both organizations, the claim was that it was too much work for me. It was finally suggested that the examination would not be completed if I did not make that decision.

I decided to leave the Farm Bureau and stay with the insurance companies for several reasons. For one thing, I was beginning to have serious questions as to whether farmers could solve their own problems without joining up with city consumers. I'm still convinced that amalgamation is inevitable. I went with the insurance companies because they represented all kinds of people and money, not just farmers and farm money. For another thing, though I did not fully appreciate it until much later, insurance is one of the few products with which there need be no consumer-producer conflict. Farmers sell grain and consumers buy bread and breakfast food. Between the farmer and the consumer stands a processor or middleman. With insurance, though, where the people who buy the product are also those who own the company, there is no middleman. It's you selling to yourself, or you buying from yourself, and if there's any producer-consumer conflict at all, it's inside yourself. To me, that's what makes insurance so important. It appears to me to be the best bet for getting all kinds of people together to fulfill their common needs.

And so the separation was made in 1948. It brought to my mind some serious thoughts about government regulation, especially insurance regulation. Now I'm not opposed to regulation, as such. Our companies have supported government regulation; we've gone to bat for the Ohio Insurance Department, for example, to get legislation to provide cabinet ranking for it, with corresponding budgetary increases. Our position is that as long as regulation is necessary, we'd like to have the best kind of regulation. My point is that regulation can be either good or bad. If it's in the public interest, it's good; if not, it's bad.

What disturbed me about our examination in the forties—and still does disturb me—was that the examiners seemed to want most of all to make us conform to their idea of what was desirable in a company. They seemed to care little or nothing about our ideals and about *why* we weren't conforming; if we didn't do as other companies did, then we did wrong.

Our investments, for instance. When we began investing, few of us had had any experience and we started out cautiously and in the most orthodox manner. We understood land, so mortgages on farms and homes were the easiest things to invest in. But as we grew bigger, I began to sense that we weren't branching out. I finally said to our investment department that it looked to me as though most investment managers were lazy. They were just following the orthodox pattern. I grant you that from the standpoint of security, investment in government bonds and the bluest of blue chips is something for which you will never be criticized. But in my opinion most blue-chip stocks are blue because companies take from the consumer more in pricing than they should. What these companies forget is that the more you take away from consumers with one hand, the more you have to give them with the other, else the profit-making machine breaks down.

It's this practice of using other people's money to deprive them of proper benefits from its use that angers me. A typical example of this practice exists in a life insurance company of which I am a director. Like most other companies, it takes money from policyholders, returns 2½ percent in dividends and benefits and then, if that money is left with the company it turns it over to someone else at 4, 5, or 6 percent for *their* use. Those people, in turn, lend that money to people who might very well hold the insurance company's policies. One small finance firm to which the money has been lent has shown a 20 to 30 percent return on its investment. We let that small loan company take as much as it can get out of people who might be our own policyholders. The point is, the people who borrow to buy cars or furniture may be borrowing their own money without realizing it. If it is their own money, it seems to me—now, I know this is unorthodox—they ought to get the greatest benefits from it themselves, and those benefits should not be reserved to the stockholders of the finance company.

Anyway, we at the Farm Bureau felt people ought to benefit from their own money, so we began to make very conservative investments in the stock or mortgages of cooperatives. This made the insurance examiners unhappy because the stock of cooperatives is not listed in Wall Street; the examiners couldn't find the value of our investments by checking the newspapers. They had to dig around to find out what these stocks were worth, and they began to raise questions. But when the examination was over and the investment values were established, they found what we had known all the time—that investments in cooperatives are equal to the best investments in conventional blue chips. If we had invested our money in some hoary and respectable railroad and lost it, it would have been perfectly orthodox to allow the loss as a proper business risk. But investment in a cooperative, whether profitable or not, is unconventional and time after time causes searching inquiry and much admonitory finger-shaking. Here, it seems to me, regulation has lost sight of its true purpose, which is to protect people who cannot protect themselves. The great danger to which government regulation is subject is that the regulated will find ways and means to regulate the regulators. Regulation thus sometimes becomes an instrument to maintain the status quo and a barrier to the creation of new enterprises that might help people.

A year or so after our 1948 examination one of our men was in New York and Robert Dineen, then the commissioner of the New York State Department of Insurance, said, "The next time that president of yours is in New York City, will you have him come in?"

I had never met Mr. Dineen, but as soon as I got in to see him, he said, "Brother, you've been having some trouble."

"Yep," I admitted.

"What is it?" he asked.

"So far as I know, they're trying to stop us. I guess we're going too fast or something like that."

"Now, start at the beginning and tell me your story."

I started in and after ten or fifteen minutes he said, "This is involved, but it's just what I thought it was. Let's set a date when we can spend plenty of time. I want to know all about it." So we set a date. We started about a quarter to seven in the evening and wound up about two o'clock in the morning. When I got through, he said: "Well, just as I thought, Murray. Before your examination started, Lee Shield, your commissioner in Ohio, called me up and told me your Farm Bureau crowd was going to get a real thorough going-over."

Why Lee Shield called Bob Dineen I'm not sure. Perhaps because New York is an important state and whatever is approved in New York is generally acceptable to insurance departments in other states. On the other hand, whatever is disallowed in New York is looked at more carefully in other states.

Bob Dineen said, "When I got that call I had a notion to call you and tell you to pull together whatever records we might need and come on down and see me. I had a feeling that maybe the reason they were after you had more implications in it than you could see on the surface. Murray, you've made one great mistake."

"What's that?" I asked.

"When you have something like this to do—justifying your sponsorship fees and the interlocking directorates—you ought to get the commissioners in the areas in which you operate all together and tell them what you're up to."

"My lawyer would never let me," I said, recalling the number of times Henry Ballard had kept me away from examiners and commissioners. "All during these negotiations with the department, Henry Ballard just told me never to go down there."

"Well, the next time you've got something like that to do," Bob said, "get them in a room and tell them your story. Some of them may not understand it, but the mere fact that you've explained it might tend to soften their opposition."

And, anyway, they're just human beings, Bob might have added, but didn't.

The separation of the insurance companies from the Farm Bureau was a severe emotional wrench for me. It took me away from the Farm Bureau after an intimate association of twenty-eight years. I felt that my departure would mean a change in the Farm Bureau itself because with my going many of the things which we had been doing would stop cold. I remember saying to somebody at the time, "Well, I'm afraid the Farm Bureau's going to degenerate into nothing but a fertilizer company because that's the thing that John Sims is mostly interested in."

I had been trying for years to demonstrate the advantage of consumer cooperatives. One of the reasons we had taken the board to Europe in 1946 was to show them how consumer and farm cooperatives were working together. But I'm sorry to say that the man who was later to become president of the Farm Bureau, and who was to install John Sims as its executive secretary when I left to go with the insurance companies, went on that trip to find out why they wouldn't work rather than why they would.

After the separation occurred I made a serious mistake. I had a candidate in mind to succeed me but I didn't offer his name because I wanted to see what the board would do itself. They did the very thing I feared they would do. They put Sims in my place and then began to cut back. The Farm Bureau had bought a bank under my urging. They got rid of it. We had set up a grocery wholesale to include city people as well as farmers. They did away with it after unsuccessfully trying to make it over into another exclusively farmer organization and finding that it competed with their own Farm Bureau cooperative. I had the feeling that they would also have given up the farm advisory councils if they hadn't proven too strong, successful, and useful.

When the insurance companies were separated from the Farm

Bureau and from the advisory councils we began to discuss ways of adapting the advisory-council concept to the insurance business. It suits the insurance business and it suits my own belief that if you ever want an answer to a human problem you must go back to the people. Don't go to those who have a vested interest in a job or who are in a position to have something to do with the solution of the problem. Don't go to the experts (unless it's a technical problem). Take a wide enough sampling from people who have no immediate selfish interest in the problem and you'll get the answer. At least you'll find out as much of an answer as people are willing to give to any problem, and once you have that you can provide them with leadership in the implementing of that answer.

The first question that arose when we started seriously thinking about setting up a system of policyholder advisory committees was whether or not people of such diverse interests would come together. It had worked for farmers in the advisory councils because, it was suggested, the farmers had common interests, desires, aims, and so on. Would it work for insurance policyholders scattered over some twelve states, all of whom were in many different occupations and many different walks of life? Well, we decided to give it a try.

It wasn't long before a bit of quiet resistance to the policyholder advisory concept began to develop. It developed because at almost every policyholder meeting some well-meaning but naïve gentleman would get up and ask, "Now, how do we elect the directors of this institution?"

In conventional stock insurance companies, policyholders have no voting rights. Only the stockholders vote. In a mutual insurance company, the policyholder has the right to vote and the right to nominate and elect directors. Historically, however, mutual policyholders have not exercised the right to nominate and elect directors. Such matters are left to management. Commonly, the management of a mutual company will take proxies from policyholders and in this way insure the election of directors it nominates. As for us, two of our companies are mutuals and, to make the nomination and election of directors somewhat more democratic, we have traditionally asked our sponsoring organizations to suggest nominees. This does three things: (1) it provides a broad geographical base for policyholder representation; (2) it gives us a group of directors that, for length of service in the leadership of people's organizations, can't be obtained under any other system I know of; and (3) it guarantees that at the place where it counts the most the consumer viewpoint gets constant and full expression.

Except for a few cooperative-minded firms like ours, and notably Mutual Service of St. Paul, few insurance companies seem to be concerned about the general absence of democratic procedure. In having our directors recommended by people's organizations we have taken at least one step to do something about it. But I am still not satisfied. It's difficult for any big mutual company, including our own, to get its policyholders together to nominate and elect directors. But I believe some apparatus has to be created to get it done because people should control the great aggregates of wealth that insurance companies represent.

As I've already written, I sit on the board of another big Midwestern life insurance company. I've not yet brought up this matter of the lack of democratic control with them. I have, however, told its president, "Society isn't going to let a few of you guys sit on top of three hundred and fifty million dollars and pass around the directorships to your friends and golf partners."

His answer was, "We're no worse than you fellows are."

"No," I admitted, "except that we're doing something about it and you're not doing anything about it."

To my way of thinking, the control of great wealth by small inside groups of self-perpetuating directors is one of the grave economic problems of our time. Its resolution won't be easy. I have seen evidence of its complexity even in our own companies. Some of our board members seem to fear that the policyholder advisory committees are, one day, going to have a say about the nomination and election of directors, and they fear that when that day arrives they may stand no chance of being nominated or elected.

Frankly, I think such fears are unfounded if a man will demonstrate that he deserves to be a leader. The leader who demands security for himself is, to my mind, no leader at all. For my own part, I have expressed it this way to the board and to the staff: "There's just one way of maintaining leadership in an institution and that's to be just so aggressive and give so much service that nobody else can catch you. I never had a contract with an institution. I don't want one. If the time ever comes that they don't want me, I don't want them. If there's ever any question about the way this company is being run, if it isn't going successfully, there's only one fellow to look to, and that's me." Of course I intend to find out what's wrong before they do. If I can't fix it, I'll quit before I let them fire me.

The unhappy truth is that people don't want to work hard. It seems to be an inevitable process that people start out working with all their hearts for a great cause. Then the cause turns into an institution and they work for that. Next thing, unfortunately, they wind up working for their own particular place in that institution. My fear is that many of us at Nationwide are, today, somewhere between the stage of working for an institution and working for a particular place in the institution. I know there are board members who say, "I'm against policyholder advisory committees because in time they may demand the right to nominate our board, and if that happens then I may not get nominated and elected." It seems to me that a man who thinks that is clearly working for his own particular place in our institution. I have told our board members that the advisory committee concept is no threat to them. I consider it the life blood of a democratic institution and I'm glad we have it because it keeps all of us on our toes a little bit.

But somewhere, somehow, the problem of giving back control of large aggregates of wealth represented by insurance companies to the people who have contributed that wealth will have to be solved. The question is rarely raised in other insurance companies. Some day I wish I could get together enough proxies to walk into a board meeting of the Metropolitan Life Insurance Company, in which I have a policy, and say to its president, "Mr. Ecker, we're going to put two new members on your board." But I don't suppose that will ever happen.

CHAPTER

16

ACTUALLY, I did once cross some words with Mr. Fred Ecker, but the occasion had nothing to do with proxies. It came about like this.

By 1950, you'll recall, Ohio's Senator Robert Taft had become a kind of swear word to organized labor. Well, in casting about for a likely candidate to run against him, both the AFL and CIO lit on me. I was approached by the national chairman of the CIO's political action committee and asked to run, and the state representatives of both unions kept the pressure on me for quite a while. I hesitated for several reasons. For one thing, Perry Green, an unreconstructed Republican, was unalterably opposed to my running and he never stopped reminding me that most of the Farm Bureau membership agreed with him. For another, I felt I was accomplishing a lot more for the good of democracy right where I was than I possibly could as a junior senator from Ohio. Still, the pressure was mounting and, in addition to labor, a lot of young people and faculty members from the university were urging me to run, and I have to confess that the idea tickled me. I finally admitted to this much—that if Joe Ferguson, a popular old-time Democrat and already an avowed candidate, would not force me into a primary fight (which I didn't believe I could win) I would consent to run against Taft. I must admit that I was deeply and secretly relieved when Joe Ferguson refused to get out of the road to let me make the race.

There was, of course, much newspaper conjecture about the prospect of my running. One day, shortly after some such story had appeared, I was in New York and decided to call on Leroy Lincoln, then president of the Metropolitan Life Insurance Company.

Leroy was a distant cousin of mine. We were born in the same part of the country and, like all of the Lincolns on my side of the family, he was tall and homely and had big feet, and I include myself in that description. He had urged me, whenever we had met at insurance conferences and the like, to drop in and see him when I was in New York. I happened to have Harry Culbreth with me at the time and we had no more than entered Leroy Lincoln's office with its old-fashioned roll-top desk piled high with clippings and correspondence, when he said, "What's this about you running for senator against Senator Taft?"

"Well," I replied, "I'm not running for anything."

"But, look at all these clippings. That's what they say you're doing. Running for the Senate."

"No," I replied. "If you'll examine them more carefully you'll find that I haven't said I would run. Other people have been urging me to run but I've made no decision."

"Well, I'm glad to hear that. We wouldn't want to lose Senator Taft or to have you oppose him."

"I thought this was a free country," I said.

"It is. But that's the kind of fellow we want in Congress."

"*You* want?" I asked. "I thought it was Ohio who was electing a senator."

"Well," he said, "we're all interested in that campaign." Which was a remark that I found greatly interesting.

Fred Ecker, who was then the executive vice president at Metropolitan (today he is the president), came into Lincoln's office and began to listen to our discussion.

"Well," I said, rather flippantly, "I suppose Taft's better than John Bricker."

"What's wrong with John Bricker?" Leroy asked.

233

"I didn't say there was anything wrong with him, I merely said that I thought Taft was better than Bricker."

"Well, those are the kind of people we want down in Congress."

"That may be your opinion," I replied, "but I am, I think, entitled to my own opinion."

We then got into an intense discussion about some of the things that both Mr. Bricker and Mr. Taft stood for and finally Fred Ecker wound up shaking his finger in my face, beet-red, shouting, "Mr. Lincoln, do you know these things you're advocating are going to destroy this democratic system!" And so we got into an argument. Leroy fluttered around trying to get the waters calmed down and I finally turned to Harry Culbreth and said, "Oh, hell, Harry, let's get out of here. We're making no progress here." I went out of that place boiling and saw a friend of mine who was in insurance and who also happened to be a Republican. I told him everything that had happened. He just grinned and said, "What do you expect out of that stuffy old office down there?"

After that experience I was tempted more than ever to run—just to prove something, I suppose. But I calmed down after a while, my cooler head prevailed, and when Joe Ferguson refused to budge and I was able to get off the hook, I was considerably relieved. There were a lot of other things buzzing in my head at the time, most of them to do with organizing new cooperatives, and I was eager to get on with them.

There are two theories as to how cooperatives should be formed. One of them is the theory of the purist and the other is something else again. Most business institutions are organized from the top down rather than from the bottom up. I mean by this that decisions are made at the top level and then sent down to the lower echelons until the last person at the bottom, generally the customer, gets the word concerning that policy, not for consideration but as an accomplished fact. Cooperatives, because they are democratically run, are organized from the bottom up in the sense that policy determination lies at the bottom of the

234

organization, among the membership; the top, the executive level, responds to and is responsible to the bottom level. Many purists of the cooperative movement insist that there is no other way of *creating* a cooperative.

Now, creating a cooperative with the bottom-up plan calls for the collection of a small group of individuals who are like-minded in their feeling about a common problem. These people then organize themselves into a cooperative and expand their size by adding other people of like-minded feelings. Now, that's fine and it has worked hundreds of times. But we in the cooperatives are moving into larger and larger areas and taking over greater economic machines. The practical problem of bringing together like-minded persons to take over a huge piece of economic equipment becomes insuperable. My own feeling is that the future of the cooperative movement lies in taking over organizations and then, working from the top down, converting them into cooperatives that will be bottom-up organizations. I hope I haven't lost you at this point, or given you the feeling that I have been double-talking you. Let me give you a good illustration of what I mean.

You have already seen the way in which a small group of farmers came together to buy their fertilizer, to buy their seed, to market their grain, and so on. You have seen how their organizations grew and how they decided to go into insurance and petroleum. When these farm groups attained an impressive size and found that they had a good deal of money, they wanted to use that money to create other cooperative ventures.

The Welch Grape Juice Company was getting its grapes from some forty-eight hundred independent farmers in five to seven different states. It would have been to the farmers' interest to buy that company and run it as a cooperative. The task of assembling these farmers, talking to them, and getting them to contribute the sixteen million dollars necessary to buy the company might seem to some of us an impossible problem. But it was done, and in an unusual fashion, with the assistance of a remarkable man, Jack

Kaplan, the former president of Welch. Because I consider the conversion of the Welch Grape Juice Company from an old-line privately owned organization into a cooperative a most electrifying example of how any company can be so converted, I want to tell the story in some detail. And because Jack Kaplan is such an enlightened American businessman, I want to tell you about him. I don't believe the conversion could have been accomplished without his unique and remarkable ability to grasp the implications of a new situation.

Jack Kaplan had been in the molasses business before the depression. Then he sold out his interests to National Distillers and Schenley and decided to sit on his money during the depression and enjoy life. He and his wife were music lovers and went each year to the music festivals at Chautauqua, New York. That is, of course, farming country and mornings when Jack went out walking he started to pay attention to what seemed to be nice old farms going to pot. One day he noticed a woman sitting on the porch of a farmhouse, looking rather bleak and depressed. Jack walked up and spoke to her. "Lady, I know it's none of my business but things don't look very prosperous around here. I have the feeling that you're letting this place run down. What's the matter?"

"Well, mister," the woman said, "there's no money in farming. We're just sitting here waiting until my husband can get a job in the city and we'll move out."

When Jack left, he was disturbed. After all, he had to eat, the same as anyone else, and it seemed to him that there was something wrong if people could not make a living out of raising the very substance that sustained life. On his way home to New York he stopped at Cornell University and asked the experts there what the answer was. They had been working on the farm problem since the 1920s and they explained it to him as best they could. Jack's conclusion was that the problem lay in merchandising, and he was one crackerjack of a merchandiser.

He decided to go back into business and began by purchasing

a small grape juice plant in New York State. His brothers-in-law, who were associated with the firm of Lehman Brothers, were, at his request, keeping their eyes open for a larger food business. It wasn't long before he got a call from one of them who said, "Hey, Jack, there's a real grape juice company for sale that some bankers down in Tennessee own. The plant's up in Westfield, New York."

Jack said he would buy it and, as I heard the story, he bought the Welch Grape Juice Company sight unseen. He then pitched into the job of merchandising the product. He's a very active and capable man with great energies and before long the company was showing a profit, but he wasn't able to get all of the farmers in the Westfield area to sell him grapes. I suppose there was some fear that he would corner the market in grapes. Jack simply couldn't understand why he couldn't buy all the grapes he wanted. Because he was involved with farmers he began to look into the problems of farm groups, and since he was a liberal he began to appreciate the possible contribution cooperatives could make to the world.

Jack Kaplan and I got together through CARE. Although our person-to-person food packages were doing a wonderful job among individuals overseas, our mission chiefs started telling us harrowing stories of how much more was needed by large groups in refugee camps, hospitals, and schools. To meet this special institutional need, we put on a limited campaign, soliciting wealthy, liberal-minded people to make lump-sum donations of a thousand dollars or more. Wally Campbell called on Jack for a contribution and during the discussion happened to mention that CARE was a cooperative.

Jack launched into a tirade. "What's the matter with you people? Why haven't you cooperatives ever gotten off the ground? You've got one of the greatest schemes in the world and you haven't gone any place. There must be something wrong with your leadership. This business of sending food packages is a nice idea—a humane idea—but is that all you're ever going to do? Haven't you got any bigger ideas than organizing relief packages?"

Wally reached back into his memory for some large idea he had heard me toss off and blurted out, "Well, sure we have. Our president wants to take over the Great Atlantic and Pacific Tea Company and make it a cooperative."

That stopped Jack for a split second. "Who is he and where is he?"

"He's a man by the name of Lincoln out in Columbus, Ohio."

Jack made it his business to come out to see me and before long we were good friends. I explained to him everything I could about the way cooperatives were run, how we were running our insurance companies and their subsidiaries.

One day Jack asked me, "Would you know how to turn Welch Grape Juice into a cooperative?"

"Sure," I replied.

"Will you help me do it?"

"Yes, I will."

That started off a series of meetings with his general management and attorneys and ourselves. Immediately I sensed trouble and hostility, recognizing the earmarks of men who are afraid of something they don't understand. The first lawyer we had hired in Columbus to set up our first livestock marketing venture completely failed to understand the principles of a cooperative, although we had explained them to him. When he was done we discovered that he had set up an old-line stock corporation with none of the principles of the cooperative in it. We tried explaining it again to him but he shook his head and said what we had in mind just wouldn't work. We had to start over with another attorney and instruct him precisely on what was to be done, without inviting his expert opinions as to whether it was going to work or not. Jack's attorneys were like that first attorney—unwilling to organize something they did not think would ever work.

The other source of hostility lay within the Welch management. They felt that once the company was converted they could

238

expect drastic salary cuts. They feared that farmers would be unwilling to pay them what Kaplan had been paying them. Their fears in that direction, I am sorry to say, were justified. The farmer never raises the hired hand or pays him what he should unless the hand threatens to quit. And, as I've said before, co-operatives in general have been less than realistic in their approach to executive compensation.

I finally went to Jack Kaplan and said, "You're not going to get this done. Your own management staff is against you."

"I own ninety percent of the stock," he said. "It doesn't matter what they say."

"But if your lawyer tells you that you can't do it, you won't do it, even though our lawyers know you can."

"These men will do anything I want them to do," Jack replied confidently.

"Well, all right," I replied and waited, hoping for the best. But the best didn't happen. The worst did. Something blew up, because Jack came in to see me, deeply upset.

"All right, I can't seem to do it myself. I don't know why. No one seems to be willing to help me. You buy the damned company for eight million and do it."

"I can't recommend to our board that we put eight million dollars into your company," I said unhappily.

"Why not?" he asked. "Haven't you got the money?"

"Yes, we've got it."

"Don't you think the company's worth it? It's worth twice that."

"I know it, Jack," I said, and started to feel uncomfortable. For one thing I didn't think I could get the board to sink that much money into one enterprise, and for another I didn't feel we were big enough at the time to warrant tying up so much money. "It isn't the kind of institution we want," I explained lamely. "I don't believe it's fundamental enough. But I hope you'll go ahead with the experiment to see whether or not we can get people to take it over."

Well, he just exploded. "You don't believe all this stuff you've been telling me!"

"Yes, I do believe it!"

"The hell you do! If you did, you'd buy it and do it!"

Disgusted with me, Jack went away on vacation for about three months, to rest his nerves or his ulcer or both, and did some quiet thinking. He came back, gathered his staff together, and told them he was going to convert the company into a cooperative. If they wanted to help him, he would be pleased. If they didn't want to, they needn't. He would go back to his friends in Ohio, or to some other group, and get it done. Because Jack is too shrewd a judge of human personality to treat his management like so many automatons, he sweetened his harsh words by arranging for his management people to have a retirement income from the proposed cooperative, and he gave them a block of stock in the old corporation. Then the farmer-suppliers took over the company, buying his stock and retaining the management.

Before the company became a cooperative, someone other than the farmers themselves set the going price for the grapes. After the change of ownership the farmers were in a position to influence prices themselves. A cooperative has a double obligation. Its first obligation, or incentive, is to give the farmer as high a price for his produce as it can without imposing any hardship upon the consumer. When the company is privately owned and operated, the impulse of the private owners is to pay the farmer as little as they can in order to enlarge the profit they make out of the consumer. The consumer, in either case, may pay the same price. But in the case of private ownership the farmer is bound to be shortchanged. When in 1951 the Welch farmers voted to pay themselves ninety dollars a ton for their grapes, they were getting what they themselves determined they should get and still enable their company to put out a competitively priced product.

At the end of the first year, 1951, the company showed a profit of $1,591,000. Each farmer then received a patronage dividend of $38 a ton additional for his grapes, making a total of $128 a ton. The profits continued to mount. In 1955 the farmer was getting $155 a ton.

The hitch in it was that the patronage dividend was not given in money but in a note from the cooperative, which was a promise to pay. Now many cooperatives, in the early days, failed to make good on similar promises, and the grape farmers who got the first notices of patronage dividends were skeptical about their real value because of past experience. The Government looked upon the dividend as income and taxed the farmer accordingly. But for the farmer the paper seemed to have no value, and some farmers sold these notes for ten and twenty cents on the dollar to some shrewd customers who figured that if they held the notes long enough the cooperative would pay off, and so it has.

Meanwhile, of course, the profit of the cooperative, because it was distributed, was not taxed by the Government. That money was kept back to pay off Jack Kaplan. As soon as 50 percent of the purchase price of the company was paid off by way of the withheld patronage dividends, the purchase of the company was then handled on a straight loan basis. The company paid Jack off in regular installments and redeemed the past patronage dividends notes little by little. For Jack, of course, being paid in this manner represented a capital gain and so his tax rate was lower; he managed to overcome a good many other problems connected with estate taxes and death taxes and so on. Of course his personal income tax bracket was so high that for him to continue in the business on salary would have been pointless. Now, you probably have the feeling that someone was slicked in the process and you may suspect it was the Internal Revenue Service. The fact is that the whole procedure was legitimate, and logical as well. You and I are taxed for a number of reasons. One is to support farm prices at certain parity figures. But the patronage dividends received from their cooperative so increased the grape farmers' income that there was no need for the Government to spend money on a program to support the price of grapes. The grape growers thus were doing for themselves what a half dozen alphabet agencies were doing for farmers of other crops. In effect, the Welch Grape Juice Company was bought and paid for by the members of the cooperative out of corporate tax savings. Of course it could not have been done without Jack Kaplan's consent and active cooperation. Setting aside the advantages which accrued to him, it was still a great gesture of community and social responsibility for one man to make.

It would be idle to suggest that the cooperative would have been the success that it is without the astute, professional management that Jack Kaplan and his executives provided. As I told Jack later on, "One of the reasons I didn't want us to take it over, even when we had the money to do it, was that I was afraid we would lose your services and the services of your executives." Farm co-ops simply were not prepared to pay the sort of salaries that Jack and his staff were accustomed to getting. Those salaries were justified, but to farmers they seemed outrageously high.

I knew that as long as Jack had his own money in the company he would stick with it and manage it to see that it made enough to pay him back. That's precisely what he did and that, I believe, is the reason this particular cooperative succeeded. It had first-rate management whether it wanted it or not.

As I see it, the Welch Grape Juice story is important because what happened there set a pattern whereby a great many other companies can be converted into cooperatives from the top down in order to function in the future from the bottom up. If we should ever seriously try to cooperatize the Great Atlantic and Pacific Tea Company, for instance, this is the way I think we'd have to go about it.

Years ago a man I'd met during the New Deal days went to work for A&P and as a sort of running joke over the years he kept asking me if I thought the Farm Bureau was big enough to take them over. My regular reply was that someday we would be big enough; the only question in my mind was whether, once we were big enough, we'd want to.

Well, today we are big enough, and I'm no longer joking. Cooperative ownership and operation of A&P would provide the world with a dramatic demonstration of the value of cooperative operation. And if the organization could be controlled by a board representing both the farmers who supplied its stores and the customers who bought the farmers' products, it would be, for me, the fulfillment of a lifelong dream—the coming together of producer and consumer interests in a common economic enterprise big enough to have nationwide influence.

A&P is probably the world's largest single private distributor of foods. It is so big that on several occasions the Government has charged it with violating the anti-trust acts. Once, I remember, the Government's inquiries into its operations so harassed and irritated John Hartford, the president, that he told a newspaperman, if the Government didn't lay off, he was going to turn A&P into a consumer cooperative. I suppose in Mr. Hartford's eyes that would have been a fate worse than death. Frankly, I can't think of anything I'd rather see happen.

I cannot stress strongly enough the importance of first-class management as it pertains to cooperatives. Cooperatives have a double burden to carry. They must educate and they must compete, whereas the old-fashioned, old-line capitalistic corporation merely has to compete. My own feeling is that effective competition comes about when the cooperative effectively educates. The desire to do good is not enough; never has been enough. Some of the sneering at "do-gooders" is malicious, but some of it is justified for they rarely "do" much of anything, however good their intentions. To illustrate what I mean:

For a long time we in the cooperative movement have been bound by the old ideas of the "starter" cooperative. The old theory was that you should get a group of people together through education, take some small, simple project that they could encompass as a result of their own efforts, and let them start it as a cooperative. Once they had that going, they would seek to start other such small units, then evenutally create a state unit and ultimately a national unit.

Now there isn't any question that back in the time of the

243

Rochdale flannel weavers this was the method that had to be followed. The cooperators were very simple people. They had never traveled, and probably they were not highly educated. They had few newspapers, no radio, certainly none of the rapid means of communicating with masses of people that are now at our disposal. This piece-by-piece, bit-by-bit, mosaic manner of building cooperatives suited the times.

But our age is quite different and the character of the people in the cooperative movement is fundamentally different. The difference was dramatically illustrated to us in 1934 when we joined the Cooperative League. The League's greatest activity was taking place on the eastern shore of the United States, with most of the activity centering about the establishment of small grocery stores.

The leadership for these stores came largely from educated people who were imbued with the desire to do something for humanity. Do-gooders, if you insist, but large-minded, well-meaning, sophisticated men and women. Few of them had had any business experience at all, and fewer still any experience in the grocery business. They were so intrigued with the chance of getting into business and playing store that they failed to pay any attention to the communities they were intending to serve. In the majority of cases they started out with great gusto and a considerable amount of funds, but failed to involve the community in which they located their store. This was the reason many of them went under.

One such group down in Baltimore called me in to tell them why they were failing. The group was largely composed of faculty members of Johns Hopkins University. They were disturbed about the economic trends in the world and wanted to do something. They had read about the cooperative movement and decided to set up a little store in a side street. The group itself had had a lot of fun cleaning up the store, painting it, fixing it, getting it stocked with groceries, setting up schedules of servicing it; but after they opened it, no one came in. They wanted to know why.

I asked them how much time and effort they had spent on an educational program aimed at the people who would patronize the store and how actively they had solicited membership. They confessed that they hadn't done anything about either. They'd thought that all they had to do was to get it set up and then the members would flock in.

Long ago we learned that if you're trying to get a group together to do something, it is always easier to get them together to do something that is *going* to be done. If it's already done and you want them to come in, the attitude seems to be: "Well, we'll just wait and see how it works out." Why that is so, I don't know. But that is the way people behave.

One of the major mistakes these groups made was that they conceived of the store as a sort of poor-looking place, stripped down to essentials, to create the impression that it was very economical in operation and so would charge less than anyone else. History has proved that supermarkets began to boom because of a certain lavishness of display. Not little stores, but huge stores. Not skimpily painted as a hand-me-down, but brightly lit, filled with chrome, looking not like the poor man's refuge but a place you'd be eager to enter because it was so bright and filled with promising things. The whole cooperative movement, with the exception of the Filene Fund, missed that point. Herb Evans, who is currently in charge of our radio stations, was helping the Filene Fund set up cooperatives. He saw the mistake being made by the little cooperative stores, but could do nothing to overcome it. They were determined to go on that way in the old tradition of the Rochdale pioneers and nothing could stop them. Good management would have stopped them, but they would not pay for good management.

As an insurance company we were on the lookout for cooperative groups to sponsor us in various states. We chose, in the East, the Eastern Cooperative Wholesale as our sponsor. Leslie Woodcock, who is on our Nationwide Board of Directors, was the devoted head of that group. He was a man who felt very strongly about cooperatives, and in his zeal to help every little group he could find, he would deliver co-op branded groceries to cooperative groups wherever they were located, irrespective of the shipping charges. He was taking groceries from New York way up to Buffalo and Schenectady in order to help out little co-op groups. But that sort of zeal and devotion was erasing whatever profit there was to be made on the groceries. It was uneconomic, even if it was well-intentioned.

The answer to these things is this: The cooperative movement must reconstitute itself, in its attitude and in its aims. If it will do that, it has a tremendous future.

What are the things it must do? It must forget the "starter" idea of cooperatives. It must face the facts of life in our economy today, and the facts are these: You can compete successfully only if you have the size necessary to compete. You must be large enough, progressive enough, and willing enough, to employ top personnel. You must have enough size to be able to carry on adequate research, and you must have enough size to bury your mistakes, because they are going to be made. The biggest and best-managed of enterprises make mistakes. There isn't time nowadays for the cooperative to go through all the bottom-up procedures that still are, to some, sacrosanct rituals. If we are going to keep our democratic form of government we must do all we can to undergird it with economic democracy, and do it as soon as possible.

Don't sit back and expect the old-line capitalists to provide us with real economic democracy. The New York Stock Exchange's expensive publicity campaign aimed at giving everyone a "share of America" by getting everyone to buy shares of common stock is no answer. While I believe stock ownership of American corporations should be as diversified as possible, I don't think we are going to increase true economic democracy by creating a few million more five-and-ten-share stockholders. The practical fact of the matter is that five shares of a common stock of an old-line stock corporation gives you nothing but a share of the earnings of that company. It gives you no say in its management, it gives you no rights of making policy. The whole dismal business of high-powered proxy solicitation agencies puts the damper on "your right" to have a voice in "your" company.

The manner in which people buy and sell stocks ought to demonstrate that they don't really feel any sense of ownership, nor even any sense of responsibility. The people scrambling about in the stock market today are trying to make one dollar grow where fifty cents grew before, and they don't really care how it's done for them. My own feeling is that they are committing economic felonies against themselves and making themselves accomplices to the erosion of their own liberties and their own form of government.

There is only one way for people to manage their own economic affairs, and so control their own economic destinies, and that is to control the economic machinery through their own cooperatives. Basic consumer cooperatives whose membership consists of individual persons (not corporations) are run on a one-member, one-vote principle. A member may have more than one share of stock in his co-op (though this is often limited to 5 percent of the total), but he may not have more than one vote in electing directors and in determining policy. The aim is to preserve the equality of individual people in the control of their cooperatives.

Of course it's not easy to do things for yourself, as you must in a cooperative. You would be asked to discuss matters of policy, you would be called upon for opinions, for recommendations. Your vote would mean something. It would not be merely another tiny fraction to be swept up by the large and energetic brooms of proxy solicitors.

We can, of course, take our money to the stockbrokers and ask them to turn over our money to big industries and let them try to make us some dough. They might, for instance, invest our money in some corporation which stands to get a lucrative contract to build a distant early-warning radar-line. We need a distant early-warning radar line, you see, because the Russians have dis-covered the world is round and might fly over the top of it to dump an H-bomb onto our heads while we're poring over the fraction of a point a stock has gained in the past twenty-four hours. But then, as we lie there, burned to a crisp, we can't really complain. All we ever asked of these companies, these fine old corporations, was that they make money, and we didn't care how they did it. If all we want to do with our lives is to make a buck, we can't really complain. But if we want to save the world and our own necks, I suggest we start thinking in terms of handling our own affairs instead of letting Big Business or Big Government or Big Anything Else do it all for us. The more we allow our Govern-ment to do for us, the less liberty we retain for ourselves, and the less opportunity we retain for saying what ought to be done about our own affairs, the closer we come to becoming a slot on someone's IBM punch card. Now an IBM punch card is a mighty useful thing. We use them in our own insurance company, but we draw the line there. Because we are a company owned by our policyholders, we want them to run us. We turn to them for all sorts of decisions—encourage them, in fact, to tell us what they want, and what they don't—for this is, literally, their business and their concern. And because it is, it is going to be run in their interest, to suit their needs, and not merely to satisfy a corpora-tion's balance sheet.

17

A FEW YEARS after I'd gotten excited over the Ford-Ferguson
tractor and the possibility of getting the world fed through mechanized agriculture, I discovered I'd been on the wrong track. That
discovery came about in a curious fashion.

Dr. Raymond Miller, who was a ranch owner in California
and had done public relations work for the Safeway Stores, was
a friend of mine. Ray held a position as lecturer on the faculty of
Harvard University's Graduate School of Business Administration, and in 1949 he had made two trips to Asia as observer and
consultant to the Director General of the Food and Agriculture
Organization of the United Nations.

In the fall of 1950 Ray came to Columbus to talk to some
national convention about the conditions he had found in Asia,
where most of the people go to bed hungry every night. Hearing
him talk, it occurred to me that what was needed was to get people themselves—not merely their governments—working on the
problem of hunger in the underdeveloped countries. After his lecture I asked Ray how he'd like to make another trip around the
world, this time to look into the prospects of a people-to-people
approach. He grew quite excited about the idea, as did I, and
that led to a long discussion, during which I must have touched
on every one of my pet subjects, from the built-in selfishness in
our economic system to the need for more international cooperatives. The upshot was that Ray invited me to come talk about

these same subjects at a Harvard seminar in Advanced Management.

I greatly enjoyed the experience at Harvard. After my talk we had dinner, and after dinner I was put in front of a fireplace in one of those old Harvard buildings and exposed to a barrage of questions. I'd been told the question-and-answer period might last an hour, but I was hardly prepared for what followed. They kept me on the firing line for nearly three hours.

I'd told them, in my address, that we were in a period of revolution, the end of which no one in the room would ever live to see. In my opinion, I said, economic, social, political, and perhaps even religious institutions would be changed before the revolution ran its course. I thought it was a revolution that the United States had started, and I thought that our country was going to have the privilege and responsibility of adapting itself to an age of plenty, the like of which we had never seen before. It was this plenty, I told them, that would change all of these institutions. Our big challenge was to learn how to live with this abundance.

I went on to tell them that if I were a member of the old oil gang which was exploiting the resources of the Middle East, I wouldn't be able to sleep nights because what I had done to earn money was going to lead the world into very serious trouble. When I said that, one fellow in front of me changed color so fast and started to splutter so badly I thought he was going to have apoplexy. If my memory can be trusted, he turned out to be a vice president of the Arabian-American Oil Company.

Another thing I touched on in my address was the matter of taxes. I asked that we not devote our whole evening to taking care of the charge that co-ops do not pay taxes. I said I know this was what they wanted to bring up, but if this was going to be their sole criticism of co-ops I could answer that charge by telling them that no American business ever paid a dime in taxes. That brought on a howl. "All right," I said, "I know you don't believe it. But if you'll think it through, you'll see that all a corporation does is to collect taxes for the Government from the customer. The only people in the world who pay taxes are individuals—you and I. The taxes you pay to the Government are included in the prices you charge, and you know it. The difference between cooperatives and old-line businesses is that we don't take so much away from our own customers, therefore we don't have to pay so much back to Uncle Sam. You can do just exactly what we do if you want to. We're in business to serve people, not to make money. We try to make profits for the individuals, not for the corporation. That's why we call it a nonprofit institution. But there's no reason on earth why you can't do the same."

Earlier, all the professors had invited me to visit their classes the next morning. But after I got back to my hotel room, I began getting phone calls, and before long I'd heard from every one of those professors except Ray Miller. They all said approximately the same thing: "If you don't mind, please stay out of my class tomorrow." The next day, they called again. "You'd better not come in at all," they said this time. "This crowd is darned mad."

Sometime later, in 1958, I attended the *Time-Life-Fortune* conference on the consumer, and a vice president of the Crown-Zellerbach Paper Company approached me. He'd been a member of the class that had heard my Harvard speech, and he said that every time he met a fellow classmate they got to talking about me and trying to figure out what it was I had said that had angered them so. He said, "In my opinion, you told us so much that was true and that we didn't want to believe, it infuriated us." He told me that he'd decided to attend the present *Time-Life-Fortune* conference only after he'd learned I was going to be there.

Anyway, it was on that visit to Harvard that I met Leigh Stevens, who was lecturing there on some subject—industrial management, I believe. Leigh was a Michigan boy who had attended Cornell University and later made some money as a reorganizer of Southern textile mills. He was an unregenerate Republican, about as far right in the Republican party as you can get without falling into the Atlantic. He didn't like the TVA, or cooperatives or anything like them, and he thought Roosevelt

251

was the worst pest ever visited on our American civilization. But Leigh Stevens had accompanied Ray Miller on his 1949 trips to the Far East, and when he heard that I had proposed another trip for Miller he said he wanted to go along.

"Well," I replied, "while I might consider financing Ray's trip, I wouldn't use any of my money to send a dyed-in-the-wool reactionary like you around."

Ray laughed at that, but Leigh said, "Oh, I'll pay my own expenses." And that's the way it was done. Our organization financed Ray's trip, but Leigh paid his own way. Soon afterward, in 1951, Ray Miller and Leigh Stevens started around the world, and they brought back some very significant information.

Leigh, who had been trained as an engineer, had studied power sources wherever he went. "Murray," he said on his return, "you're all wrong trying to mechanize agriculture at this time in the world. The Ferguson tractor may be the greatest thing since Crackerjack, but it has limited use."

"What do you mean?" I asked.

"Ox power is what runs agriculture in most of the world."

"Well, of course," I said. "That's what we want to get rid of and that's what the Ferguson tractor will do."

"But before you can use tractors you've got to have roads, you've got to have gas stations, you've got to have mechanics. You've got to have an industrialized society before you can have a mechanized agriculture. Do you know what's wanted now— *right* now? Plows with steel points to replace the twenty-two million wooden plows that are being pulled by oxen. With a steel point you can plow up more land and plow it deeper and release a lot of those nutriments under the soil which those farmers haven't been able to reach with their wooden plows."

Leigh and Ray had brought back with them one of those old wooden plows. After I heard their story, I took another look at it and made up my mind.

"All right," I said, "let's get 'em some steel plows."

And that's what inspired the famous CARE plow. There was

quite a fuss on the CARE board before we were all agreed to try it; it meant a basic shift from our policy of providing relief only to one of helping people help themselves. Eventually, though, we were able not only to work out a CARE package containing a simple steel plow but another that was equally needed—a kit of farm handtools.

These kits usually contain a shovel, fork, hoe, and rake, but they vary according to the needs of the countries where they're being sent. The Resettlers Kit, which contains a machete, shovel, and pick, has given thousands of people who were resettling in a strange land a chance to open up new farming areas. In a good many cases that simple little kit has spelled the difference between raising their own food and starvation.

And it's the same with the CARE plow. Almost eighteen thousand of these plows have been shipped to twenty-eight countries, giving poverty-stricken rural peoples a chance for a better life by improving their crop yields. We began the program in India where the use of wooden plows for tillage makes it impossible for that country to raise enough food for two-thirds of its three hundred and sixty million people. We shipped six or seven different types of plows to India before we settled on the right one, or ones, for the soil in each area. Mutual Service Insurance Companies of St. Paul, Minnesota, one of our sister cooperatives, launched a campaign for contributions and raised thirteen thousand dollars, enough to send thirteen hundred plows to farmers in scores of Indian villages.

One of the first plows shipped to India was shared by a whole village. The villagers followed the simple instructions CARE gave them for using the plow and the right seed and fertilizer, and they were wide-eyed at the first season's results. Their dried-out old soil produced more food than they had seen in a half-dozen seasons combined, and it was better-quality food than even the oldest man in the village had ever eaten. What's more, the use of the plow released the children from the fields and gave them a chance to go to school. And this has more or less been the case all over

India and wherever else the CARE plow has been shipped—Pakistan, Greece, Korea, Latin America, to name a few.

The trip that Miller and Stevens made around the world had another interesting result. The two men were invited to appear before members of the House Foreign Relations Committee which was discussing the question of wheat for India. Now I had some definite ideas on this matter and I encouraged Miller and Stevens to propose to the committee that the wheat be shipped on a loan basis, sold by the Indian government to its citizens, as was customary in such cases, and that the money received from the sale be put into a fund for the development of agricultural research and applied farming techniques. The proposal was accepted, and the Wheat Loan Fund in India became one of the most important developments in the whole program of American assistance in Asia. Incidentally, Leigh Stevens is now in India, working on some projects he started while on that trip with Ray.

Sometime in the fall of 1951, several months after Ray and Leigh had returned, I got a second invitation to visit Harvard. My appearance this time was relatively calm. In fact, what I remember most about that trip was a quiet and very pleasant dinner with about six or eight of the professors. What particularly sticks in my mind is a story Ray told us.

On one of his trips for the UN Food and Agriculture Organization, Ray had stopped off in Ireland to talk with a Catholic priest. Toward the end of their conversation, Ray said, "Father, I've always heard the argument, made principally by Catholics, that Catholicism is the best bulwark against communism. But I wonder if that's quite true."

"Why do you ask?" Father Byrne said.

"Well, you're ninety percent Catholic here in Ireland, and you're having no trouble with communism."

"Ninety-two percent," Father Byrne said, correcting him.

"All right, ninety-two percent. That would seem to prove the argument. But in Italy you're eighty percent Catholic and—"

"Eighty-eight percent," Father Byrne corrected.

254

"Eighty-eight percent," Ray went on, "and yet there you're having all kind of trouble with communism. Now, why?"

Father Byrne looked at him. "Don't you know? Here in Ireland we forced land reform on the English Crown a good many years ago. We got them to divide up the estates of the great landlords and then we set up the Irish cooperatives."

At this point one of the Harvard professors interrupted to say, "Yes, they introduced land reform, all right. But you know how they did it, don't you? They took fifteen hundred landlords out and shot them." That brought on some discussion as to whether this was a good way of getting land redistributed. We agreed that while it was a forthright method, it seemed slightly undemocratic.

Ray continued with his story. Father Byrne said, "Now, down in Italy, that hasn't been done. As a result, those people have a legitimate economic grievance which hasn't been resolved and so they have turned to communism as an answer."

Ray turned to us then and said, "Now, do you want to know the best answer to licking communism in Asia?"

"Of course," we answered.

"General MacArthur showed the way. It's one of the things I found out, Murray, when I was traveling around for you this year. Did you ever wonder why MacArthur could remove the bulk of the American army from Japan for the Korean War without worrying that the Japanese would kick over the traces?"

"Yes," I said.

"Because during his administration, MacArthur, as the military commander, forced land reform on the Japanese. He brought in a crowd of economic specialists and helped form thirty-seven thousand cooperatives in Japan. As Father Byrne over in Ireland told me, there's this to remember—when you overthrow a feudalistic form of government you create a vacuum. Now, you can fill that vacuum with a democratic form of government, but if you do not at the same time provide the people with an economic system they can control, the ruling classes that ran the government before will begin to run the economy and in the long run undermine the political government that has been installed. In time the old ruling class will be back in the saddle, both politically and economically. Now," Ray went on, "I was told that if MacArthur had explained this to the American people as a way of combatting communism, instead of trying to override President Truman's directives on running the army, he might have continued in command and might have become a major figure in the world. As it is, he was recalled and relieved of his command and not properly thanked for the real contribution he made in the true war against communism—which is not a war of shot and shell, but a war of ideas and ideals."

I was fascinated by what Ray told us. Then a little later a man came into my office who said he was between two government assignments and wanted a part-time job. I asked him what he had been doing and he said, "I've been in Japan on MacArthur's staff, setting up cooperatives." Now I had never seen any mention of this in American newspapers or commentators' columns or in government reports of the Japanese occupation, so we hired him for ninety days to write up a full description of what had been done with the Japanese economy under MacArthur. The world still does not know the full story of that phase of the American military administration of Japan, and does not know that what MacArthur accomplished in the economic field may be the most significant thing we have ever done in Asia to win that continent to democracy's cause. I feel it is a story that should be widely known. My own hunch is that someone is consciously suppressing it.

Ray Miller did us a great service. Leigh Stevens also did us a great service, because he went abroad with his eyes open, wanting to learn. I think this capacity to examine the world and the things that surround us with new eyes is one of the most valuable any man can have. I will never despair of a man who is curious enough to look again at something he has previously discarded, to see whether or not he has missed something in it. I believe that Wendell Willkie became a liberal—a great liberal—because he went around the world and looked at it—not as the president of Commonwealth and Southern, not as a businessman seeking to exploit an economic situation, but as a human being, trying to find out what the human problems of our world are. He came to the conclusion that we ought to think of ourselves as part of one world.

This business of looking at the world and its needs, and finding out how to satisfy those needs without thinking first of how best to make two dollars grow where one grew before, is the idea behind our whole program of establishing affiliated and sub-sidiary companies. One of the best examples of what I mean is something called Tectum.

Sometime in 1948 we were approached by Games Slayter and Howard Collins of Newark, Ohio. They had been engaged in the production of Fiberglas, with Slayter as vice president in charge of research. In the course of their research, they discovered that certain wood products could be chemically combined to create a new material which resembled wood but was superior in that it was virtually fireproof, had remarkable insulating properties, had improved soundproofing characteristics, would not rot or warp, and was immune to fungus and vermin. They called this phe-nomenal new material Tectum, from the Latin word meaning "roof," or, figuratively, "house."

What we at once saw was that Tectum provided farmers with an opportunity to find a market for their surplus wood products. We also saw it as an opportunity for builders of homes and schools and farm buildings to build well for much less money than prevailing costs of materials permitted.

At first we only had a cash investment in Tectum, about half a million dollars. Darrell Jones was president of the company, and the man who had had a hand in the development of the material, Howard Collins, was in charge of operations. Charles Sawyer, a former lieutenant governor of Ohio and later Secretary of Commerce under President Truman, was a principal investor.

After we made our investment, the plant started to get into

257

trouble. The material was not coming out as they said it would. Collins, an erratic sort, would run the plant making one thing for half a day and then shut it down, rearrange machinery, and make something else and then stop it and go on to something else. Collins and Jones began to argue between themselves a good bit.

We had employed the firm of Rogers, Slade and Hill as a management consultant team to look into other matters for us. Now we asked them to look into Tectum. They reported that the material could be made, but they made no recommendations as to what costs would be involved in machinery and other equipment. Then, when management of the company continued to disagree, we became so concerned that we proposed that one of us buy the other out. Collins and Jones refused to put any more money into it, so we took over the stock and put Lee Hill, of our management consultant firm, in charge. He brought in some engineers who did do a lot toward straightening out the technical operation of the plant, but it wasn't until Carl Frye was put in charge that things really began to look up. Once Carl got matters settled down, Tectum was used in building a group of homes in Amsden Heights in northern Ohio. Later the plan for Lincoln Village in Columbus was developed, and Tectum was used extensively in those homes and in its school.

Tectum's acceptance came about for several reasons. In addition to those features already mentioned, it had superior acoustical qualities, and it could be manufactured in large panels that were light and easily handled. A large-area roof can be constructed with Tectum in a matter of hours.

The vice president in charge of research for the Austin Company discovered Tectum and started using it in industrial building. Because of its fireproof qualities, it soon proved to have special value in the construction of new school buildings. Some 50 percent of Tectum production has been going into school construction, and in some instances its use has resulted in considerable savings to local school boards.

A second plant has been built in Arkadelphia, Arkansas, now that Tectum is nationally accepted and demands for it are increasing. But Tectum itself was just a beginning, because it has led to Tec-Pan. Before I describe Tec-Pan I should say a word or two about Don Kramer, the young man whose interest led to our working on it.

Don's career with us was interrupted twice by calls to service in the Marines, once in World War II and the second time in Korea. While he was in Korea he could not help but notice the hideous housing conditions under which most Koreans lived. He had followed the development of Tectum here and came back wondering if some cheap, strong, fireproof material could be developed from a little-used product of Korean agriculture. Their principal agricultural waste was rice straw. He spoke to the research people at Tectum, and they went to work on the problem. Their first experiments with local straw were disappointing. They then tried rice straw. Despite the fact that the U.S. Department of Agriculture had been pursuing this problem without success for many years, our chemists and engineers hit upon the correct chemical and mechanical combinations to make rice straw a useful building material, which we call Tec-Pan. We believe that it may revolutionize housing in those areas of the world where rice is a staple of the diet. At the moment two of our men are preparing to set up a Tec-Pan plant in Korea. It will be the first new private industry in Korea's history as a republic, all the others having been introduced under government sponsorship. The harvesting and preparing of the rice straw will be done by Korean cooperatives and the plant itself will be managed entirely by Koreans just as soon as they're satisfied they can run it successfully. In time, Tec-Pan, or materials like it developed from other native fibers, promises to provide low-cost shelter for underprivileged people throughout the world. At this writing, talks are under way with representatives of six different countries, each of which wants to go into partnership with us.

But discussing Tectum and Tec-Pan takes me ahead of my

story, for they are only a part of our whole subsidiary program, which got started much earlier. That program didn't, like Topsy, just grow. It came out of some very definite impulses on my own part and out of some definite feelings I had about the progress of a people's institution.

If I have read history correctly, no great revolution and no great advance in human society has come out of the broad mass of people. It has generally come about because a few people have had an idea, exposed it to others, and it was either accepted or rejected. And the idea that people ought to control their own finances, I figured, was not an idea that was going to be born spontaneously among all the people. Someone would have to express the idea and show them how it could be done and what benefits it would bring them.

I have always been interested in the power money wields and I don't think we will ever be a world safe from hunger, disease, poverty, and war until people have greater control of that power. But money is a touchy subject, and I've always said that the powers-that-be would let us fool with fertilizer and seed and insurance and electricity, but when we started to mobilize our own finances—well, look out! Because that act threatens the very citadel of power, economic power, and in this democratic land of ours economic power also means political power.

I would like to have seen farmers set up their own banks rather than go into the production credit program. In the early days of our Farm Bureau Credit Association, some of our members, particularly those who were sitting on boards of production credit agencies created and sponsored by the Government, were very critical of our developing our own credit sources. They were lulled into a sense of security because the Government had put up some capital for those production credit associations. I don't want to discount the importance or the effectiveness of those agencies, but I predict that the farmers will never have full control even after they've put up their own capital. The Government will never relinquish final control of these agencies. This, of course, is just my own opinion and time will prove me right or wrong.

In the early days of the Farm Bureau I wanted us to set up our own financial institutions, but Uncle George Cooley and some of the others didn't cotton to my ideas. When I met that opposition I remember thinking to myself, "Well, all right, if we can't do it directly, we'll do it indirectly." One of those important indirect steps was the formation of insurance companies.

We have, since the end of the war, embarked on a subsidiary program with very definite and specific objectives. We've been trying to invest some of our policyholders' money on a conservative basis in projects and industries that will make some important contribution, or so we hope, to their own welfare. Food, housing, finance, communications, oil, and electronics have been our major fields of interest. We had a fling in electronics, and we'd like to get into petro-chemicals, proprietary drugs, plastics, and a few other things.

One of our first subsidiaries, Peoples Broadcasting Corporation, took us into communications.

Fred Palmer, a radio consultant who lives in Columbus, said to me one day, "I don't know what you're up to, but it must be good or you wouldn't have got as far as you have." I had seen Mr. Palmer only a few times, knew him only casually, and was under the impression that he knew next to nothing about cooperatives. But what he said next rang a bell in my mind.

"I've just returned," Mr. Palmer said, "from a meeting of the National Association of Broadcasters, and the president of one of the leading networks got up and said: 'Gentlemen, we who control the airwaves can come nearer to telling the American people what to eat, what to drink, what kind of pills to take, and what to think than any other group in this country.' " Mr. Palmer paused to allow the importance of that remark to sink in and then went on to say, "Mr. Lincoln, if what you're up to is good, and I'm assuming it is, how can you ignore having your foot in the door of communications where you can reach people?"

261

What sprang into my mind was the recollection of the difficulty we had once had when the Cooperative League sought to do a radio program on a national network. Although we were prepared to pay the regular commercial advertising rates, both NBC and CBS refused us air time on the grounds that our program was too controversial. I recalled, too, a bitter newspaper campaign launched in Columbus against the Farm Bureau and myself. I remembered the campaign the National Tax Equality Association led against cooperatives and against me when I spoke at the Cooperative League in the presence of a prominent labor leader. I remembered Fulton Lewis's attacks on us over the Mutual Broadcasting System, to which we were never granted equal time to reply. All these things were in my mind when I said to Mr. Palmer, "Well, I guess you're right. How do we do it?"

My own feeling has always been that if *anything* belongs to the people it's the air and the airwaves. But there is no way they are ever going to control them unless they have some machinery to use. When we organized the Peoples Broadcasting Corporation in 1946, which now has five radio stations and one television station, we began to set up that machinery. It is an interesting fact that no really savage attack has been launched against me or any company within the Nationwide organization since we acquired our radio stations. There may be no significant connection, but I have a hunch there is.

It was our idea to use some of our money to put together these packages of communication machinery with the hope of eventually selling them to the listeners in each area. We could then have a network that covered the whole country the same way that NBC and CBS do. By some sort of joint association or joint management the stations could be formed into a cohesive communications system owned and controlled by the listeners. We haven't yet got this started but that's our ultimate purpose. It seems to me that this would be one sure way to diversify radio and television programing so that a broader range of listener preference might be served. I don't think our airwaves ought to be turned entirely over to the rock-and-roll majority, and it distresses me that so little time nowadays is being devoted to serving minority tastes. Since the rise of television, radio has practically abandoned any sustained attempt at serious adult programing. I'd like to see our PBC stations be an exception. The Canadian Broadcasting Company, government-owned, has tied its stations to listener advisory councils. I'd like to think that any network we might help establish could be guided by similar advisory councils. In fact one of our stations, WTTM in Trenton, New Jersey, has developed its programing with the aid of a "listeners' advisory committee," composed of educators and civic leaders.

I used to think if we got control of machinery then we could do the things we said we've always wanted to do. And we have, to a certain extent. While many other stations have adopted a program formula of rock-and-roll music and sketchy news reporting, our PBC programing has been oriented primarily at adults, and our stations have sent their own newsmen to cover such world events as the Lebanon crisis, the United Nations Atomic Energy Conferences in 1955 and 1958, and Vice President Nixon's tour to Russia. Our PBC newsmen also have gone to South America and Alaska on reporting junkets.

But in spite of all this, we've run into the oddest resistance to saying on the air just what the motives were behind the purchase of our stations. Let me give you an example.

Soon after we bought station WGAR in Cleveland, Ohio, I went up there to attend a meeting of the staff, from the general manager down to the janitor. I wanted to explain why we had established a Peoples Broadcasting Corporation, why we believed in cooperatives, and why we were in business at all.

After I'd told my story, a man who was then the program director said to me, "Well, now, you don't expect me to say some of those things over the air, do you?"

"Well, why not?" I asked, surprised.

"We'd lose all our sponsors if we did," he said.

"Look, mister," I told him, "I've been saying these things for thirty years and we got two million dollars together to buy you out, so what's the matter with saying it?"

This problem of trying to get our advertising and communications people to say what we were up to had been plaguing me for some time. Henry Ballard, as I've mentioned, thought that the less we told what we were up to, the better off we would be—in the insurance business, anyway. Now here was this program director, convinced that unless we kept what we were up to to ourselves, we'd be hurting the advertising billings on the station we now owned.

I had been talking about this problem with a writer. We were staying at the Hotel Cleveland. About eleven o'clock he rang my room. "Get up and listen to WGAR," he said.

I turned on the radio and caught the news broadcast. The show was sponsored by a building and loan association in Cleveland, and the president of that company was advertising his business thus: "We're a people's institution. You own us. You elect the board of directors and the profits go back to you."

The next morning we went over to the station to see the program director. I said, "Do you ever listen to your own news program at eleven o'clock at night?"

"Sure," he said.

"Let's get out the recording of last night's show and play it." And so we did.

"Now, do you hear what the president of that savings and loan association is saying?" I asked.

"Yes," he said.

"Have you any reason to believe that that's any different than what I said at my meeting last night?"

"Oh, that's what you mean, is it?"

No comment.

We had another such incident sometime later when Kaiser and Company, which had just purchased Willow Run in Detroit, invited Carl Frye and me up to inspect the three hundred acres they'd purchased around the plant. They intended to have homes built for their employees.

The man in charge of real estate and development for Kaiser showed us around. They had already built some thirty-eight homes for key personnel and wanted our opinion as to the costs and feasibility of our building houses for the rest of their employees.

"Now, we don't want any of this cooperative stuff," the real estate man said. "We just want you to build houses for these employees." We said okay and followed him about.

He took us to where the thirty-eight homes had been finished and with great glee told us how the group presently living there, physically separated from the city of Detroit, had hired one man to take care of all the lawns, another to come around and collect the trash and garbage. With great pride he explained how this group of thirty-eight families was working together to get certain specific things done for the group. Carl and I listened with secret amusement and finally could not resist joshing him.

"You don't know what you're doing. You apparently don't know what you're saying."

"What do you mean?" he asked, startled and confused.

"That's all we're talking about when we talk about a cooperative. People get together and help themselves just as these people have."

"Is that what you mean?" he asked.

No comment.

Housing, because of its shortage in the post-war period, seemed to us a human need that ought to be filled, and we did what we could about it. The Government had built a series of apartment houses in Bridgeport, Connecticut, in 1918 and 1919. They had been designed by one of the leading architects in the country, the man who was later asked by the Rockefellers to do the restoration of Williamsburg, Virginia. These properties were later sold out at about half the Government's cost to a local lawyer. He kept them as long as he could take depreciation savings out of them on taxes and then he was ready to sell them.

We had been looking for some real-estate property that we could buy and turn over to the tenants, as a demonstration of the way a cooperative could work in the housing field. We discovered these apartments and bought them for $1,200,000, then turned around and sold them to the tenants for $2,700,000. The total cost of buying and selling was $200,000. While the difference between our cost and the selling price appears to be a pretty good profit for one year of ownership, we sold the apartments to the tenants so cheaply that their mortgage payments were less than the rents they'd been paying. Not only that, the last tenant who resold his apartment made $5,000 profit.

To date at Nationwide we haven't begun to do anything that would compare with the splendid co-ops built in New York City under Abraham Kazan's leadership. Someday, though, I'd like to see us develop something similar to the Swedish housing co-operatives. In Sweden the co-ops not only have tremendous apartments, they also provide single-family dwellings. If you want a house, you go to the cooperative. You may either bring your own plans for them to build the house, or they will provide you with a plan. They will supervise the building for you as an architect would if you had your own plan. They will lend you the money. Not only will they build the house and finance it, they will furnish it right down to the last bit of shelving material. All of this on a cooperative basis.

We haven't gone as far in housing on a cooperative basis as we would like because it requires an enormous investment. Ten thousand dollars is the minimum investment on single units, and when you start to think in multiples of hundreds the totals run up very fast to surprisingly large figures.

In 1948 we set up Peoples Development Company (now called Nationwide Development Company) to see what could be done about better and lower-cost housing. Our purpose was to find out, experimentally, how much house we could give for a dollar, not how many dollars we could make out of a house. Our first experiment was in northeastern Ohio, where the Farm Bureau had a farm machinery company. For the employees we built eighteen or twenty homes in Amsden Heights, at Bellevue, Ohio.

That first attempt wasn't on a large enough scale to give us much proof. When Westinghouse came to Columbus and built a large factory there, it approached John W. Galbreath to see if he would build homes for its employees. Westinghouse finally decided it didn't want to be both landlord and employer to the people who would live in the homes, so it proposed that Galbreath build the houses on his own.

John and I had known one another for some time, although I don't think he knew a great deal about what we stood for as an organization. When he approached me about the eleven hundred acres surrounding the Westinghouse plant, we bought it and started to develop Lincoln Village.

People who understand housing values tell me that there is more value per dollar in Lincoln Village homes than there is in any other house now for sale at the same price. But these are largely hidden values, difficult to demonstrate to prospective buyers. There are opportunities for an unscrupulous builder to make his profit out of the hidden materials—the thickness of the concrete, the quality of plumbing and fixtures, the size of electric wiring, the weight of roof shingling, the amount of insulation, and so on. We have not found a convincing way of demonstrating to the average home-buyer the true worth of these hidden values.

For instance, I bought a house out in my own neighborhood, in Gahanna, for one of my farm employees. We found, for one thing, that there was no tile ditch to carry off the water from the downspouts. The builder had put one tile into the ground but then the water built up against the cellar wall and leaked through. We found that the house had no proper drainage so that every time a big storm came up the cellar would be wet. Of course we bought the house on a bright sunshiny day and assumed that nobody would build or sell a house unless such things were taken care of. In house-buying one learns by unpleasant and sometimes costly experiences.

We have to date earned money on the acreage at Lincoln Village, enough to cover our cost, but have not found a way of demonstrating the value in the houses. Eventually, we will.

We started Approved Finance in 1951. We started it, first, to establish another vehicle for the use of people's money so that they could borrow from themselves at a lower rate of interest than they were currently having to pay. Second, we started it to maintain our auto insurance. What was happening was that people with our auto insurance would decide to buy a new car. They would go to a dealer and he would deliver a fresh new product of Detroit, insured for collision, fire, and theft. He would also give them an installment plan on which they could buy the car out of current income. Our policyholders would discover either that they had double coverage or that their coverages with us had been canceled by the dealer or the new insurance company. In a number of cases Nationwide policyholders found to their chagrin, after they had been in an accident, that not only had their auto collision coverages on their own car been canceled, but also their Nationwide coverage for liability for personal and property damage. What *we* discovered was that many times there was more money to be made by the dealer on the car loan and insurance commission than on the sale of the car. We figured that if we could set up a company which would lend the policyholder the money to go buy a new car for cash, he would probably save some money on the car in terms of the interest charges he would have to pay if he bought on credit. At the same time he could retain his insurance with us.

While the plan is working out reasonably well today, the average man, so far, seems to feel that it is easier to buy the whole package—car, financing, and insurance—from the auto dealer than it is to go through the various steps of calling his agent, making an arrangement for the loan, and then going to the auto dealer and dickering with him.

We can, in dollars and cents, prove substantial savings in most cases if the car-buyer will go through these steps, but many people seem to have an emotional attitude toward car-buying and not a practical dollars-and-cents attitude. The recognition of this problem has led us to investigate the possibility of going into the car-leasing business. We've found that through mass purchasing, financing, and insuring, we can make it to the average driver's considerable advantage to lease a car rather than buy one. The problem that we've run up against, and we're struggling with it right now, is the amount of money involved.

We made a survey and found that the potential leasing market in the Columbus area is about five thousand cars. If that figure is extended nationally, we discover that the American public would want to lease more than a million new cars per year. At three thousand dollars a car, the cost runs into billions. We've continued to investigate but haven't yet found the answer as to where to find the money to finance the plan for our policyholders.

In 1952 Approved Finance acquired ownership of a mutual fund management company, and in 1957, by reorganization, created Heritage Securities as the national distributor for an investment trust, Mutual Income Foundation. Ownership of shares of this mutual fund is, as I see it, a natural and necessary complement to life insurance. Use of a mutual fund in this way is a real innovation in planning a lifetime financial program.

Over the years I had been somewhat disturbed at our inability to produce innovations in life insurance as we had with our casualty lines. Before we separated farmers from other types of drivers, few casualty insurance companies had ever classified one group of drivers as being different from another for purposes of insurability and risk. Because we started out as a farm group to insure our own members, we discovered, almost by chance, that farmers, because they were not exposed to the hazards of traffic as often, were likely to get into fewer accidents. In a sense, we pioneered the classification system in casualty insurance.

Because we were trying to meet the needs of the farmer in the early days, we started insuring them for six-month periods for their convenience, without fully understanding at the beginning how effective an insurance plan this was. In short, some of the basic innovations in casualty insurance came our way simply because circumstances forced us into them. Later innovations, however, arrived more by design. For example, our fourth Nationwide insurance company, Nationwide General, was organized in 1957 in response to a need expressed by our policyholders for merit-rated auto insurance. This means that the premium charged for the insurance depends upon the policyholder's traffic accident record. Accident-free years mean lower premiums, accidents mean higher premiums.

I turned to insurance, in my personal life, because all I had when I was married was a wife and no property, and the only way I knew of leaving her an income at all was to buy life insurance. I never fully looked into the whole question of term insurance and mutual funds because in those early days mutual funds weren't well known. However, a book my brother gave me many years ago explained the mutual-fund principle so that it made a lasting impression. In most insurance circles term insurance was deprecated because it was pure protection and particularly because it paid the agent very little in the way of a commission.

As I began to acquire property I always added term insurance to my existing life insurance so that my widow would have enough to cover all my indebtedness. In addition, I carried a policy for my daughter's education and a policy for retirement.

I was a victim of being oversold on life insurance. I wanted to accumulate an estate and this seemed the only apparent way of doing it. Fortunately, I knew something about land, particularly farm land. Sometime during the 1920s Roger Babson said, "If you want to make as safe an investment as anybody knows how to make at the present time, buy suburban property in the Middle-western United States around a college town." Well, Columbus happened to fit those conditions exactly. With Babson's advice in mind, I began to buy farm land and farm it in the areas around Columbus. Now, if I hadn't done that, I wouldn't have had enough money today for my retirement. (The Farm Bureau never paid large salaries.) But because I took the cash value out of my insurance and invested it in suburban property I'm going to do all right. If I had had the foresight to buy only term insurance and save the difference between the cost of term and old-line life, and then invested that difference—astutely, in average good investments— I would today be getting three times, in returns, the amount I am receiving on matured life insurance policies. Now, please don't misunderstand me—I am not disparaging life insurance in any way. We sell it and I believe in it and the fact remains, most people are *under*insured. The average man just doesn't know how to invest money unless he has some special knowledge. He would, quite likely, have lost that money and, faced with the necessity of making up the loss in his investments, would have dropped payments on his term insurance and would have been left without an investment and without protection.

My own feeling has been that life insurance is not enough and that the erosion of the dollar is going to continue. Despite the fact that the face amount of your insurance policy is ten thousand dollars, and you or your heirs will receive the face amount as stipulated, inflation is going to bring the purchasing power of that ten thousand dollars down twenty years hence.

It was the desire to protect our policyholders against inflation that interested me in a man named Galen Van Meter. He had been one of the officials of the Investors Diversified Services, a Minneapolis corporation, and had resigned when Bob Young took it over. He then went to New York to resume his career as a financial consultant, which he is today.

Van Meter had made some money in the 1920s but lost it during the depression. He became interested in trying to do something to protect the investments of small investors and people with modest savings. On the basis of his achievement, we appointed Galen Van Meter and Company, the investment manager of our Mutual Income Foundation.

More than half of our five thousand agents have been licensed as security salesmen to sell MIF shares. Their licensing, and our going into the mutual-fund field, occasioned a great deal of controversy. In the early days we were told that a part-time agent, as most of our agents were, wasn't qualified to sell insurance. We proved that he was. Then we were told, "The same fellow who sells casualty insurance can't sell life insurance." We proved that he could. Now our agents sell over a hundred different varieties of insurance and mutual-fund shares as well.

Here, I think, is where we're beginning to see how our companies can make a distinct contribution in the field of personal financial planning. Insurance has become a part of the average individual's lifetime financial program. Because we have the mutual fund to offer our policyholders, our agents can make money selling shares in it as well as selling life insurance. Because this is so, after they've sold a customer the right amount of life insurance (and sold it in a combination that's right *for the customer,* which could be any combination of term, ordinary life, and endowment), they don't feel urged to keep piling more life insurance on top of him simply because they have nothing else to sell. I am pleased that we have given the Nationwide agent a full complement of financial tools so that as he becomes sufficiently acquainted with a policyholder to help him plan his whole financial program, he can offer that policyholder, through mutual-fund shares, something life insurance alone cannot provide—a share in the natural growth of our country and a hedge against inflation. We've given a new term to this Nationwide concept of family financial planning—Securance. The word insurance is obviously too limited.

In 1956 we organized Nationwide Corporation, a holding company that gives Nationwide Insurance sizable stock interests in other life insurance companies. Ownership of the corporation is shared between private investors and Nationwide's auto and fire insurance companies.

The Nationwide Corporation is unique. The laws of New York, for example, provide that only a certain percentage of the surplus of a casualty company can be invested in insurance. In the main, a life company in Ohio can't buy the shares of a casualty company. Just why, I don't know. Casualty companies have the freedom to make insurance investments, but only under certain limitations. Before we organized Nationwide Corporation, our casualty company invested in our own life company and in other insurance companies to the permitted limit. We formed Nationwide Corporation to increase our ability to acquire stocks of other companies.

Organization of the board of Nationwide Corporation is also unusual. Half the board is composed of people who have nothing to do with cooperatives or our own particular effort. The other half is controlled by the directors of our casualty company. Now, we did this deliberately to encourage investments among people who aren't particularly interested in cooperatives. Because we control only half the corporation we believe it constitutes a fair situation for them. We fully recognize the danger that if the two groups don't agree, we can't do anything since the control is so evenly divided. But our feeling is that this even division prevents any small group from gaining control. As it stands, the worst thing that could happen is that nothing would be done.

But in the long run we're not going to sit and do nothing with our investments valued at more than fifty million dollars. To date the setup has worked well. We've had complete agreement on everything we've ever done.

We believe that this is a good device—one we will use again to attract outside investors. Through Nationwide Corporation we've begun to acquire stocks in other insurance companies, mainly in life companies. We now own major interest in Michigan Life, National Casualty, Pacific Life, as well as our own Nationwide Life, and we own 51 percent of the stock interest of the Northwestern National Life Insurance Company of Minneapolis.

I do not want to give the impression that our subsidiary program was launched without problems. There were many. In the beginning, hardly any of the subsidiaries were making any money. The grapevine, which I always say works as well for the president as it does for others, said to me at the time: "If this blankety-blank president of ours hadn't kicked us into so many of these subsidiaries, everything would be all right, because insurance is doing well."

Well, about 1953, casualty insurance companies as a whole, not only ours, started to have more difficult times, because the cost of settling claims and our general administrative expenses were rising faster than rates could be raised. Up until 1957 or 1958, when the curve began to turn upward again, our subsidiaries were what really enabled us to continue to make a contribution to surplus. Not only did they support themselves; they showed profits. Since then the grapevine has been rather quiet.

I think the subsidiary program has done more than provide us with a surplus. The more people we got acquainted with through our subsidiary activities, the more areas we got into, the larger our potential was for finding customers for our insurance business. We figured that if we could prove to the operating heads of our insurance companies that we were doing more than rendering additional service—that we were bringing them additional business by such programs of additional service—they might be happier about the subsidiary program. My own feeling has always been that a man who starts out to help people and succeeds in doing that makes money whether he means to or not.

Part Five

18

OIL HAS ALWAYS BEEN, to me, one of the most exciting commodities produced. It is, of course, one of the great sources of energy. I believe that a very convincing argument can be made to demonstrate that whoever controls sources of energy can control the most vital aspects of human life.

Because the internal-combustion engine is so much a part of our daily life, it has become literally impossible for the majority of us to live without oil. Now I'm not speaking of oil only as a fuel. I know that when I was in London on my first trip shortly after V-E day, cars and trucks and buses were being driven by all sorts of weird combinations of steam and electric batteries and what not. But sooner or later these machines getting along without gasoline would have ground to a halt without lubricating oils to keep their metal parts from grinding, heating, and breaking. Charles Van Bergen told me that both Germany and Japan finally had to give up offensive war because they both ran out of lubricants. You may do without fuel oil and without gasoline and without a dozen derivatives of crude oil, but you cannot do without lubricants, and until some smart chemist comes up with a substitute for lubricating oil, crude oil is going to be king. And the nation that controls the largest supply of crude oil is going to wind up dominating the world, either as a solitary power or as the leader of a combination of other powers. It is my hope that no nation will ever again truly dominate the world, and that includes my own. The nation that stands astride the world invites its own downfall, and that's a fact of history that runs true from antiquity to the present day.

Until the oil resources of the Middle East were uncovered, our own reserves of petroleum were the largest in the world. Then too, we had the industrial capacity for refining the greatest quantity of oil. Now there is a race on in the Middle East for control of those vast reserves, with the juggling of smaller nations by both the Western and Eastern powers. We know now that there is oil everywhere in the world, but the cost of bringing it to the surface varies dramatically. The oil in the Middle East lies so near the surface that the cost of bringing it up runs to some figure like twenty cents a barrel, whereas here in the United States it costs us several dollars a barrel. Oil from the Middle East can be brought here at a transportation cost of eighty or ninety cents a barrel. It would compete seriously with our domestic product. In the light of the importance of preserving our own reserves, we ought to be buying Middle Eastern oil but we are not. We do not buy it, in my opinion, largely because our domestic oil companies have great sums of money tied up in their fields and because our country has a new class of oil millionaires who would not take kindly to such "unfair" competition. These millionaires were created by a fantastic act of tax generosity upon the part of the United States Government. Someday, I hope, the Congress of the United States will pass a bill to reassess the depletion principle as applied to crude oil.

From the standpoint of national security, I have long advocated that we hoard our oil resources and buy as much in the foreign market as we can. I don't mean that we should bid up the price of Middle Eastern oil so as to freeze our own allies out of the chance to buy what they need, but I do advocate that we buy as much as we can and keep in mind that Russia may be biding her time until that moment arises when our dwindling oil reserves may prevent us from waging a major war in our own defense. Russia's interest in the Middle East has nothing to do with the consumption of Middle Eastern oil. She certainly has abundant reserves of her own, and in her satellites, to care for her somewhat limited needs. Her interest in that area is to deny us and our allies the oil that we desperately need. I have heard it said that if England could not get her allotment of Middle Eastern oil her total economy would grind to a standstill within days—not years but days—and that her people would be reduced to the most primitive living conditions within six months. We, of course, would not allow that to happen to England, but we could only support them out of our own reserves.

There has now been heard throughout the world a demand for the end of colonialism, for the end of the feudal regimes which have ruled backward nations. Now, these are cries we ought to hear sympathetically, for they evoke memories of our earliest history—days when we were a colonial possession, when we wanted self-determination. The call for an end to colonialism and the right of self-determination is certain to have its impact upon the old-line oil companies. In the end, I believe we will lose all our foreign oil investments by expropriation.

What we ought to be doing now is encouraging the peoples of the oil-rich Middle East to handle their own resources, to help them develop their own refineries. We should be their chief customers. We should have begun doing all this twenty years ago. That's what Watson Snyder had in mind when he asked me to help establish a cooperative refinery in Iran. I was excited by the prospect, but in the Farm Bureau we weren't ready. I couldn't find anyone in the oil cooperatives who was ready. The opportunity was missed. I could not know then how prophetic Snyder's remark, "You could change the course of history," would turn out to be.

A few years ago I represented the International Cooperative

Alliance on the United Nations Economic and Social Council. I remember the time the International Cooperative Petroleum Association (Howard Cowden's baby) proposed that the Middle East oil reserves be placed under United Nations control. What a howl arose from the old-line oil companies!

Mohammed Mossadegh, then the premier of Iran, heard of the proposal and it evidently made sense to him. He came to the United States with a group of his government advisers to see what could be done about pushing the proposal through. This was, as I recall, before his showdown fight with the Anglo-Iranian Oil Company. The day Mossadegh and his group were to land, Howard Cowden, who normally would have been the one to do the honors, had another meeting on his hands and I was asked, as president of the Co-op League, to go in his stead to welcome and meet with them in New York. Jerry Voorhis, the League's hard-working executive director, who is especially good at sensing delicate relationships, thought the Iranian premier would expect to be met by someone high in cooperative circles and might even be offended if he weren't. I canceled some appointments, readjusted my schedule, and went to talk with Mossadegh and his staff.

Dr. Hussein Fatemi, Mossadegh's deputy minister, spent several days discussing with us the Iranian grievances against the Anglo-Iranian Oil Company. He was never satisfied with the company's financial statements; he thought they were unnecessarily complex and incomplete. As a result, the Iranians were working in the dark when they asked for a greater share in the profits: they did not know whether the monies they were receiving approached an equitable share or even represented the percentages agreed upon.

When I left Dr. Fatemi he and his delegation were in agreement that we should go ahead and establish a cooperative for them on a beginning basis of a fifty-fifty division of profits, with the cooperative ultimately reverting to total Iranian control. Although this was to be done under United Nations auspices or directly with the International Oil Cooperative, nothing came of the plan, unfortunately. Instead, we were treated later on to the spectacle of the English squeezing the Iranians to the wall and insisting upon the observance of the original contracts which had been imposed upon the Iranians in earlier years.

The old-line oil companies have recently been showing signs of what I would like to look upon as realism in this matter of exploiting Middle Eastern countries. Some companies are entering into new arrangements with the ruler of Saudi Arabia, splitting profits fifty-fifty all the way from the well to the consumer. I know there are many people who believe that this is not only right but that it will help to save the situation for us, and I certainly recognize that this whole matter of Middle Eastern oil is a complex one with direct bearing on our oil needs and on America's role in international relations. But no amount of benevolence upon the part of these companies is going to save the old-style method of doing business. I believe it is doomed, and no arm of the United States Government ought to be employed to try and stave off that doom. For our Government to be required to aid and support feudal princes, in an age when princes are being overthrown, is an unthinkable perversion of the democratic idea.

Fortune magazine publishes annually a list of the five hundred largest American business organizations. If you will cover the list with your hand and read the companies' grosses and compare them with the net incomes, after taxes, you probably will discover that you can spot the oil companies without any trouble at all. Because of the depletion and depreciation allowances, the oil companies are the only companies paying as little as 21 percent as a tax rate. The margin of profit in oil is so great that few people realize how much many oil companies can make above and beyond their original investment. We make a fetish of efficiency in business; the average businessman is fond of saying that business is more efficient than government and that only efficient businesses thrive. Yet look at the oil industry. It permits four gasoline stations to be built on the four corners of numerous crossroads in America, at an average investment of forty thousand dollars per station. All four stations are selling substantially the same product. What we have learned is that it does not make any difference how many gas stations are put up, nor how many compete in the same street for the same trade—the oil companies still make money. I am not speaking of the individual station owner or lessee. I am speaking of the company that supplies him with his product. If a company cannot only survive but thrive on such unbusinesslike methods, the margin of profit must be substantial. We as consumers have no need of four gas stations at our crossroad corners. Yet we pay for them. When you add to the immense margin of profit, a tax gift each year from the people of the United States, I think you can begin to see why I feel that the oil industry of this country is not being conducted in the best interests of the people who buy petroleum products.

As I've said, our own interest in oil goes back to the early 1930s. When we entered the gasoline business, Henry Knight tipped us off to a way we could lessen distribution costs. "You can do something that nobody else can do in the petroleum business," he said. "The average dump per gasoline truck to any one farmer is about fifty-seven gallons. He doesn't take any more than that, because when he needs more, all he does is hang a red flag on his mailbox and any one of three or four tank trucks driving past his place will stop and give him another dump. But you people are owned by your own customers. Why don't you talk them into putting in larger tanks on their places and taking an average dump of two hundred gallons? That way you'd up your sale considerably and reduce the cost of it to your members at the same time."

The idea seemed sound to us, so we started to put on a campaign. That was the beginning of our success in gasoline. Before long we bought out the Pure Oil gas station in Wilmington, Ohio, which turned out to be the first of our retail gas stations, and Pure Oil moved its own station up the street. Henry Knight was meeting regularly with the board of directors of Pure Oil, and partly out of his old irritation with them and partly because it became a sort of game, he used to furnish us with the figures on their sales at Wilmington, Ohio, so we could compare them with ours. That new station Pure Oil set up never did catch up with ours in sales because we were getting all the farm customers plus a few from town. It turned out to be one of the most profitable single retail enterprises run by any county Farm Bureau in Ohio.

Our interest in gasoline led to a lasting and valuable friendship with Cyrus Eaton. It came about through Tracy Herrick, a distant cousin of my old boss at the Society for Savings, Myron T. Herrick.

Harry Collin, a Toledo broker with the firm of Collin, Norton and Company, used to make trips to Columbus to see us at our insurance companies, trying to sell us government bonds, gilt-edged securities, and the like. One day, Lee Taylor, who was my assistant, said, "We can buy these things of anybody. Why don't you get us something we want?"

"Well," he said, "what do you want?"

"A petroleum company with a refinery."

"I know where you can get one," Collin said.

"Where?"

"The National Refinery of Cleveland. Some of their officers were killed in a private plane accident. The president was badly hurt, but he's alive and that thing is up for sale."

We grew interested.

About this time, Tracy Herrick, a vice president of the Cleveland Trust Company, was out in Lorain, Ohio, to solicit the investment account of a wealthy farmer in that area. The farmer was out in the field when Mr. Herrick called and while his wife was out getting him, Mr. Herrick picked up a copy of the *Ohio Farm Bureau News* that was lying on the table. He thumbed through it and came across the startling statement that the Farm Bureau was selling more gasoline to Ohio farmers than any national oil company in the state.

When the farmer entered, Herrick asked him, "Do you belong to this Ohio Farm Bureau?"

"Yes," the farmer replied.

"Do you think they're all right?" Evidently the farmer gave him a fairly enthusiastic account, for when he returned to Cleveland, the first question he asked of his associates was whether anyone knew anything about the Ohio Farm Bureau. "They claim they've sold more gasoline in the state to farmers than any private company." Someone volunteered the information that a man who used to work for the Society for Savings (referring to me) was connected with the Bureau in some capacity or other. The man who told Herrick this was on the Board of Trustees of Hiram College, and Perry Green, who was president of the Farm Bureau, was also a trustee of Hiram, so, next thing, Perry got a visit from Tracy Herrick. He started asking Perry a lot of questions and Perry finally told him to go down to Columbus and see me.

Mr. Herrick came down and was reasonably impressed with what he saw of our budding insurance company and our other activities. His purpose in coming, of course, was to secure our investment account, but we were having so much fun doing our own investing we didn't feel like giving it up to a stranger. We'd never had so much money before and we were just feeling our oats. Herrick, though, was very persistent and prevailed on me to come up to Cleveland to meet the officers of the bank.

When Harry Collin told us about the National Refinery in Cleveland, we decided to see if we couldn't buy it. Mr. Collin took me up to Cleveland and into the Cleveland Trust Company to meet the chairman of the board, Judge Isadore Freiberger. The judge had been on the bench at one time, and was prominent in civic affairs. He was a little chap, with a great air of being brief and to the point. After the introductions were made and Collin had told the judge who we were, I said I would like to talk about the National Refinery.

Judge Freiberger shot me a severe look of the sort he had probably given prisoners in the dock. "Have you got fourteen million dollars?"

"No," I replied.

"Well, what are you bothering me for?" he asked a bit snappishly.

I got up and said, "Well, I guess I came to the wrong place."

Before I left the bank I decided to see Tracy Herrick to say hello and tell him what had happened. He heard me out and then shook his head. "Well, that's a great howdy-do. Here I've been trying to get your account and convince you that we've got the most forward-looking banking crowd in the state, and when you do come in with a piece of business you get treated like that." He shook his head again. "Do you really want that company?" he asked.

"Well, we'd certainly like to look into it."

"All right," he said, "get your hat and coat and follow me."

Herrick took me to the office of Cyrus Eaton, who was on the board of the National Refinery. I told Mr. Eaton who we were and what we were trying to do and why we were interested in buying the refinery.

Mr. Eaton thought for a moment and then said, "Well, have you got the money to buy it?"

"We've got some money, but not fourteen million dollars."

"Have you got eight million?"

"If we had that much I doubt whether we'd want to put all of it into one company."

"Well, have you got five?"

"Well," I said, rubbing my neck, "I'm not sure."

"Have you got two?"

"We might make it, but I'm not sure," I said doubtfully.

Eaton sat up in his chair. "Mr. Lincoln, this is a twenty-five- or thirty-million-dollar company. You don't expect to buy it for nothing, do you?"

"Mr. Eaton, I've always heard that you're a person who can perform miracles. I didn't know but what you could perform one for us."

He laughed at that and said, "Well, I'll do my best, but you'll have to have some money."

I went back to Columbus and got the board to look over the physical assets of National Refinery. They had a chain of service stations throughout the country and an enormous statement of assets. The sheer size of the organization scared us. The staff began to tremble in their boots and both Lee Taylor and John Sims began to oppose our proposed purchase.

One day Mr. Herrick called up and said he'd bought it. "Well, I've got it. Now come on up here and we'll make a deal."

I went up to Cleveland with the committee and my assistant but the opposition was so strong that the negotiations finally soured. One of the pieces of real property the company had was a refinery in Coffeyville, Kansas. Howard Cowden, who'd gone into the oil business sometime before, was looking for a Western refinery. When I saw that we couldn't agree among ourselves whether to go ahead or not with the purchase of the whole company, I called Cowden and said, "Do you want that refinery you're talking about?" He said he did. "Well, why don't you get together with Cyrus Eaton? I think he's got one for you." Cowden bought the Coffeyville refinery and that refinery really started him on the outstanding accomplishments for which he's known today.

I didn't realize how profitable a transaction I had dumped into the laps of the owners of the National Refinery until some years later when I happened to be in Boston, meeting with an attorney to consider the purchase of the Columbian National Life Insurance Company. There was something on my business card that scratched the lawyer's memory.

"You don't happen to be the Murray Lincoln who used to be with the Farm Bureau, do you?"

"Yes, I am. Why?"

"Didn't you have something to do with the National Refinery at one time or another?"

"Yes, we tried to buy it."

"Well, why in the world didn't you?" he asked, surprised.

"We just couldn't come to an agreement," I said.

"You missed something there," he said. "That was the doggonedest junk deal that this country's ever seen."

"What do you mean, 'junk deal'?"

"Well, they decided against selling the whole company with all its service stations and refineries as a unit and started, instead, to sell it off in pieces—the refineries to one group, the service stations to another group, and so on. They made a mint of money out of it doing it that way."

It wasn't news I exactly welcomed hearing, but I carried it back to our board and staff. It was an opportunity missed and every opportunity we miss makes it easier, for me anyway, to get them to latch on to the next opportunity. I don't know if anyone ever determined that the proverb "Opportunity knocks but once" has any real truth in it. If it had, I suppose we would never have grown to our present size and influence. Opportunity hammers at the door time and time again, and that is something for which I have been eternally grateful.

Certainly the opportunity of gaining control of the oil business in this country could not lie with farmers alone. Lee Taylor, who had opposed our entering the Cooperative League, wanted to keep our oil business confined to farmers. I told him then, "You can take this gas business yourself and I'll keep out of it, but I want to warn you that you'll get your tail burned faster than anybody else."

"Why?" he asked.

"Because we're in business through the sufferance of the big oil companies. Our sales represent nothing more than a fleabite does to an elephant. Any time they want to put us out of business, they can. After all, we have to deliver the gasoline to the farmer. The bulk of the business is done in the city where the city fellow drives up to the pump and takes it away himself."

Lee Taylor never believed that, but I know now that that is the truth. Its truth is borne out by the figures on sales made by some of our own cooperatives. For instance, the Cuyahoga County Farm Bureau Cooperative, which has fewer farmers in its membership than any other county farm bureau in the state, has one of the best sales records and shows some of the highest savings for its members. The reason is that its principal business is the sale of heating oil to people who live in the suburbs of Cleveland. The Southern States Cooperative of Richmond, Virginia, has found out that its biggest customer for petroleum products is the group of Greenbelt cooperative stores around Washington. The oil cooperatives still in existence in Indiana have found that their sales of home-heating oils to suburban customers far outreach the sales of all petroleum products to farmers. The discovery of the power of the consumer is being made, little by little, by some farm groups.

There is only one way for a cooperative to go into the oil business today and that is directly at the source of crude oil, and this fact is confirmed by a conversation reported to me some years ago by an old New Dealer named Jake Baker. Jake had left the Government to go into some sort of private economic survey service, and in the course of his new job he had occasion to meet the presidents of the large American oil companies. During one conversation, Jake brought up the question of cooperatives in the oil business.

"Oh, the cooperatives don't amount to anything," the oilman said. "We don't worry about them because the profit's gone out of retailing. There isn't even much money to be made out of refining. The real money lies in crude oil, and if cooperatives ever started to be bothersome we'd make them pay through the nose for crude oil. That would stop them quick enough."

"I don't know what you're going to do about it," Jake told me later, "but at least it's something you'd better look into."

That's when I began to collect my scrapbook on oil and began to search carefully into the meanings and implications of what control of this vital source of energy meant to us as Americans, as members of a democratic country and citizens of the world. I do not say that if oil companies were democratically controlled by the people who used their oil that they would be run more efficiently, more cheaply, or more profitably. I do say that oil is too vital a commodity in our civilized society and in our upset world to allow it to be controlled by some old-time corporations

286

whose business aims go no further than establishing the difference between their costs and their income.

I do not believe the Government ought to own oil companies. I believe the users ought to own them, and own them under the limitations of a cooperative, which would keep them from being brought under the control of a small group of people. Now, it might happen that a large group of people, using and owning the oil companies and dictating their policies, would say, "Let's get on with it. Let's force our Government to throw its weight around abroad to get us better prices. Let's support undemocratic and authoritarian governments to protect our sources of supply. Let's bleed our own domestic resources to keep the prices up. Let's risk a third world war to get profits rolling into the company." The projected cooperatives might conceivably behave in that fashion. But I have known enough Americans in my life, having spoken to thousands upon thousands of them, that I can say they would not behave in that fashion. Of course there is a streak of greed in all of us. But when the stakes are so high—another world war and all of the devastation atomic research has made possible, against the small increase of dollars each individual user of oil would receive—few men are going to be so greedy as to take the chance. But the fact is there are a few men now in control of some oil companies who may be reckless enough to take the chance.

19

In all the business biographies I've read, there is usually something said about the nature of the ideal executive. Now, that's a legitimate concern of any businessman, and of any business. And because cooperatives are also a business, although a relatively new kind of business, I'm concerned with executives and managers in the same way as the old-line capitalist. In many ways, his problems are simpler than mine.

In the old days, men produced under the threat of the economic lash. A man succeeded or he was kicked out. Society was simpler, more brutal, and more direct. Those are the "good old days" I'm talking about. Now and then you run across such free-wheeling entrepreneurs still doing business in the same old way. By and large, however, our complex society has involved us in a whole network of different ways and means of dealing with people. No corporation president would allow his foreman to treat his employees in a rough and ready manner, because his unionized employees are ready, willing, and able to meet rough and ready tactics with rough and ready responses. Since no one wants strikes or lockouts, big businessmen have resigned themselves to the whole ritual of labor relations experts, personnel specialists, psychologists, and so on. Then, too, the modern businessman is more civilized than his mutton-chopped predecessor whose portrait glares down in the board room. He has come to look upon his fellow human beings as being more complicated, more sensitive. I suppose we owe all that to Freud and his disciples. In any case, the methods employed in the nineteenth century won't do in the twentieth, and most of us are glad of it.

On the executive level, matters have always been a trifle more refined. I suppose the old-line operator kicked workmen out when he pleased but couldn't quite bring himself to apply the boot to the seats of the pants of his executives. Partly, I suppose, because the executive was apt to be his social equal and you don't treat your equals as you do your inferiors. Partly (and perhaps this was the most important consideration), because an executive holds a complicated position in an organization and is not so easy to replace. First-rate executives have never been in abundant supply and even the wildest of free-enterprisers understands that much.

Today, the old-line capitalist businessman has plenty of problems choosing executives and, having chosen them, training them; and having trained them, keeping them; and having kept them, managing to keep them happy. The greatest tool he uses in this regard is compensation. The basis of his business is the earning of money and nothing else. That's his philosophy and his reason for existence. Life in these United States is so arranged that most people think that's an eminently respectable and worthy goal in life. I'm not going to argue that matter much here. If you want the argument, go see your minister. If he can't dig up a half-dozen arguments as to why that *isn't* much of a goal in life, you'd better shop around for another minister.

Since there are so many young men about who feel as our old-line capitalist feels, he can afford to be choosey about the young men he selects for his executive pyramid. He can say that they must be Protestants, and immediately discard about forty or fifty million Catholics and about four or five million Jews and another million or so other young people of different creeds. He can say that they must be white, and so discard another twenty or thirty million people of other colors. He can say that they must be Anglo-Saxon in origin, and discard another couple of million Protestants. He can say that they've got to have Ivy League college training, and that discards another few million of the comparative handful of Protestants who are left. Then he's got to discard the deviates, anarchists, drunkards, thieves, and so on, and what he winds up with is a pinch of pure, crystallized dust in the palm of his hand. And when he looks at this dust, he has to stir it about with a pair of hair-thin tweezers to pluck out of it those one or two paragons of white, Anglo-Saxon, Ivy-League, Protestant young manhood to be chosen for education as executives. No wonder he has trouble finding executives! But even if he were broad-minded enough, democratic enough to say, "I do not care what color, religion, or background my executives have," he would still find the pickings slim since the executive mind is not common and men of executive ability are not easily come by.

His problems are great enough. My problems as a cooperative executive encompass his and several others of which he has no knowledge. But to me, these other problems are a constant headache.

Before I can discuss what sort of management, executives, or personnel best suit our kind of organizations, let's examine what we believe.

For one thing, I believe the human race was placed upon the earth for some purpose. I am not yet sure what that purpose is, but to accomplish any end at all, we've got to get along with one another. And in this pursuit of life, liberty, and happiness, it seems to me we ought to be able to live without the strife and war in which we have heretofore found ourselves. I believe that the democratic process, with all its admitted imperfections, is the best way for the greatest number of people to get along with one another while they try to find out what purpose there is in life. I believe that if we extended this democratic process to the rest of the world (and I am always speaking of the democratic process in its economic and social sense as well as its political sense) we would have very much less to worry about in the appearance of authoritarianism or statism in one country or another.

I believe that science has provided us with the tools, both in industry and in agriculture, to ease—if not literally erase—some of the age-old scourges of man: hunger, disease, improper housing, unemployment—and war.

War, whatever its ideological colorations, is still a form of competition between nations that have and nations that have not. War will never be put aside until we find a more equitable distribution of the world's goods and its opportunities. Even if we cannot, tomorrow, re-distribute the goods and opportunities of the earth, we can, tomorrow, let the world know that this is our intention. If the world believes us—and it would believe us if we began to put our slogans into practice—I believe that the road to war would start to grow narrower and narrower and the aggressor who started to travel it would find himself alone. Does anyone believe that Russia would go to war tomorrow if she knew that every other nation on earth would oppose her? Why does she now, in all her current strength, court the favor of small nations? Because she cannot travel that road alone. War could be made a lonely proposition if the underlying causes of war could be removed.

When we in the Farm Bureau started out to solve the farmer's problems we discovered, little by little, that the farmer's problems cannot be solved until the problems of the whole of society are worked upon. The problem of our society cannot be worked upon without working upon the problems of the world in general.

I believe that people have the duty to work upon these problems. I not only consider it a duty but a privilege. Large groups of people are not spontaneously going to turn their lives toward the solution of those problems unless they get adequate leadership to direct—and, yes, to inspire—them.

Nearly every great revolution, whatever its final effect, has been planned and rationalized and led by a comparatively small group of people. As a rule, the plotters and planners were men who were better educated, more widely traveled, or broader in vision (good or bad as the vision was) than the people they led.

Now we have come to an age, the first in history that I know of, when the greatest revolution of all is possible—the revolution that will change the lives not merely of the people of one state or one country, but of the world. It is the revolution that will not merely overthrow one kind of prince to bring to power another form of government, but the revolution that will overthrow the international monarchies of hunger, disease, illiteracy, poverty.

We now live in a nation that has the tools for this revolution in its hands. We Americans can show others how to use these tools, how to fashion their own destinies with what they have. I say that we have the duty, the obligation, and the privilege of doing this for the whole world. And incidentally, we should do it in our own interest as well.

I'm firmly convinced that there is more to life and to living than just making as much profit as you can. I don't feel that any business should be run at a loss; neither do I feel that profit should be the mainspring of that business. I believe that the profit to be made in any business should be merely incidental to the business so long as the business meets human needs. In our own business we have tried to conduct ourselves in this fashion. It has worked.

When people work together to help one another, they discover in the process that each individual improves his own lot. Now, I do not claim that this works to perfection. No human institution is ever going to be perfect and work without some injustices, some errors, some back-slidings, some confusions, some instances of selfishness. We in the Farm Bureau did not start out to do anything nobler than to find out how the farmer could get more for what he produced than he had been getting. In the process we discovered that he could get more for his money if he bought cooperatively. Going further into the matter, we discovered that the farmer was not alone in the economy. When we made that discovery and acted accordingly, we left behind a great many people and farm organizations who insisted upon isolating the farmer from his fellow Americans. These men and organizations are still in existence, still issue press releases, still behave as though they have all the power and influence, but the fact of the matter is that they are lost in history, and as the world rolls on and becomes smaller and smaller, they are going to shrink out of sight and out of earshot and then disappear entirely.

I have believed for some time now that what we must do is help people run their own economic machinery. They must run it as democratically as they are willing to accept the responsibility for so doing. They must be ready to meet all the ordinary hazards of competitive business, without extraordinary governmental protection or subsidy. And when they do this, they are going to guarantee both to themselves and their associates material gains they had not believed possible. But what is more important, they will in this fashion strengthen the political democracy in which we live. If political democracy is strengthened by this means in any other part of the world, it strengthens our political democracy at home. We in the Farm Bureau, and later in Nationwide Insurance and its related companies, have proved that it can be done. We have competed successfully with the old-line, old-time capitalists and have done it not once but dozens of times and have done it on a scale that leads us to believe that it can be done by others in the same way, in other fields.

Since these are the things we believe, and these are the bases of the organizations we have established and are running, our problems in finding personnel for them are unique.

One of the basic principles of management, I believe, is to staff your organization with people who have a fundamental belief in the underlying philosophy of your organization. Now, the orthodox, profit-motivated businessman doesn't have much trouble on that score. He can always find plenty of people who believe that making money is the greatest thing in the world. We don't believe that, and so we have a difficult time finding people. What we must do largely is to take people into our organization from the same pool of trained and available executives from which the old-line capitalist does his fishing. The candidate comes into our organization and hears our story and because he's a polite person, nods his head and tells us we've got a great idea. He sees that we are successful. He can see that we have surrounded ourselves with all the trappings and trimmings of big business, and that we seem to be doing business in the same way everyone else does. We seem to get as excited about profit and loss as anyone else. Very soon he comes to the conclusion that we are doing as everyone else is doing and this business about serving people, catering to human wants, and so on, is a sort of meaningless ritual of the sort service organizations go through. It is easy for him to make this assumption because we are not always perfect, because we do not always live up to our own ideals. I never mean to suggest that we are not a human organization. We are. We are prone to all the human frailties. Because we resemble other big business organizations we're often treated like them, and what's worse, if we aren't careful, we sometimes behave like them.

We have had a great deal of trouble trying to make advertising agencies understand what it is we want to do with our businesses. We have employed management consultants and have worked hard to make them understand what it is we are up to but they have not always understood. Shortly after we'd hired Rogers, Slade and Hill, I put this question to Art Slade: "How do you compensate people for doing *for* people, in the same manner that they have been compensated for doing things *to* people? Obviously you cannot compensate them upon the basis of the profits they make, since they are not working for profits. They are working to serve others. They are working to induce others to help themselves. What basis of compensation can you find for that sort of work?" Art Slade never did find a specific answer to my question, nor has anyone else. The answer we have finally settled upon, and I do not believe it is the proper one, is to pay people on the basis of what they would be paid in comparable business organizations.

Our similarity to other big business organizations is superficially so great that many people, including some who work within the organization itself, never understand that there is a difference. The difference is one of direction.

My favorite illustration of this difference is this: I go down the road in the same kind of automobile a regular businessman is driving. He and I use oil in our engines, gasoline to power our motors, we use the same road system, obey the same traffic signs, the same speed limits, and we stop at the same hotels. But he and I are going in different directions. He's on his way toward making all the money he possibly can, and I don't disagree with his right to do it. The road I am traveling is toward the satisfaction of human needs. Only incidentally am I trying to find out how to make enough money to pay for my trip and for my car expenses. The difference is, for me, all the difference in the world, but I'm not so sure that everyone else understands the difference as I do.

What sort of people must we have in our organizations? First of all, they must have all the technical efficiency and skills that would be demanded by any business organization. In addition, they must be strongly convinced that we are headed down the right road, in the right direction. This conviction has to be basic to them, because there are so many opportunities for men to ignore that direction and instead follow the old-time business concepts in a fruitless, foolish paper chase. Ours is one sort of business in which you can make all the money in the world and still be a failure. It is also a business in which you can break even and still be a crashing success.

What is the prime requirement, in a general way, for the sort of executives we need in our kind of organizations? I don't know what it is, but one of my executives seems to have an uncanny knack for choosing men who fit in well and get ahead. One day I asked him how he chose his associates. He told me, "Well, I've come to the conclusion that a man who has a liberal political viewpoint is apt to be happy in this kind of an institution. He's already convinced himself that people are more important than things, and that changing institutions is not a shameful thing. His convictions are apt to be strong enough for him to withstand ridicule. He's not made unhappy by the sense that he is out of step with most everyone else."

This question of ridicule is a serious one. I don't suppose any executive working for an old-time capitalist has ever had to defend his company's desire to make money. But our executives do have to defend our policies and philosophy. I am sorry to say that I have heard, from time to time, that some of our people have refused to make any defense. Some of our top executives, challenged by friends or acquaintances with the charge that they were working for an organization that seemed to be leftist or utopian, have remarked, as Gene Hensel once did, "Oh, I don't believe in all that stuff. I'm just working there." They've refused the challenge put by outsiders who, while they don't agree with what we're doing, feel that a man owes loyalty to the organization from which he earns his living. Those outsiders, shocked by such behavior, have come and told me of these encounters.

Now, I've not been as shocked by such behavior. I understand something of what it means to defend what you believe in. Not everyone has the capacity for putting up a strong defense. Not everyone has the ability to present a reasoned rebuttal to an argument or a charge.

I quit attending the Kiwanis Club a long time ago for the simple reason that I grew sick and tired of having a squabble about what I believed in between the soup and salad every Wednesday noon. I took the easy way out by quitting.

But even within our own organization we are confronted with the necessity of arguing the validity of the cooperative approach with people who get their salaries from a cooperative institution. I hate to have to argue that Christianity is worth while with a minister who is paid to preach it. I have had that argument and it is distasteful to me. It is equally distasteful for me to have to argue that the cooperative approach is going to work with people who are being employed by a cooperative. But I find that we are constantly forced into the position of having to prove its worth to our own people. Every time we've entered a new field, some of our people have mistrusted our ability to compete with conventional businesses. Well, we have competed, and successfully—on every occasion—and yet the old fear that we're not going to succeed crops up whenever there is a recommendation that we start something new. I almost wish we'd have an enormous failure sometime, just to see how we'd react.

I used to think that once I had charge of an institution I could make it do anything I wanted it to do. But after an organization grows to a certain size it has a life of its own and you can't *make* it do much of anything, however much power you have to hire and fire. You must work constantly through education, persuasion, and demonstration to get your own people to do what you think ought to be done.

Any organization, once it becomes successful, is apt to lose its original drive and vision. Despite their idealism, or perhaps on account of it, cooperatives are no less vulnerable to this kind of erosion. Because this is so, I've often suggested that we have a vice president in charge of revolution. He'd be one man not responsible for any operations. He'd stand to one side, with whatever staff he needed, to pick holes in whatever we were doing and remind us of our basic philosophy, our fundamental concepts. His job would be to stir up everything and everybody, to criticize and challenge everything being done—objectives, methods, programs, results. He'd keep us so discontented with the status quo there'd never be any doubt of our desire to seek new ways to meet people's needs. He'd keep us on the right track.

People change whether institutions change or not, and institutions that forget this are left behind. Executives get into ruts. Many people don't want to think. Most people are afraid to tackle something new. Then, too, they get a vested interest in what they are doing and try to defend it to the death. I believe that many people oppose a new idea because they don't feel capable of jumping in and handling it. They would rather oppose it and keep their little jobs down pat as they've got them organized,

297

than try to tackle something that might throw them out of their routines—and possibly out of their jobs. I would want my vice president in charge of revolution to spend time throwing us off balance, shaking us out of our coziness, making us feel a little insecure and uncertain.

Many a young man, after he has heard about the cooperative concept, has come in to see me with a desire to save the world. But the moment he gets a private office, a good-looking secretary, and a title, he wants to hang onto those things rather than go ahead and save the world by taking some dramatic but hazardous steps in that direction. I suppose this is a failure that occurs as often in old-line businesses as it does in cooperatives. My own feeling is that anyone who accepts a job with a cooperative ought to be more willing to risk his position than a man who has joined an old-line business. The man who joins the old-line business does his best to dig in; the man who joins our organization ought to do his best to dig up. The difference is the difference between consolidation and exploration.

Part of our trouble has always rested with what I call the "palace guard." These are the technicians who have come in to help us lick certain problems and have then been kept on in positions where they can make policy. They are, on the whole, conservative, more interested in maintaining the status quo than in extending the work of the cooperative into larger fields. They are absolutely necessary as technicians, but they do represent a drag upon the imaginative powers of the organization. I suppose this is true even in orthodox corporations. The problem, of course, is that they cannot easily be replaced. Time and again I have said to my staff, "There isn't one of you around here, including myself, that I wouldn't fire if I knew for sure I could get somebody else to replace you who was just a little bit better." However, whatever their drawbacks, they are competent. If they balk and kick and obstruct, out of whatever legitimate or illegitimate fears and reservations they may have, they are really no worse than any comparable group that may replace them. You have to get used to the faults of the horse you have and learn how to adjust your thinking and instruction to his limitations. It does no good to get rid of him and get another horse. Another horse presents you with another set of problems.

There's no way of judging what characteristics a man ought to have to work in a cooperative. I've suggested that he ought to have a liberal political outlook to begin with. But if you want to take me as an example, well, I did not. It took many years before my political outlook became liberal. Most successful businessmen who publish their biographies hint rather broadly that they were the models of the ideal executive. Now, while I am no less eager to pat myself on the back than the next man, I cannot, in all honesty find any reason to stretch my arm for this one.

Sometime ago, we brought in psychologists to give us analyses of our executives, in hopes we could find some patterns for selecting future executives. Since everyone else was taking the quiz, it was suggested that I take it too. After I'd gone through my life history with the examiner, he said to me, "Do you know what your outstanding characteristic is, according to my analysis?"

"No," I replied. "I haven't the slightest idea."

"Persistence. The majority of people who have run up against the things you've met would have said, 'Oh, it can't be done,' and would have given it up. You did not."

I had never really measured myself against other people on this matter but I did know that I was ever ready to wriggle and twist and try another way and yet another way until I could get going again.

The psychologist went on to say that my greatest handicap— it was a fault in my personality—was that I was not patient enough with the people about me, that I was not aware enough of their limitations, and that I was apt to destroy a team because I pushed too hard.

Now while that was quite interesting, I couldn't quite credit it. There are more than a few people who started their careers with us many, many years ago and who, if my behavior could have

299

discouraged them, would have left long ago. The fact that they're still with us indicates to me that either I'm not too tough on them, or that they're tough enough to stand up to me when the need arises.

As for my impatience—well, in the early days I would talk and talk and talk, going over the same ground so many times that the sound of my own voice began to hurt my ears. But I kept seeing evidence that my listeners did not understand what I was saying. I think my fault, then, was that I was too patient, too willing to go over the same ground.

What I've learned from working in a cooperative is that you have to like working with people to get along well. Now that is one of my strong points and I need no psychologist to tell me so. I like to be associated with people in a common enterprise, but when I want to do some thinking I get off in a corner by myself.

I like to work on teams, even though I may get impatient when people don't move as fast as I think they should. But no matter how impatient I get at times, and no matter how often my ego would trap me into believing I can go it alone, or that I've done something grand all by myself, I know that without the support of a devoted team my accomplishments would amount to little. It is my nature to be restless and dissatisfied, and I have never found it the easiest thing in the world to tell people I like them, or that I'm pleased with what they're doing. It's the New Englander in me, I suppose. All the same, I know that without the close in-fighting of some loyal and sometimes anonymous field men all over Ohio I would have lost many a battle in the old Farm Bureau days, and I know that our insurance companies could not be in the enviable competitive position that they are today if it were not for the innovations in product and procedures developed by a gifted group of specialists. I have cause to be grateful to all these people, as well as to the members of our several boards, our executives, and our agency force. I not only believe in the group, I am dependent on it.

But one of the things I have learned painfully over the course of many years is that the top executive is in a lonely position and that little by little he has to restrict his friendships both within and without the organization.

Friendships within the organization are tricky and delicate and sometimes dangerous. In the early days of the Farm Bureau my wife and I, as reasonably friendly people, tried to get close to members of the staff, and I encouraged Anne to hold social meetings with the wives of other staff members. None of us, in those early days, were making much money and none of us had large houses or servants of any kind, so the social get-together for the ladies was something of a burden on Anne, as it would have been on any one of the other ladies. But some women don't reckon burdens when it comes to matters of social status. During the course of the meetings the women began to compare the salaries their respective husbands earned, and there ensued a good deal of jockeying for position. One day one of the women asked Anne, "Well, who has a right to call this meeting?" Anne, who knew nothing about status or the political maneuverings within the Farm Bureau, didn't know how to answer the question. It became fairly obvious to me then that these meetings would soon cause more trouble than amity. They were quietly dropped.

Anne and I continued seeing members of the staff and their wives on a social basis, but even this had unfortunate results. It seemed to become a rule that as soon as we became friendly with a man and his wife, sooner or later I would be forced to fire the man, or he would resign in a huff. It didn't happen once or twice, but several times. So often, in fact, that it would have been funny if it hadn't been so puzzling and, in one or two cases, so unhappy an experience that I could draw no humor from it. I have always been interested in learning why this should be the case. I don't know. I only know that in the interests of peace and harmony and good order within an organization, the top executive almost has to shun close personal relationships with his executives and his staff. It is not a situation about which I am happy but it is one I have had to accept as a fact of executive life until I can find a better answer.

As president, I like to drive with a loose rein. It suits me. Unfortunately, it does not suit others. When you're breaking through new ground, finding new approaches to old problems, I believe in being allowed to pick out your own way. Many executives don't like that freedom. It upsets them. They come to me for confirmation, for reassurance that they are doing right. They do not do this openly, but obliquely. Many times have I heard a man say to me, "I don't think I'm really doing a job on this." He doesn't believe that. He wants reassurance from me that he is doing a good job. Many times I don't know whether he is doing a good job or not. No one knows. I don't care what sort of a job a man is doing so long as he is plowing ahead and trying one way and then another. My own feeling is that inertia never did anything. A body at rest remains at rest. A body in motion remains in motion and is liable to get somewhere. Who knows if a man is headed in the right direction? He may charge off and do the wrong thing. I never condemn a man for making a mistake. I will condemn a man who plays it cozy, who refuses to expose himself to failure. Such a man is worse than useless. He tends to spread the paralysis of caution up and down and across an organization. Such a man has no faith in himself or in others. And faith in people, I believe, is an important requirement in an executive.

I have heard the statistics and arguments about the mentality of the average American and I deplore, as I'm sure you do, the low grade we score. But we are working with large groups of people and their decisions at any particular moment represent the limit to which they will move. With time they will come along further. It does try one's patience to see people refusing to accept something they should accept. But in time, with the proper education and persuasion and motivation, they will move. People act spontaneously to help one another in moments of great stress, of tragedy and catastrophe. At other times, they must have competent, honest, and vigorous leadership. The management of a cooperative must have faith in people, realizing that while they are not always right, they can only be led in steps to their own salvation and the pace must be the one they set for themselves. At the same time, the executives of a cooperative must never forget the goal toward which they are aiming and must not let up.

There are virtues in driving with a loose rein but there are also serious drawbacks. It is difficult for me to let people go ahead without restriction. Sometimes they do nothing, which bothers me. And sometimes they go on too long and too far. Then the problem of discipline arises. It comes as a shock when I must stop my associates and say, "You're not doing right." I know that I have caused the organization a great deal of loss and injury because I won't stop a man the first instant I learn he is doing something wrong. I would rather allow him to discover for himself that he has gone wrong. I know it is a costly method, but I believe it is the only acceptable one for at least two reasons. The first reason is that I'm sure it takes a fairly arrogant man to assume that he knows better than anyone else how a job should be done. I do not pretend to know more than the next man. I hesitate to correct him in the performance of a job which is, after all, his responsibility. The second reason is that if the man in question has gone far enough wrong to satisfy me that he is wrong but not far enough to satisfy himself, a correction from me or from his superior is going to destroy a fraction of his independence. In addition, it's going to instill in him a resentment based cn the feeling that he was right and would have been able to demonstrate it if he had not been prematurely checked. An expensive process, I admit, but one that does save executives from being ruined, that does save people from becoming embittered and unhappy and ultimately useless. After all, an organization that is designed to meet people's needs ought to take into account the needs of the people who work for it.

20

When you behave unconventionally you have to expect people to mistrust you, misunderstand your motives, and generally regard you as a dangerous character. I think part of our trouble in the Farm Bureau and in its related organizations had to do with our public relations. People did not, could not, or would not understand what we were doing. I think we should have done more than we did in trying to make them understand, at least those who were open-minded enough to listen. Those who *will* not understand, of course, are a dead loss. Nothing will convince them and I believe it is a waste of energy even to try.

John W. Galbreath, one of the foremost real-estate men in the United States, lives in Columbus and has a been a friend of mine ever since we and others set up a poor man's riding club in 1934. One day out on the farm he asked, "Murray, what are you up to? I hear that you don't make much money, but you've got a great big institution. What are you trying to do?"

"Trying to save the world," I said.

"Well, how are you going to save it? We'd all like to do that."

"By making everybody a capitalist," I said without a smile.

He looked at me for a long moment and then said, "Now you know a lot of people don't think that's what you're up to, don't you?"

"Yep."

"You know what they think you are, don't you?"

"Yep," I replied. "A damn Communist. I've heard it. But if I live long enough, I bet you we'll prove that we've made more of a contribution to saving the capitalist system that any of these people who have been running us down. And what's more, we'll prove that we've helped save private capitalism from becoming state capitalism."

This failure to understand the core of our thinking and of our philosophy, if you want to put as grand a word as that on what we believe in, comes in many different ways. When I spoke before the Cooperative League with a CIO leader in the audience and used the word *revolution* in my speech, the National Tax Equality Association printed hundreds of thousands of leaflets, screaming that the co-ops and the CIO were getting together to take over the country. This kind of failure to understand is willful. It is, in fact, no failure at all in the sense that someone has honestly tried to do something and could not. No one in the National Tax Equality Association is interested in learning what we are doing. Ben McCabe, who was once the president of the National Tax Equality Association, took great delight in giving out cash prizes to high-school girls who wrote dutiful essays showing that the wicked co-ops do not pay taxes. He used to be an important grain-elevator operator up in Minneapolis, and it tickled me to live to see Ben McCabe sell his string of fifty grain elevators to the Farmers Union Grain Terminal Association, a group of co-operatives managed by Bill Thatcher. Well, I doubt that Ben McCabe and his group will ever understand what we are doing. He and they don't want to. I'll be honest enough to say that I don't care if they ever do understand. I resent the misinterpretation they have placed upon our motives and our methods, but I don't believe, in the long run, they are ever going to convince any independent thinker that cooperatives are wicked inventions of tax dodgers.

Sometimes the failure to understand what we are saying comes from a whole background of thinking one way and being incapable of shifting to another point of view. When we were entering upon our rural electrification program in the 1930s and the private utilities sought to bring us under the utility act, we appeared before a committee of the Ohio State Legislature to explain why we should not be subjected to that act. We maintained that we didn't need to be regulated by any governmental body because *we were serving ourselves.* I never saw such confusion in my life. Those men literally could not understand how people serving themselves would not cheat themselves. The very idea was so new and strange to them they could not make the mental shift necessary to understand what, to us, is a simple thing. But this failure to understand is not peculiar to people outside the cooperative movement. It also occurs to members within cooperatives.

Farmers were never as interested in what they could be saved by purchasing cooperatively as what they could get, by way of an increase in price, from marketing cooperatively. "I don't care what I have to pay for fertilizer and feed. Just get me more for my livestock and wheat and poultry and eggs." Perhaps those farmers failed to understand because the acquisitive instinct was too strong in them. It seems odd, but I found it to be true, that the dollar you have in your hand is more important than the dollar you do not need to spend. And yet in both cases you have a dollar more. I am not arguing that the dollar in hand is more tangible. Of course you can see it and feel it, but the dollar you save has a reality as well. Why that reality is not as important as the reality you can touch at the moment, is something I do not understand. Perhaps in this business of realities lies the reason that consumer cooperatives, which are potentially so immensely powerful, are not so popular. Our society is interested in the dynamic business of making money and much less interested in saving it. Someday someone is going to be able to explain this characteristic, and when he does we are going to unlock the power of the consumer.

At the moment, the only way I know of convincing people that they can, by their strength as consumers, take over large pieces of economic machinery to make them work for themselves is by a process of demonstration. In 1926 a small group of Ohio farmers invested ten thousand dollars and set up a new mutual insurance company, designed to meet the special needs of its members by operating as a cooperative. Today, the children of that company, the Nationwide Insurance Companies, have total assets of over three hundred and fifty million dollars. Part of that growth reflected the growth of *all* insurance companies, but a large part of it can be attributed to our uniqueness as an organization. It is an organization geared to serve the people who use it, it is an organization expressly made to serve its owner-patrons. How is it different from any other insurance company? *It is different from any other insurance company because it is not in business primarily to make a profit out of its services.* Please read that sentence again. I think if you once understand that simple idea, you will have caught the sense of what we have been doing, and what I have been trying to do ever since I had the feeling that the farmer ought to be paid as much as a schoolteacher.

With few exceptions, insurance companies are profit-making institutions. They are businesses designed to run on an absolute minimum of risk. They are run on actuarial tables, and mainly they rely on the average man's sense of inadequacy, fear, and apprehension to bring them their customers. They put their monies only in safe and sound conventional investments to get a certain percentage return, and seldom do their interests extend into other fields. They have protected themselves by disclaimers, waivers, and releases to keep from being snowed under by claims. For instance, the greatest fear any of us has now is of a total war—an atomic, hydrogen-bomb war between ourselves and the Soviet Union. What have the conventional life insurance companies done about that risk, that fear? Read your policy. Somewhere in the fine print you will find that in such an event all bets are off and you won't collect on your insurance. I am not saying that you will not find the same notice in the provisions of Nationwide's life insurance policies. That provision is there for the simple reason that any company that tried to pay off all the claims of persons killed in a major war would be out of business within a day. To insure you against such a risk would mean that the company would have to ask you for a premium roughly equal to the face amount of the policy *before* the first bomb fell. In short, the company insures you against the *average* hazard of the male or female of a certain age reaching a certain age. This hazard is computed by measuring how many males and females of any particular age live to be a certain particular age. To make sure that their risk is an average risk, you are asked to take a physical examination to determine if you are in average good health. Then you are asked if you engage in certain hazardous occupations that show a bad record. If you are not so engaged, you used to be asked if you planned to take any flights in airplanes. Now that commercial airliners have piled up an impressive record of air safety, insurance companies no longer take the matter of ordinary travel on commercial, scheduled carriers into account as a hazard. The point I am making is that insurance companies try carefully to hedge their bets. They are betting that you will live longer than you believe. It would be in their interest to see that you do, and there are a few companies that spend money trying to get people to keep slim, advising them on diet and health care and what not. In this case business interest and social welfare coincide. But of the major hazards of the world, for which they give no insurance, what do the average insurance companies do? Precisely nothing.

Nationwide, on the other hand, is serious when it says that it wants to save the world. It was the only insurance company to send observers to the Geneva conference on atoms for peace. It helped sponsor the anniversary dinner meeting of American Nobel Prize Winners in 1957 in the hope that the views of these great men would stimulate discussions on a governmental level leading to some form of disarmament and mutual understanding. We do not pretend that we know a simple remedy for war. But we are using some part of our assets, some part of our resources, to see what we can do about insuring everyone against the hideous peril of an all-out war. I don't think any businessman in this country is doing his duty unless he devotes some part of his time and some part of his company's earnings to promoting peace. I don't accept the argument that because he pays taxes to the Government, and because the Government uses his tax dollars to buy armaments, and because armaments are supposed to be the best insurance of peace, he *is* doing his part. No nation ever prepared for war that did not sooner or later go to war. And I don't believe that letting someone else do it is the way to get anything done. You must do it yourself. We're doing it at Nationwide. I am not saying that we deserve medals for what we are doing, but if you ask me what the difference is between Nationwide Insurance and any other insurance company—one difference is our persistent and organized concern for peace.

One way we're trying to demonstrate that difference is through sponsorship of radio and television programs that aim for something more than pure entertainment or escape. This is not to say that everything we put on is grim or serious, or that I've been invariably proud of it all. I do think, however, that when we sponsor a show that's supposed to be entertaining it's pure entertainment, and not the kind of blood-and-thunder sadism that fills so much of the air these days. For instance, once they were released for syndication, we sponsored episodes of the television series, *Mama*. I thought the series a charming recollection of bygone days, but I also thought it an innocuous program for Nationwide Insurance to spend money on. But then, I am only the president of the company, and I think you understand by now that I don't run it alone. I have been much prouder of a special series of radio programs that we sponsored over the CBS network in the winter of 1958–59, and again in 1959–60. This series was narrated by Edward R. Murrow and it was called *The Hidden Revolution*. It offered a thoughtful review of some of the basic issues facing mankind today, and it won the Peabody Award for outstanding radio public service.

One program, I recall, had to do with the effect of automation upon American working people. Someday we are going to have a twenty-hour work week. Eighty years ago, a man had to work about sixty-three hours a week to provide for himself and his family—and even so, he could provide them with nothing more than the bare necessities. Today a man can provide his family with a great many luxuries by working only forty-two hours a week. What will the increasingly shorter work week mean to us? I think it will change our way of life, our whole society.

Another problem *The Hidden Revolution* took up was the way in which our freedoms have been whittled away, both by the Government and by business. In a special discussion guide prepared for the series by faculty members of Ohio State University, the problem was stated this way: "Freedom to work where and how one desires is being drastically abridged by modern job requirements." You don't believe that? Ever hear of a young fellow working for a big corporation who refused to take a transfer from one city to another part of the country? He was either fired or passed up on the next promotion. Big companies keep thousands of families moving like gypsies across the United States each year. "Freedom to buy and consume what one wants is being overwhelmed by mass marketing practices. Freedom to form independent judgments is under heavy assault by television, radio, and the popular press. Worst of all, the individual is likely not to recognize such threats to his freedom because his thoughts and opinions have been molded for him by 'the group.' The fellow who does protest these subtler but no less vital invasions of freedoms may be labeled a crank or destructive influence. His very act of protest has been reduced to the pathetic gesture: the unhappy car buyer decorates his purchase with lemons; the objector to nuclear-bomb-testing attempts to sail his leaky boat into the Eniwetok blast area." Now I think that point is especially well made. We can hardly kick about anything any more without being called a crab or something worse—usually a Communist. We've got a buttoned-up and buttoned-down society. Everybody plays with the team or he doesn't play at all.

Other problems discussed on our radio series have centered around national loyalties, what sort of schools we have and what sort we want, the United Nations, and the whole question of war: Are we frightened enough to give it up as a political weapon? How do we know when we ought to go to war if we go at all? Who ought to decide when the buttons are pushed? And so on.

We were proud to sponsor this series and we intend to sponsor more like it. We think it's the sort of thing other insurance companies ought to be doing.

In 1958, in a speech to the American Management Association, I said, "Adolf Berle, corporation specialist and former State Department official, points out that insurance and financial executives control vast billions of what he calls 'masterless' money—money that belongs to other people—and that the way in which those executives use that money can well determine the fate of this nation, if not of civilization itself. Investments in the Middle East are a case in point." As you can see, I was riding my old hobbyhorse again—Middle Eastern oil. I don't think there is any insurance company in this country, with the exception of Nationwide, that consciously and consistently invests some of its assets with the knowledge that their use may have something to do with the fate of our nation and of our civilization. *That's* a difference between Nationwide and other insurance companies.

In that same speech I included a few excerpts from an article published in the September, 1958, issue of *Fortune,* and written by that brilliant scholar, Dr. Louis Finkelstein. He wrote:

"The U.S. businessman is preoccupied chiefly with gain, coasting on the spiritual momentum of the past. . . . History shows that when we become success-dominated, we lose sight of our real reasons for living.

"No institution will survive if it is dedicated *only* to self-preservation. A business is not a biological organism whose survival is a virtue in itself. Rather, it is a man-created institution, an integral part of our culture, and as such must make a contribution of service to society (as well as a profit for itself) if it hopes to survive. It cannot do this out of a focus on self-gain or pride."

The difference between Nationwide and most other insurance

company in this country? We are *not* dedicated solely to our own self-preservation.

Some people find it hard to believe that we mean what we say. They don't believe us because for one reason or another they mistrust all business and businessmen. But it's not only in the business world that selfish interest lies. Selfish interest is to be found in government, in science, in the military world, and in every phase of our society. We have become so huckster-minded, so profit-motivated, that we instinctively put our hands over our wallets when someone sidles up and says, "Brother, I'm going to give you something absolutely free." P. T. Barnum introduced the saying "There's a sucker born every minute." I regard him as a flamboyant old promoter who had the courtesy to tell the truth about himself and the people he flimflammed. He said something in an impolite fashion that was true of polite society and of the polite world of nineteenth-century business. No one wants to be played for a sucker. As a result, we tend to look with a jaundiced eye upon people who seem to be altruistic. I know that when I went down to the Ohio Democratic Committee headquarters some time ago, it was generally assumed that I was angling for something. I told them, "No, I don't want any job or contract or favor. I want to see to it that you fellows put up candidates I can vote for with a clear conscience and some enthusiasm." They all announced in loud, brave, bucko voices that that was exactly what they thought Democrats ought to be doing. They praised me for being a good citizen and a good Democrat. But what they said so bravely and loudly and publicly they forgot when some of them got me into a quiet corner and nudged me and asked with a wink, "Okay, Murray, what do you *really* want?" I gave them the same answer in private that I had given them in front of the other members. I wanted nothing for myself. "I've got a good job and I'm happy with it. I'm too old to start running for elective office. I merely want to see that you men put up decent candidates." It bewildered them. It surprised them. Some of them still don't believe me. I went to one of the county Democratic chairmen who had been in that office for some time and asked him about this reluctance to believe me. His suggestion was this: "Murray, you'd better say you want something, because when you say you don't want anything they think you're hiding something."

"How about telling them that I want good government in order to get fair and adequate insurance examinations?" I asked.

"That's all right," he said. "You tell them that and they'll quit worrying about what you've got up your sleeve."

Not long ago we considered a proposal to go into business in the Philippines with a group of Filipino businessmen who were interested in developing their oil resources. A leading Filipino businessman came to the United States looking for help on the project. Someone in Washington recommended me and Nation-wide. He came to Columbus and told me who he was and what he wanted to do. He knew very little about me except that I was the head of an insurance company and the size of our building seemed to indicate that we had a respectable business. "Have you got any answer to this problem, Mr. Lincoln?" he asked.

No, I didn't have any answer but I did have an idea. It was that we would help the Filipinos get started with an oil company, then once our original investment was returned we'd pull out of it completely and let them run it. Or, if they preferred, we'd stay in it to provide management services.

The visitor looked at me for a long moment, evidently trying to decide where the hook lay in the bait. "Now, you do know what you're saying, do you?" he asked.

"Yes," I said, "I know what I've been saying because I've been doing and saying the same thing for thirty years."

"I've seen a few other businessmen and none of them has put up that kind of proposition," he said.

"No," I replied, "and I don't believe you'll find anybody else who will."

When he was finally convinced that I had no hook to conceal and that I was offering him no bait he said something I will never forget. "Well, Mr. Lincoln, if you'll help us make this one experiment, then we who are brown can go to our brothers who are yellow and black and say, 'Here's something new in the world. Here's a big company in a big country that's willing to help us instead of exploit us. Here's a big business that wants to help us set up, and get the benefits from, our own institution.' "

Now this man is an honorable gentleman and I presume he believes me when he says he does, but he will be only human if he wonders now and then if I mean what I say. For, unhappily, we were unable to grant a loan on terms that would have made it possible for us to go into business with him. Someday, though, I hope we'll have another opportunity, because I know that the only way I'll be able to prove that I really mean what I say is to demonstrate that I do. It was what old Pop Hart had told me to do when I was training myself to become nothing more than a nursemaid to a herd of dairy cows: "Show 'em the right way and they'll follow you."

What is the plain truth of what we're doing? We're trying to acquire the machinery through which people can help themselves. We are trying to build a consumer society—the one kind of society where the welfare of everybody is put before the welfare of special groups. Do we at Nationwide want to do it all by ourselves? Not at all. We are willing to help anyone—as we were willing to help Jack Kaplan and the forty-eight hundred farmers who supplied the Welch Grape Juice Company to make that company a cooperative. We are not advancing a complicated and foreign social ideology. Farmers, Midwestern farmers at that, are the most cautious and conservative group of citizens in our country. They believe in cooperatives. If some of them don't want to admit city people into their cooperatives then they've missed the boat. But they haven't bought a complicated and foreign social ideology, because economic democracy is no more foreign and complicated than political democracy. Did someone remark that cooperatives were born abroad? Where do you think the principles of the Declaration of Independence and of the Bill of Rights were born? Abroad, out of the memory of oppression through the special privilege of princes of royal and economic power.

This is the heart of the thing we keep referring to as "our story." We want to extend democracy to its logical limits within our own country and ultimately to the rest of the world. Whether we want it or not, whether we like it or not, the world sits in our back yard and on our front lawn and looks in the parlor windows. And if you can eat while starving Indian children watch you, you've got a stronger stomach than I think you have. And if you can take your leisure while you watch millions of human slaves struggle for an animal's existence you're a colder fish than I think you are, and if you can watch millions turning in their desperation to the false promises of demagogues then, brother or sister, there is little hope for you. Because they will come after you, through the back door, through the front door, and right through the parlor windows, and what will happen to you and your comfort is something I leave to your imagination.

But I don't believe you're callous and cold and dense. I believe that most Americans are finally realizing that they can't live in a little island of abundance while the world starves, that they can't keep the benefits of democracy to themselves while the rest of the world, nation by nation, falls under the hammer of statism or collectivism. The answer doesn't lie in bigger and better H-bombs or missiles. Such things only kill people—they don't convince them. We have to do a lot of convincing and the best way of convincing people that democracy has something to offer them is to demonstrate it. Show 'em the right way and they'll follow.

Part Six

21

Some men's lives involve more of the present and the future than they do the past. By that I mean that men who are intensely interested in some vision or idea are apt to be racing into the future so fast that they rarely look back. My own life has been so busy, so filled with storm and strife, with so much reaching for the next corner, the next hill, that I'm generally living ahead of myself. I am grateful that God gave me a large, vigorous body, and I am grateful that as a boy the rigors of farm life gave me a rugged constitution. They've allowed me to live the sort of life I have lived and the sort I'll probably go on living. I still work my farm on weekends and that satisfies the muscles and bones of my body. I am not a contemplative man. I think that's something you may already have guessed from reading this book. But I do think about the future and, despite the heartaches and the terrible perils that lie ahead, I do envy the youngsters who are going to live to be part of it.

The first week of every month we set aside for board meetings of our insurance companies and the subsidiaries. Every Wednesday morning of that week, for years now, I have been speaking to the board on a variety of subjects. Someone once referred to

316

them as my "Wednesday morning sermons." My over-all subject has been the state of the world. Time and again I have said something like this: "The world today is balanced precariously. The situation is dangerous, interesting. You people ought to do something about it. You've got kids and grandchildren. You've got them to consider. I'm out of the picture. I won't be around when the holocaust strikes—and from the way things look it is *going* to strike and nothing on earth seems to be rising up to stop it. That means you men have got to stop it, to change it."

The board members have listened, laughed at what jokes I could scrape up, and nodded at the things they knew were true. Someone once complained to me that it didn't look as though I was making much of an impression. But I know differently. I know those talks have had a cumulative effect. Education is the acquisition of knowledge in bits and pieces. When a child is sent to kindergarten, he learns to play with other children. No one expects him to learn higher mathematics in kindergarten. He has to learn about the world in bits and pieces. He has to learn about it through his primitive animal senses first. He tastes objects that are not meant to be eaten because this is the first way in which a baby learns what kind of world lies about him. Bit by bit he learns to read simple sentences and to write letters and words, and then he learns the world of numbers. When you consider what a child is capable of learning between the ages of infancy and five, you begin to appreciate that if he were capable of learning the same amount in every five-year period thereafter we'd have a race of gods. But the learning process begins to run downhill almost before it reaches its peak. Happily, the learning process, even if it slows down a good deal, never stops. And when I repeat and repeat and repeat myself, I am teaching others, and, by the way, teaching myself as well. And I have seen the effect of my talks on the board. I have also seen the effect of our common experience. They've learned, just as I have, and some of them faster than I. If there is anything to say about the future that I can base on what I know from direct experience, it is this: Men can learn and have learned and will learn from their experience. They may move ahead by fits and starts and they may fall back one step for every two they take forward, but the world will improve.

On September 1, 1955, we changed our name from Farm Bureau Insurance to Nationwide Insurance. That was because we planned to add to our thirteen-state operating territory all the other states. We couldn't do it as Farm Bureau because in a number of those other states insurance companies already were doing business under that name. So the change was a rather important milestone and the day it became effective we held a big meeting of our Columbus employees. All sorts of personal feelings were tied up in the name Farm Bureau. It could have been an occasion for sentiment and nostalgia. But I didn't talk about the past that day. I talked about the future. I was a little afraid that some of our people might interpret the change in name as a change in purpose, and what I wanted to make clear was that the truth was just the opposite, that we were obliged to change our name in order to carry out our purpose. This naturally led me into trying to define our purpose, and I wound up plowing deeper than I ever remember doing in a speech, before or since.

"If the vision of science prevails," I said, "the society of 1975 will be planned and engineered to provide a material abundance far beyond anything man has ever dreamed. There will be no wars, and no depressions. Weather and climate will be controlled on a global basis. You'll be on a thirty-six-hour week, maybe on a thirty-four-hour week. You'll either fly to work in your own personal helicopter, or ride to work in a pilotless, wireless trolley, or drive to work on a one-way street at a hundred miles an hour, in perfect safety; traffic will be electronically directed. You'll get your mail by guided missile, and you'll live in a house that uses electricity generated from atomic fuel. You'll have no fear of cancer, polio, tuberculosis, or any of the other currently common diseases; you'll either be immune or you'll have a quick and effective cure. You can expect to live to be a hundred.

"In 1975 today's deserts will be lush, flourishing farmlands, irrigated by fresh water converted from salt water. We will have found the way to capture energy from the sun itself. We will probably be using it to melt the ice of Greenland and Antarctica, turning those barren wastes into fertile, productive areas."

These remarks were delivered late in 1955. I am writing this four years later. How about some of the predictions? We've begun to lick polio, thanks to Dr. Jonas Salk and his vaccine. Thousands of homes are using electricity generated by an atomic-energy plant at Shippingport, Pennsylvania. Some of those predictions are coming true, already. But I also had a warning to give in 1955 that I want you to read.

"Technologically, we have found the key to plenty. But notice that I say 'technologically.' For here is the hedge. Here enters the great big 'if.'

"We can have this promised world of abundance *if* we have wisdom—*if* we have the good sense to use our new techniques in our own best interest. For let's make no mistake. In the last analysis, people—not science, not technology, but people—will determine the kind of world we live in—*if* we live—in 1975.

"For, like all times that try men's souls, the future has two faces. There is the future of peace and plenty, assured us by the statesman who says, 'The atom and the electron have made modern war as disastrous for the winner as for the loser—a form of race suicide. This fact cancels out war as an instrument of national policy.' But there is also the future of war and death, which some philosophers see as inevitable. The atom and electron, these philosophers remind us, have been released in a divided world, where there is no responsible authority to deal with irresponsible aggression. If we escape destruction, they say, it will be by the grace of God and the skin of our teeth.

"Indeed, any sensitive man must take pause when he reviews the record of the past twenty-five years. Yes, this was the period that brought us television and the jet airplane and the frozen lima bean and the air-conditioned ranch house. But it was during this

319

same period that mass murder was introduced as a matter of national strategy, that medieval torture methods were refined by the systematic application of modern psychology, and that the freedoms of almost a billion persons were sacrificed to the police state.

"Let's face it, then. There *is* the possibility that we will not survive. There is the real and present danger that in our ignorance, in our pettiness, in our greed, in our distrust we might turn this new force against ourselves. There is the real possibility that the same awesome power which could make this an earth of milk and honey will instead reduce it to radioactive rubbish. This, too, is one of the facts of life in the mid-twentieth century, and we can hardly forget it.

"And yet, I cannot bring myself to despair. In fact, *I* feel optimistic about the future. It seems to me that once we've taken a good, cold look at the contradictory 'yes, but' nature of the times we live in, we have to proceed on faith. I start with the assumption, as problematical as it may be, that we *will* have a chance to build this fabulous world of 1975 and that there'll be no war to stop us. I do not spend my time, therefore, brooding about the possibilities of extermination. On the contrary, I am spending my time trying to figure out solutions to the human and social problems that this new technology is creating.

"Obviously, it is not enough to build a world of no disease and little pain, of long life and physical comfort, of short working hours and big pay. Such a world would reduce the average man to the status of a vegetable—or, at best, that of a placid, satisfied infant. I personally don't look forward to a world where every man's a gurgling baby any more than I do to a world where every man's an eggplant.

"The world that technology can build, then, is only a half-world. For us to build a complete world, fit for men, we must ask ourselves questions that can't be answered with a slide rule, or with Dr. Einstein's magic formula. We must be concerned with the meaning of things, and not merely their function. We must be concerned not only with man's plumbing but with his spirit. It's good to look forward to a clean, comfortable world, but it's even more important that we start building guarantees that it be a free world. What are we going to do with this abundance when we get it? What are we going to do with all this newly won leisure? Suppose we do live to be a hundred, what are we going to do with all those extra hours? Right now, the way mutual investment funds are growing and the way pension funds are being turned back into the economy, it seems almost inevitable that in twenty years or so every man—and possibly every woman and child, too—will have a share, literally, in the ownership of American business. But what are we going to do with our shares? Give our proxies to a bunch of managers and let them run our businesses as they see fit? Is ownership to be in name only? Or will we exercise our rights and actively participate in the decisions that govern the businesses we own? How much say will we be allowed in this world of tomorrow?

"How we answer these questions now will determine the world of the future. *How* we build the world of 1975 is as important as *what* we're building. As a matter of fact, in terms of man's welfare, the how may be even more important than the what. For, as we all know, inconsistent means have a way of corrupting the end.

"It seems to me that the greatest danger in the years ahead is that man will become the servant of his own machines. He will be a well cared for servant, to be sure, but he will have lost the one thing that has always distinguished him from the lower animals, the unique thing that has made him man—and this, of course, is his ability to control his own destiny.

"It is easy for us to be intimidated by these new machines. None of us, I'm sure, could win in a computing contest with the IBM 650, the new electronic thinking machine we're installing this month in our accounting department. Similarly, few of us feel prepared to cope with the political and social questions that our machine-age culture has raised. Should we, or should we not, give up some of our dubious right to wage war—in order to establish an effective world police force? Can we afford to disarm? Can we afford not to disarm? How can we develop an educational system that will help make whole individuals, rather than functional counterparts to machines? How can we attain a sensitivity to moral standards which will withstand the emphasis on self-interest now so evident in business and political life?

"Faced with such questions, most of us are inclined to assume one of two postures. Either we throw up our hands or we bury our heads in the sand. The questions seem too big for us, the answers beyond us. The tendency is, more and more, to leave the answers to the experts. The danger is that we will give up and forfeit our right of decision to the specialists, to a small and soulless group of professional decision-makers.

"We simply cannot let this happen. That's why our greatest challenge today is to preserve and extend the people's right to control their own institutions. And this is the job we've cut out for ourselves here at Nationwide. This is where cooperatives, and this institution in particular can make their greatest contribution to man's future. . . .

"The individual can learn responsibility only by exercising responsibility. The intrusion of government into economic affairs is only one way—and often not the best way—of extending democratic control over business. . . . Another way is extension from 'beneath'—the consumers, the employees, the union members, the stockholders. For too long we have pretended that our economic system was a separate compartment of life. We can afford to do so no longer.

"This is what we've been doing at Farm Bureau Insurance. This is what we're going to be doing even more at Nationwide Insurance. *This* is what we're trying to do—to give individuals the responsibility of governing their economic affairs; to encourage wider ownership of business enterprises, thereby helping to extend democratic control; to encourage greater consumer participation in business activities; to create more wealth, see that it is fairly distributed, and thereby increase freedom for the individual. *This* is what we're up to.

"This is why we work through sponsoring organizations. This is why we're supporting the programs of the Cooperative League. This is why we're trying to get policyholders organized and active in advisory committees. This is why we're investing in cooperatives, and why we're putting as much money as we can into new people-oriented enterprises like Tectum and Peoples Development and Mutual Income Foundation.

"We mean to do what we can to guarantee that *people*, and not just a few powerful managers, have a hand in shaping the future."

The material I have quoted shows my conviction that the future will present both the greatest dangers mankind has ever faced, and the greatest opportunities we have ever had to surmount those dangers and make a better world for all. I believe we will never have a peaceful world until all nations give up their right to wage war to an international body. When we have eliminated the threat of war, the economic reorganization of our world will be relatively an easy matter. What we ought to do, for instance, is encourage every country to produce or develop those things which it is best qualified to produce. For instance, isn't it sheer economic waste for England to raise wheat when we and Argentina and Canada have the capacity to produce enough wheat for England and most of the world? Today, England will not give up raising wheat because it is a staple of her diet that war and blockade might cut off. Without the threat of war or blockade, she would have no need to continue a wasteful and uneconomic activity and could turn her manpower and energies and investments in more fruitful directions.

To put the matter simply, the world will have to form some type of confederation so that all of us can be satisfied in better ways than by the present method, which calls for my trying to take something away from you or your trying to take something away from me. The removal of the threat of war is the only way we are ever going to lift from our backs this enormous burden of a military program which takes billions and billions of dollars a year out of the world's productive capacity. Not only is this money being spent by us, but by the English and the French and the Russians. But all this money and manpower and energy is being consumed toward no purpose, toward no end. Our ordinary sense of self-preservation tells us that this ought not to be. But it is. Our problem, then, is to see that it stops.

What we *will* do in the future is one thing, what we *can* do in the future is another, and what we *ought* to do in the future is still another. What we can do is go on doing what we have been doing, and that is letting Uncle do too much for us. We can do this and pray to God regularly that it doesn't land us in a world war after we've lost every friend we've ever had on the face of the earth. We can do this. I hope we don't. What we ought to do in the future is stop treating democracy as though it were simply an historic document to be preserved between sheets of glass in a specially guarded case in Washington. We ought to treat democracy as a fresh, sharp working tool and start digging into our own economy with it to break up economic privileges, to free the nutriments from the soil of our economy so that it can grow—so that it will thrive, not on a basis of scarcity, but on a basis of abundance. Not only ought we to be doing this to our economy, we ought to pass the tool to people about the world, showing them how to use it, encouraging them to dig into their economies, encouraging them to raise their own standards of living. The economy of the world is a tough, impacted ground filled with a network of roots that feed mighty few people well and a lot of people poorly. Economic democracy, through cooperative ownership, can change matters drastically. I am not afraid of democracy and I don't think any American worthy of the name ought to be afraid of extending it world-wide. This is what we ought to be doing in the future. I have been trying to do it for over thirty years and will go on doing it as long as I can.

Summing Up

I DON'T KNOW whether I really want to do any summing up. I recall the story of the wealthy and successful businessman who was given a dinner on the occasion of his eightieth birthday. Speaker after speaker had risen to give tribute to this pillar of society, this paragon of virtue, this man of many accomplishments and honors. He sat and listened to what was said about him, trying to appear as modest as he could. Inwardly he was delighted with the words spoken about him. He was still active in the company he had founded and was still putting in a full workday. And this, too, was commented upon with awe by those who had come to pay him tribute. The time came for the old man to rise and speak. He thanked those who had spoken so fulsomely about him and about his accomplishments. He then launched into a speech touching upon those things he didn't think the previous speakers had covered in sufficient detail. While he was speaking he saw, in the rear of the room, sitting at a small table, alone, the Angel of Death. It suddenly struck him that the Angel had come for him. As he spoke, he grew more and more frightened and he began to ramble. The Angel of Death yawned slightly. The guest of honor began to realize that his listeners were growing bored and restless. Deciding to wind up his speech, the businessman skipped down to the last paragraphs: "Well, in the final summing up, I have this to say—" The Angel of Death rose from his chair with an expectant smile and started forward. The speaker, no fool, switched in mid-sentence: "—that I'm not ready for the final summing up."

I feel much as he did. I'm not ready for the final summing up because I keep on learning new things about the world, about the people who live in it, and about myself. Just when you think you've understood your life someone comes along and knocks you for a row of pins by revealing something you had never known. It happened to me.

In 1944, Claude Wickard was Secretary of Agriculture. David Niles, President Roosevelt's administrative assistant, asked me if I would like to serve under Wickard as Assistant Secretary of Agriculture. I didn't know if I wanted to do that, but Dave insisted that I speak to Wickard. The best place to talk to him happened to be on a train trip.

I met Claude Wickard and found him a nice, estimable fellow from Indiana. I talked about world events and the farm program and a lot of other matters that seemed important, and just didn't get any rise out of Claude. But as soon as I got to talking about pigs, he really opened up, because he was a good farmer and a good hog breeder.

I remember thinking to myself: My gosh, can this kind of a guy sit in the chair of the Secretary of Agriculture? His job was the one governmental job, I think, that I would have taken had it been offered to me. I finally brought up the subject.

I said, "I suppose you know why I'm riding with you."

He said, "Yes. I would be very happy if you would come down and be the Assistant Secretary of Agriculture."

"Did you have anything to do with the offer?" I asked.

Wickard shook his head. "No. But I'd be very happy to have you working with me as an assistant."

I phoned Dave Niles to report on our conversation. He said

he wanted me to talk with Marvin Jones, Mr. Roosevelt's Food Administrator. Although I agreed, I wasn't enthusiastic about the prospect. None of my Farm Bureau associates thought I ought to accept the job. Most of them were Republicans, remember, and although it may be a little hard to understand, considering what the AAA and REA had done for them, they didn't want me associating with the New Deal.

Marvin Jones had been chairman of the United Nations Food and Agriculture Conference at Hot Springs, so we weren't altogether unacquainted. When I next went to Washington I phoned him but suggested maybe I ought to go see Claude Wickard first.

"You don't need to," he said. "Come right over here."

"Look, Marvin," I said when I met him in his office, "I'm anxious to know what's going on here."

He said, "I don't know. We were just told to get you down here to meet with the President about accepting this job."

"Marvin," I said, "may I ask—did you have anything to do with this?"

"No," he admitted, "I'm very happy to see you down here, but I had nothing to do with it."

He took me over to the White House, and I found Jimmy Byrnes, then the head of the War Production Board and an assistant to Mr. Roosevelt, waiting to take me in to see the President. Major General Edward "Pa" Watson, acting as the chief protocol man around there, got a phone call and said that our appointment was to be delayed a few minutes.

Byrnes and I went out on the southern porch of the White House to wait until the President could see us. By that time I was getting a little nervous, and I said, "I appreciate my having this opportunity and my being considered down here, but I'd like to know what's back of it. I think one thing you folks down here ought to know is that I pasted the living daylights out of your agricultural program. I think you ought to know it before you give me any consideration for an official job."

"We know that, Mr. Lincoln," Jimmy Byrnes said, "but we

also know some other things. You're one of the people in agriculture who's been wise enough not to get at cross purposes with labor. We also find that you tell the same story everywhere. You don't tell us one story and then go out in the country and tell another, and we admire you for it." He went on to say, "Confidentially, some of us think that you're more right than wrong in your opposition to the present farm program."

"You didn't have anything to do with my coming down here?" I asked.

"No, this comes from higher up."

A few minutes later we went in to see the President. He wanted to know if I'd be interested in taking the job. I said I thought I could be more real use to the country if I kept on with my job of helping farmers to organize to do things to help themselves.

"No, that's not right," President Roosevelt said. He went on to say, in effect, that the affairs of the world would probably be dictated or influenced by our government for years to come. "There are many things to do here and there's going to be a lot of fun doing it," he said. "You ought to come down and be one of the crowd."

I knew better than to argue with the President, so I said, "Well, I'll be glad to consider it," and bowed out.

I couldn't get anyone around our institution to agree that I should take the position, and my wife had some kind of horror at the idea of my going to Washington. Finally, through Dave Niles, I turned it down.

In 1946, when we were getting into the radio business, I happened to be in New York with our radio consultant, Fred Palmer. I was staying at the Roosevelt Hotel. From past experience I knew that Dave Niles kept a room there, so when we ran into Dave in the lobby I wasn't surprised.

I started to introduce him to Fred Palmer, and Fred, surprised, asked, "Do you know Murray Lincoln?"

"I ought to," Dave said. "He's the only man I ever knew who

turned down the opportunity to be President of the United States."

"What?" I said.

"Yes," he replied, "you're the one man I know that turned down the opportunity to be President of the United States."

"What in the world do you mean, Dave?"

"You remember the time we asked you to be Assistant Secretary of Agriculture?"

"Yes," I said.

"We were going to move you up to Wickard's place and give you a chance to get out amongst the electorate and make speeches and see if you could catch on. And if you had, you might have been the vice president instead of Harry Truman."

Well, there it was and I was floored. Maybe he was kidding me, I don't know. But that's what happened. I've sometimes said that was the nearest claim to fame I've ever had.

The longer I live the more I learn about things I thought I fully understood to begin with. I'm grateful for this learning process. I think only the young are ever very sure that they've got every problem licked, every detail buttoned down, every angle covered. As we grow older, the more thoughtful of us begin to wonder if we are so sure, if perhaps we haven't overlooked something, if perhaps we haven't been on the wrong track about this, that, or the other thing. As I grow older I find fewer and fewer certainties in the world, and the simpler solutions look harder all the time.

There are many questions I would like to see answered. Why does material wealth destroy societies? It has, in the past. I've always believed that if a nation was freed of the drudgery of providing a bare animal existence it would go on to the cultivation of the higher, more civilized arts. Yet we in the United States, enjoying a material wealth the like of which the world has never seen, seem to be falling into the danger of deteriorating morals, public and private, and a decaying sense of personal responsibility. Here we are, endeavoring to take over the leadership of the world while many American parents can't keep their children out of bands of juvenile delinquents. Our expenditure for liquor rises faster than the money we spend for schools.

Why do we hold human life as cheaply as we do? The rate of traffic accidents on our highways is shocking. Safety experts tell us we have the means at hand to cut that death and accident rate in half—by stricter law enforcement, by the elimination of road hazards, by stricter licensing, by safety education, by the arousal of community support to such programs. And yet people do not rise to the occasion. They will not control themselves or one another, and the death rate continues in its hideous upward curve.

Why do we continue to consider war a possible instrument of national policy when we have abundant evidence that it does not work? Why do we even suggest that it could be a solution to our problems when every reputable scientist warns us that the hydrogen bombs necessary to fight an all-out war would erase the bulk of human life from the face of the earth and reduce the remainder to the most primitive standards of the early tribes?

I could, of course, go on and on in this vein. I think there are answers to all these problems and that one day we will find them. Perhaps not through design, nor even through thought, but through accident or necessity. We're preparing now to start exploring our solar system, sending men to the moon and some of the closer planets. The question that arises in my mind is, Why are we bothering? Is the world as perfect as we would like it to be? Have we done all we could here? I know man is restless and inquisitive and tackles one problem before he has licked another, and I can appreciate the interest and excitement that contact with other planets can stimulate. But our own problems, without leaving earth, are so staggering, and so critical, it seems to me that we are directing a lot of our energies in the wrong direction. The first nation to send a living man to the moon will be honored—until it builds a missile launching site on the moon. And then what will happen to the tensions we have not yet resolved on earth? Will they be relieved? I think the answer fairly obvious—

and deadly. We seem to be compounding our sins, not reducing them. Is it the eternal cussedness of man that makes him keep on this way? Or is it, rather, the whole business of trying to keep the good things in life to ourselves?

We are failing in our fight to win the cold war. We are losing it every day because we are trying to win it with a program of missiles rather than a program for mankind. When are we going to make the change? Every day that goes by that we haven't made the change shortens our chances for survival. Are we going to lose the world, which is a living, breathing, populated planet, because we're too busy fiddling around trying to reach a dead planet? If it's dead planets that interest us, a little more of this research into missiles and less into people and human relations, and a dead planet will be a lot closer than many of us would like to see. Ours will be the dead planet.

Why are the majority of people indifferent to their fate? They seem to be shucking off their democratic responsibilities, letting Uncle Sam and Uncle Business run things. Are they so satisfied with the way the big Uncles are running things that they haven't any complaints? Or are they so cowed and intimidated and con-formity-minded that they can't bring themselves to speak out, to act up? Robert Osborn, the social-minded illustrator, has suggested that we ought to drop the bald eagle—that fierce, inde-pendent, bad-tempered bird—as our national emblem and choose, instead, a flock of sheep. Drew Pearson and Jack Anderson, in their book *USA—Second Class Power?*, insist that one reason we have been falling behind in the race for world leadership is that those who are in authority in our country hate new ideas. Note that word *hate*. Not distrust or suspicion—hate. We hate the things that threaten us because we do not understand them, do not know how to cope with them. But have we come so far along the path to being vegetables that we are actually afraid of new ideas to the point of hating them?

Each of us has come to where he now is by his own long and winding road. My journey to understanding has been a slow one.

331

As you have now discovered, I've had mighty few brilliant inspirations during my life, and when I've had them I've been wrong as often as not. But I've clung to the basic idea that people ought to be helping themselves and that the way they ought to be doing it is in groups. So, all my life I've worked with groups of people, urging them to organize themselves to help themselves, egging them on to solve their own problems instead of running to Uncle. I've said over and over that people have within their own hands the tools to fashion their own destiny—if they'll only use them. I have from time to time despaired that they ever would use them, even if they could see them. But I've overcome that despair and plugged away at it, nagging, talking, demonstrating, pushing, hauling, doing everything and anything that was in my power to show people (1) that they must control their own destinies if they are not going to be cheated of their birthright; (2) that they can control their destinies as soon as they use the tools at hand; (3) that the forces which seem so great and powerful are powerful only because they are using the machinery that millions of ordinary, seemingly powerless folk make possible; (4) that they can fashion for themselves and for generations to come—not only in our own country but in the whole world—a better life than they were born into without science advancing another step beyond its present level of knowledge.

The tools are here, the need is here, the promise of fulfillment lies just beyond the horizon, the rewards can extend until the end of the race of man on earth, and that end can be extended for millions and millions of years.

I have dedicated my life to urging people to take those tools in hand. I didn't do it consciously. That dedication sort of sneaked up on me and now, as I look at my life, I realize that that is what I have spent it doing. I will go on spending it in the same direction because I've learned one great thing: *If you really want fun out of life, align yourself with some worthy but unpopular human cause.*

I've been called all sorts of names by all sorts of people. Some people have thought well of me. And some people who have not agreed with me have conceded that I am sincere. If I had seriously worried about what people thought of me, I suppose I wouldn't have pursued an unpopular cause much of my life. Even the people who were in the same boat with me have at times treated me as if they wished I weren't along. But however right a man feels he is, however determined he is to ignore criticism, however indifferent he appears to be to praise, he does, wistfully, wish that more people understood what he was talking about. I recall two occasions in particular when I was touched by the realization that somehow I'd gotten through to people. The first was that time, years ago, when Ray Ascham said to me, "I don't know what you're talking about, but it's great." I had communicated to him something of my excitement, my sense of urgency, the need to save the world and the way of life we hold most precious. To set a man on fire with the desire to do something for himself and for his fellow man is a great privilege. And it is a tough thing to do in an age when everything but the human mind seems to be combustible.

The second of these occasions when I was deeply touched, and made humble and proud at the same time, was the night I got a call from Mrs. John Dewey, the widow of the great American philosopher and teacher.

She told me that she had a problem with some small business she owned. The problem had arisen when her husband had had his last illness, and because he knew she was concerned, he tried to tell her what to do. Although I had hardly met Mr. Dewey and could claim no honor of his knowing me, he must have heard something of me at one time or another during his life and formed some opinion of me. Almost his last words on earth were: "Call Murray Lincoln. He's an honest man and knows something about business."

I'm not making any plans to have an epitaph written for myself, but that's how I'd like to be remembered.

Index

AAA Program, 103, 105–108, 150, 152, 327
A&P Tea Company, 228, 242, 243
Advisory Committee of Policyholders, 228–230
Advisory Councils, 96, 118–121, 228–230
Agricultural Adjustment Act, 106, 107
Aiken, George, 85
Alabama Farm Bureau, 105
Amalgamated Clothing Workers, 170
American Bankers Association, 90
American Council of Voluntary Organizations for Foreign Service, 205
American Cyanamid Company, 59
American Farm Bureau Federation, 56, 57, 59, 60, 87, 97, 103–105, 124, 154, 211
American Friends Service Committee, 205, 210
American Guernsey Breeders Association, 24
American Institute of Cooperation, 150
American Jewish Distribution Committee, 210
American Management Association, 311
Amsden Heights, 258, 267
Anderson, Jack, 331
Andrews, Grandmother, 28, 30, 33, 81
Anglo-Iranian Oil Company, 278
Antigonish Movement, 114, 116–118, 120
Approved Finance, 268, 269
Arabian-American Oil Company, 250
Arnold, Mary, 112
Ascham, Ray, 91–112, 333

Atlantic Coast Fisheries, 48
Atoms-for-peace Conference, 308
Austin Company, 258
Avery Company, 109

Babcock, Ed, 152–155
Babson, Roger, 270, 271
Baker, Jake, 286, 287
Baker, Newton, 51
Ballard, Henry, 134, 135, 137, 138, 155, 157, 186, 222, 226, 264
Barnum, P. T., 312
Beale, Harry G., 68
Beaverbrook, Lord, 198
Benjamin, Roland, 202
Berle, Adolf, 311
Bradfute, O. E., 57
Bricker, John, 233, 234
Bridgeport Housing Project, 265, 266
"Brockton Enterprise," 44
Bromfield, Louis, 176–178, 181
Brosseau, A. J., 78–80, 196
Bryan, William Jennings, 160
Bunau-Varilla, Philipe, 88, 89
Byrne, Father, 254, 255
Byrnes, Jimmy, 327, 328

Campbell, Wallace, 205–207, 237
Canadian Broadcasting Company, 263
CARE, 204–216, 237, 253, 254
Carmody, John, 145, 163, 164
Carson, John, 200, 204
Cash, D. M., 121, 128
Catholic War Relief Services, 205, 210
Chicago Theological Seminary, 115
Churchill, Winston, 173
CIO, 169, 206, 211, 232, 305

Clark, Dr. Lincoln, 204–208
Clark, Mrs. Lincoln, 206
Cleveland Electric Illuminating Company, 47, 54, 83
Cleveland Trust Company, 281
Coady, Father M. M., 114, 116, 117
Collin, Harry, 281, 282
Collins, Howard, 257, 258
Columbia Broadcasting Company (CBS), 262, 312
Columbian National Life Insurance Company, 284
"Columbus Dispatch," 169
Commission on Higher Education, 113
Commonwealth and Southern, 257
Congregational Christian Service Committee, 214
Connecticut Farm Bureau, 217
Consumers Cooperative Association of Kansas City, 193
Consumers Cooperative Services, 112
Cooke, Morris L., 132, 138, 142, 145
Cooley, G. L., 55–58, 77, 137, 261
Cooperative for American Relief Everywhere (*see* CARE)
Cooperative League of the U.S.A., 40, 108–112, 148, 152, 155, 168, 193, 204–206, 211, 244, 262, 278, 285, 323
Cooperative Movement in Great Britain, The, 109
Cornell University, 35, 56, 107, 155, 236, 251
Country Life Commission, 30, 44
Cowden, Howard, 193, 194, 200, 201, 278, 285
Credit Union National Association, 211
Cripps, Sir Stafford, 197, 198
Culbreth, Harry, 157, 193, 197, 198, 233, 234
Cuyahoga County Agricultural Association, 55
Cuyahoga County Farm Bureau, 55, 285

Davis, Mr., 15–17
Dayton Power and Light Company, 133
Democratic Party, 1, 90, 168, 312
Deressa, Lidj Ylma, 173, 174
Deterding, Sir Henry, 194
Dexter, John, 47, 49, 50, 52–54
Dewey, John, 333
Dewey, Mrs. John, 333
Dichter, Ernest, 188
Dickinson, L. J., 60
Dineen, Robert, 225–277
"Discovery of the Consumer, The," 71, 99–101
Dodge, Lawrence, 22, 23, 25, 26
"Dollars from Ditches" Program, 55
Doolittle, Jimmy, 173
Douglas, Paul, 109
Duncan Electric Company, 138
Dunlap, George, 202
Dyer, Chester A., 58, 64

Eastern Cooperative Wholesale, 245
Eaton, Cyrus, 98, 281, 283, 284
Ecker, Fred, 231–234
Einstein, Dr. Albert, 320
Elsinger, Verna, 95, 99
Erf, Oscar, 67
Evans, Herbert, 157, 245
Extension Service, Ohio State University, 25, 61, 63, 66, 90, 91, 93

Farley, George, 30
Farm Bureau Agricultural Credit Association, 77, 163, 260
Farm Bureau Automobile Mutual Insurance Company, 6, 72–75, 84, 85, 102, 217–223, 225–228, 241, 318, 322
Farm Bureau Federation, American, 56, 57, 59, 60, 87, 103–105, 124, 154, 211
Farm Bureau Federation, Ohio, 56–58, 61–66, 68–74, 76–78, 81, 91–96, 102–105, 112–113, 118–123, 127,

132, 134, 146, 149, 155, 156, 161, 163, 165, 170, 176, 181, 184–186, 202, 217, 219–223, 225–227, 232, 261, 262, 267, 271, 281, 282, 284, 291–293, 300, 301, 304

Farm Bureau Life Insurance Company, 202

Farm Bureau Mutual Fire Insurance Company, 202

Farm Credit Administration, 163

Farmers Alliance, 160

Farmers Commercial Service Company, 68

Farmers Union Grain Terminal Association, 308

Fatemi, Dr. Hussein, 278

Federal Farm Board, 91, 92, 97

Ferguson, Harry, 178–182

Ferguson, Mrs. Harry, 178, 182

Ferguson, Joe, 232, 234

Ferguson Company, 183–185

Field, Fred, 44

Field Shoe Company, 44

Filene Fund, 245

Finkelstein, Dr. Louis, 311

Flagg, Horace, 41

Foch, Marshal, 51

Food and Agricultural Organization of the United Nations, 249, 254

Ford, Henry, 61, 180–182

Ford-Ferguson Tractor, 181–182, 184, 185, 199, 249, 252

Ford Motor Company, 178, 184, 185

Forristall, Elwin, 8, 9

Forristall, Mrs. Elwin, 9

Fort, Franklin W., 97, 98

"Fortune," 280, 311

Fountain, Clayton, 168

Four-H Clubs, 213

Franklin County Farm Bureau, 61

Freedom Fund, 205

Freiberger, Judge Isadore, 282

French, Paul, 209, 212

Frye, Carl, 133, 138, 141, 144, 258, 264, 265

Galbreath, John W., 267, 304

Gamble, Arthur, 210

Garet, Garrett, 89

General Motors Corporation, 124, 179, 181

Geneva Conference, 308

Gilmore, Paul, 141

Gooding, Frank R., 60

Grange, 19–21, 58, 64, 102, 111, 152, 160, 211, 212

Grange League Federation, 149, 152, 201

Great Atlantic and Pacific Tea Company (*see* A&P Tea Company)

Green, Fred, 68

Green, Perry L., 105, 112, 156, 157, 160–163, 176, 177, 232, 282

Greenbelt Cooperative, 86, 288

Grimm, Caspar, 124

Gulbenkian, Carlouste, 199, 200, 202, 203

Hall, E. C., 36

Hanna, W. H., 56

Hart, Professor William, 13–15, 18, 26, 27, 36, 37, 314

Hartford, John, 243

Harvard University School of Business Administration, 249

Harvard University, Department of Economics, 84

Haskell, General William N., 207, 209

Hawes, Alex, 208

Haywood, Carlton, 28, 29

Henry, Clarence A., 58

Hensel, Gene, 155–157, 296

Heritage Securities, Inc., 269

Herrick, Myron T., 30, 44, 45, 47, 49, 50–55, 58, 78, 82, 83, 88, 89, 281

Herrick, Tracy, 281–284

"Hidden Revolution, The," 310

Hill, Lee, 258

Hiram College, 160, 282

"Hoard's Dairyman," 32

Hodson, John, 183

Holland, C. P., 30, 31, 35–38, 41, 42, 45, 48, 78, 82
Hoover, Herbert, 91, 97, 98, 204
Horchow, Joe, 122
Howard, James R., 57, 59
Howard, Louis, 10–12
Howard, William N., 33, 34, 43
Hull, Harvey, 123, 124
Hurst, Rhoda, 28
Hutchinson, Carl, 115, 116, 120
Hutchinson, Howard, 76

Illinois Agricultural Association, 104
Indiana Farm Bureau, 123, 124
International Cooperative Alliance, 181, 202, 277
International Cooperative Petroleum Association, 278
International Harvester Company, 91
International Oil Cooperative, 278
Investors Diversified Services, Inc., 271

Jarvis, C. D., 19, 20
Jewett, Elmer, 23
Jewett, Mrs. Elmer, 23
Johns Hopkins University, 244
Jones, Darrell, 257, 258
Jones, Marvin, 327

Kaiser and Company, 264, 265
Kaplan, Jack, 235–242, 314
Kazan, Abraham, 266
Kelly, Zeno, 3
Keltner, Ed, 220
Kentucky Tobacco Growers Association, 94, 95
Kerr, Dean, 219
Ketner, Forrest G., 58, 64, 92, 93
Kiwanis Club, 165, 166, 296
Knight, Henry, 124–126, 182, 184, 185
Knott, Dr., 24
Kramer, Don, 259

La Follette, Robert M., 60
Lang, Frank, 218
Lasher, G. E., 68
Laski, Harold, 198
Latchaw, Charlie, 67
Legge, Alexander, 91, 92
Lehman, Herbert, 207
Lewis, Fulton, 262
Lewis, John L., 164, 165, 173
Licking County Farm Bureau, 119, 120
Liimatainen, Bill, 148
Lincoln, Abraham, 171, 172
Lincoln, Anne Hurst, 27–29, 33, 47, 48, 50, 81, 82, 106, 107, 114, 133, 136–138, 152, 153, 177, 183, 301
Lincoln, Arthur, 2
Lincoln, Betty, 47, 48, 50, 158, 159
Lincoln, Charles, 16, 17, 24
Lincoln, Edith, 2
Lincoln, Edward, 4
Lincoln, Helen Andrews (mother), 2, 27
Lincoln, grandfather, 1–3, 6, 7, 16
Lincoln, Joseph, 171
Lincoln, Leroy, 233, 234
Lincoln, Minot J. (father), 1, 2, 4, 6, 7
Lincoln Village, 267, 268
Louisville Refinery, 127, 128

MacArthur, General Douglas, 255, 256
MacLaury, Dorr, 32–35
Mack Truck Company, 78
Malabar Farm, 177, 180, 181
"Mama," 309
Manley, Weston, 41–44
Massachusetts Agricultural College, 8, 12, 18, 30
McCabe, Ben, 305
McIlvain, R. W., 126, 127
McLean, Dr. John, 18
Mercier, Cardinal, 51

Metropolitan Life Insurance Company, 231–233
Michigan Life, 273
Miles, General Fred, 127
Miles, George, 205
Miller, Dr. Raymond, 249, 251, 252, 254–256
Monks, Mr., 48
Morse, Doris, 29
Mossadegh, Mohammed, 278
Murrow, Edward R., 309
Muscle Shoals, 59, 60
Musselman, Charles, 49, 50, 52
Musser, Karl, 24, 25
Mussolini, Benito, 173
Mutual Broadcasting Company, 262
Mutual Income Foundation, 269, 271, 323
Mutual Service Insurance Companies, 229, 253

Nasser, Gamal Abdel, 203
National Association of Broadcasters, 261
National Association of Manufacturers, 57
National Broadcasting Company, 262
National Casualty, 273
National Catholic Welfare Conference, 205, 210
National Cooperatives, Inc., 149
National Council of Cooperatives, 151, 152
National Council of Farmer Cooperatives, 152
National Council of Negro Women, 211
National Dairy Products Corporation, 41
National Education Association, 213
National Farmers Union, 211
National Fertilizer Association, 62
National Grange, 211
National Refinery, 281, 283–285

National Tax Equality Association, 169, 170, 262, 305
National Wool Pool, 91, 92
Nationwide Corporation, 272, 273
Nationwide Development Company, 266, 267
Nationwide Insurance Companies, 75, 187–190, 266, 272, 293, 307, 308, 311, 314–316, 318, 322
Nationwide Life Insurance Companies, 75, 270, 273, 274, 308
Nationwide Mutual Fire Insurance Company, 75, 273
Nelson, Cleve, 93
Nelson, Donald, 207
New Deal, 99, 103, 105, 132, 145, 191, 242, 286, 327
"New England Homestead," 16
New London County Improvement League, 18, 19, 24
New London County Pomona Grange, 20
New York Stock Exchange, 246
"New York Times," 115
Niles, David, 153–155, 326, 328, 329
Nixon, Richard, 264
Nobel Anniversary Dinner, 308
Norris, George W., 60
Northwestern National Life Insurance Company, 274

Odaffer, David M., 68
Ohio Bell Telephone Company, 76–78
Ohio Farm Bureau Federation, 25, 56–58, 61–66, 68–74, 76–78, 81, 91–96, 102–105, 112, 113, 118–121, 123, 127, 132, 134, 146, 149, 155, 156, 161, 165, 170, 176, 181, 184–186, 202, 217, 219–223, 225–227, 232, 261, 262, 267, 271, 281, 282, 284, 292, 293, 300, 301, 304
"Ohio Farm Bureau News," 281
Ohio Farm Bureau Service Company, 68

Ohio State Grange, 58, 64, 67, 68
Ohio State Legislature, 78, 90, 134, 135, 161, 306
Ohio State University, 67, 310
Ohio State University Extension Service, 25, 61, 63, 66, 90, 91, 93
Ohio Wool Pool, 91, 92
O'Meara, Joseph, 222
O'Neal, Edward A., 104–106, 153, 154
Open Formula Feed, 69, 86
Owen, Charlotte, 205

Pacific Life, 273
Packard, Arthur, 104, 106
Palmer, Fred, 261, 263, 328
Palmer, L. B., 91, 93, 95
Panama Canal, 88, 89
PARCELUS, 208
Peabody Award, 309
Pearson, Drew, 331
Peoples Broadcasting Corporation, 157, 202, 261–263
Peoples Development Company, 266–267, 323
Pig Club, 30–31, 47
Plymouth County Trust Company, 27, 45, 48–49, 78
Policyholders Advisory Committee, 228–230
Populists, 160
Portage County Farm Bureau, 161
Portage County Improvement Association, 161
Powers Tabulating Machine Company, 53
Pure Food and Drug Act, 84
Pure Oil Company, 124, 125, 127, 280, 281

Ramsower, Harry C., 66, 90, 91
REA, 78, 132, 133, 136, 145, 146, 163, 327
Rector, Edward A., 93
Republican Party, 1, 90, 97–98, 251
Reuter, Richard, 212–213
Reuther, Victor, 168

Reuther, Walter, 168
Ringland, Arthur, 204
Rittenour, Everett, 202
Robison, Mrs. Harold, 202
Rochdale Society of Equitable Pioneers, 40, 71, 100, 101, 102, 244–245
Rockefeller, John D., 121, 122
Rogers, Mr., 24
Rogers, Slade and Hill, 184, 294
Roosevelt, Franklin D., 134, 153, 154, 191, 207, 251, 328, 329
Roosevelt, Mrs. Franklin D., 172
Roosevelt, Theodore, 89
Rubinow, Sidney, 103
Rural Electrification Administration, 78, 132, 133, 136, 145, 146, 163, 327
"Rural New Yorker," 16

Safeway Stores, 249
Safford, Bill, 72, 156, 157, 222
St. Francis Xavier University, 114
Salk, Dr. Jonas, 319
Sangamo Electric Company, 138
Sapiro, Aaron, 94
Sawyer, Charles, 257
Save the Children Federation, 207
Scarff, Max, 157
Schoenberger, Fred, 161, 162
Scovil, Samuel, 47, 54, 55
Securance, 272
Shaw, Norman, 162
Sheffield Farms, 41
Sherman-Clayton Anti-Trust Act, 84
Shield, Lee, 226
Silver, Gray, 60, 88
Sims, John, 227, 284
Slade, Art, 294
Slayter, Games, 257
Smith, Earl, 104
Smoots, Herbert, 119, 144
Snyder, Watson, 200, 201, 277
Society for Savings, Cleveland, 30, 44, 46–47, 49–50, 52–54, 78, 281, 282

Sollars, Walter, 91
Solvay Process Companies, 59
Southern States Cooperative, 149, 286
State Farm Mutual Automobile Insurance Company, 72
State Farmers Elevator Association, 67, 68
Stevens, Leigh, 251–252, 254–256
Stough, Ed, 157, 183, 184

Tabor, L. J. (Lou), 58, 90, 110, 111, 153
Taft, Robert, 232–233
Taylor, Lee, 146, 155, 157, 281, 284, 285
Tec-Pan, 259
Tectum, 257–259
Tectum Corporation, 258, 323
Thatcher, Bill, 305
Thayer, Mr., 28
Thomas, M. C., 58
Thrift, Tim, 52
Time-Life-Fortune Conference on the Consumer, 251
Tompkins, Father J. J., 114, 116, 117
Thompson, Eastburn, 205
Thompson, Mr., 9, 10
Truman, Harry S., 113, 191, 257, 329
Tuttle, Jean, 51, 53
Twain, Mark, 7

United Automobile Workers of America, 168
United Cooperatives, Inc., 149
United HIAS (Hebrew Immigrant Aid Society), 210
United Nations, 203, 278, 311
United Nations Atomic Energy Conferences, 263
United Nations Conference on Food and Agriculture, 171, 172, 176, 327
United Nations Economic, Social, and Cultural Council, 278
United Nations Housing Center for Central America, 213

United Nations Relief and Rehabilitation Administration, 204, 207
United States Bureau of Standards, 84
United States Chamber of Commerce, 56, 57
United States Department of Agriculture, 19, 22–23, 25–26, 211, 259
United States Steel Corporation, 59

Van Bergen, Charles, 194–195, 199, 200, 202, 275
Vance, Silas, 121, 128
Vandenbark, W. G., 67
Van Meter, Galen, 271–272
Varilla, Philippe Bunau-, 88, 89
Vermont Farm Bureau, 104
Voorhis, Jerry, 278

Walker, Jap, 91
Warbington, Lewis, 119
Warbasse, Dr. James P., 108, 109, 148
War Production Board, 207, 327
War Relief Control Board, 204
Warren, Dr. George, 107
Watson, Major General Edward, 327
Watson, Neil, 126
Webb, Beatrice, 71, 99–102, 109, 150
Welch, J. T., 62
Welch Chemical Company, 62
Welch Grape Juice Company, 235–242, 314, 317
West, James, 202
WGAR, 263–264
Wheat Loan Fund, 254
Whitman, C. D., 24
Wicher, Mr., 33
Wickard, Claude, 326, 327, 329
Willkie, Wendell, 256
Wilson, Mr., 135
Wilson, Woodrow, 44
Woodcock, Leslie, 245
World Veterans Federation, 213
WTTM, 263

Young, Bob, 271

Acknowledgment

The writing of a book of this kind involves many more people than are represented by the names appearing on the jacket. I wish to take this opportunity to thank the members of the book committee of the Board of Directors of Nationwide Insurance, Messrs. David Scull, Edward Stough, Roy Wood, and Leslie Woodcock. Thanks also to Calvin Kytle, Vice President–Public Relations for Nationwide Insurance companies, for hard labors extending back some two years to the day when we first met for an unlikely breakfast conference to first discuss the book to the present moment of the writing of this acknowledgment. Thanks, too, to Don Kramer, Vice President–General Manager of the Tectum Corporation and former assistant to Murray Lincoln, for many valuable insights into the character of my subject. Equal thanks, too, to George Campbell, former assistant to Murray Lincoln, for the same kind of aid. Thanks to Mr. Dean Kerr, director of government relations, and Mr. J. E. Keltner, Vice President–Controller of the Nationwide Insurance companies, for invaluable material relative to the critical insurance examinations of the 1940s. Thanks to Mr. Harry Culbreth, Vice President–Human Relations, for patient explanation of cooperative

341

theories and practices; to Forest Lombaer, Vice President–Personnel, for discussions concerning personnel selection; to C. W. Leftwich, Vice President–Actuarial, Carl Bair, formerly director of policyholder relations, and Robert Rennie, Vice President–Research, for their patience in checking historical material; to Herbert Evans, President of the Peoples Broadcasting Corporation, for many talks on his experiences with the Filene Fund and analysis of Nationwide as a unique business organization; to Mr. Bowman Doss, First Vice President of Nationwide, for his reminiscences of service with the companies; to Davis Douthit for his considerable editorial aid; to Martha Sliter for a hard, unrewarding task of checking facts and figures, spellings, etc.; to Miss Kathryn Gee, secretary to the President, for her many secretarial aids, for finding so many things when no one else could find them; to Mrs. Jane Spinks for her truly enormous labor of transcription of many, many hours of taped conversations and for the hundreds of odd jobs which I thrust upon her so often in two years of work; to Richard Bull, assistant to the President, whose companionship and assistance in many different ways made my work pleasanter and easier; and a special debt of gratitude must be acknowledged to the late Perry Green from whose unpublished history of the Ohio Farm Bureau I have drawn a great deal of invaluable information and insight. Because I was a stranger at work in Columbus for many weeks, I deeply appreciate the hospitality and kindness of those who made a lonely job more tolerable, especially Calvin and Elizabeth Kytle, Davis and Ruth Douthit, George and Jean Campbell, Harry and Betty Culbreth, Richard and Shirley Bull, and, of course, Murray and Anne Lincoln. My thanks, too, to all the people at Nationwide who helped me in too many ways on too many occasions to record here.

David Karp

Great Neck, New York

McNulty

√ Prayer - for they horse - 5

√ ___ ___ ___ - ___

√ ___ ___ 16 2

√ Commun___ ___ } 174

√ Democracy - weakness of }

√ Peace in economic as well as
of other democracy 175
other democ

√ Draft not all - 191, 190,
ef. 311

√ Peace - thru cooperatives 202

√ Caring - CARE 212 - 214

√ Cooperatives work when have
ideas and there - 214

√ Group action 249

√ Cooperatives - way of life ofher 248

√ Peace - thru " 234

√ communism cant beat
cooperatives if 254